'A BREATHLESS HUSH . . .'

'A BREATHLESS HUSH…'

The MCC anthology of cricket verse

~

EDITED BY DAVID RAYVERN ALLEN
WITH HUBERT DOGGART

Methuen

First Methuen paperback edition, 2007

Copyright in this selection © 2004 David Rayvern Allen and Hubert Doggart
Copyright in the introductions © 2004 David Rayvern Allen
Copyright in the chapter headings © 2004 Hubert Doggart

The right of David Rayvern Allen and Hubert Doggart to be identified as the editors of this work has
been asserted by them in accordance with the Copyright, Designs and Patents Act 1988

First published in Great Britain in 2004 by Methuen
Methuen Publishing Ltd
11–12 Buckingham Gate
London SW1E 6LB

www.methuen.co.uk

Methuen Publishing Limited Reg. No. 3543167

A CIP catalogue record for this book is available from the British Library

ISBN 10: 0-413-775917
ISBN 13: 9780-413-775917

Typeset by SX Composing DTP, Rayleigh, Essex
Printed and bound in Great Britain by
MPG Books Ltd, Bodmin, Cornwall

As readers will see from the preface and editor's preamble, this volume of verse was the brainchild of Lord Alexander of Weedon. Sadly, since the original publication, Bob – always, charmingly, he introduced himself as Bob to whomever he met – has died. The inspiration and enthusiasm he provided in the creation of the anthology will never be forgotten. Therefore this new edition is dedicated with much affection to his memory.

David Rayvern Allen

CONTENTS

~

III.   CRICKET'S APPEAL

(How's This? How's That?)

IV.   TIME REMEMBERED

(The Broad Sweep)

V.   THE POWER OF PLACE AND PROTEST

(Points of View)

VI.   CHARACTER RECAPTURED

(Straight Drive or Square Cut)

VII.   HOME AND AWAY

(National Boundaries)

VIII.   THE HUMOUR OF CRICKET

(Short-legs and Long-stops)

IX. CRICKET PARODIES

(On-and-Off-Beat)

X. CRICKET IN NARRATIVE

(Timeless Tests)

XI. PRACTICALLY SPEAKING

(Ins and Outs of the Game)

XII.   CLOSE OF PLAY
(End of Season)

CODA

PREFACE

There are legions of great writers who have loved cricket. Some were masters of prose who have made the drums beat to their words, from Neville Cardus to John Woodcock. It is less well known that Samuel Beckett, the noted playwright, is the only winner of the Nobel Prize for Literature to figure in Wisden as a member of a team. But it is not surprising that the charms, skills, drama and above all infinite variety of our game have inspired fine poetry.

This exciting voyage of discovery from the works of Keats and Wordsworth to those of Betjeman and Masefield should delight cricket lovers everywhere. We owe this remarkable anthology to David Rayvern Allen and Hubert Doggart, two passionate and sensitive cricketing scholars. David says that when I was Chair of the MCC Arts and Library Sub-Committee, whose enjoyable task is to cherish our Museum and Publications, I suggested that it was time we had an anthology of verse. If so, I am thrilled to have been even the smallest catalyst for the treasure house which they have brought together and for which we owe them a great debt.

Lord Alexander of Weedon QC

FOREWORD

The time has long gone when MCC controlled not only English cricket, but also had the most powerful voice in cricket anywhere in the world. However, the great Marylebone club still has many important roles to fulfil, in addition to its guardianship of the Laws of the game. It remains a vital part of the fabric of English cricket, fielding hundreds of teams every summer, thereby encouraging thousands of young (and some a little older) players, continuing to spread the word, the spirit and the enjoyment of the sport as it has for over two hundred years. In other English seasons the MCC flag is flown in many far-flung places where more commercial cricket organisations rarely go.

It is not only on the field of play or even solely in the present day that MCC flourishes. Its headquarters, the matchless Lord's ground, is a marvellous combination of history and modernity, both through its architecture that embraces Victorian confidence with twenty-first-century imagination, and within its museum and library, where the greatest contributors to the game are never to be forgotten.

Cricket literature has no equal in sport. Perhaps, however, cricket verse and cricket poetry have been given less than their due over the centuries by publishers and historians. This anthology, edited on behalf of MCC by the eminent cricket writer David Rayvern Allen with the assistance of one of its past Presidents, Hubert Doggart, will help to correct any such imbalance. Like MCC itself, the collection bestrides the centuries with aplomb.

Some verses herein could only have been written as the Victorians constructed the pavilion, others must have been composed in the metaphorical shadow of the Media Centre. Some are funny, some are sad, some are portraits of formidable players, or (by and large the autobiographical ones) of players not over-burdened with talent. Some acclaim great deeds and games, some record the most obscure of fixtures, all live on.

Surely no other game could muster such an array of contributors to an anthology of this kind. Byron, Keats, Wodehouse, Hughes, Betjeman, Masefield, Arlott, Chesterton, Housman, Wordsworth and Milne make a pretty good first XI chosen from those now in Heaven's grandstand, but the selectors have equally strong reserves from many other eras. Indeed, one of the fundamental reasons for this book was to include a comprehensive selection of recent verse alongside the tried and trusted.

I was fortunate in that the editors' diligent compilation took place during my Presidency of MCC. I am not bragging when I say that my lyrical skills are superior to my very limited cricketing ones – I am sure this is not true of many other past Presidents and in a spirit of feeling appropriate I am delighted to recommend this fascinating collection.

Sir Tim Rice
November 2003

EDITOR'S PREAMBLE

'I think we should do a book of cricket poetry.' Bob Alexander's casual remark at a meeting of MCC Arts and Library Sub-Committee met with an enthusiastic response. Before long there was another teasing delivery across the table: 'David, would you like to take it on?' There are many offers that cannot be refused and this was one of them. Verse of every kind had been an enthusiasm since schooldays.

Soon Hubert Doggart joined the project as co-editor and more or less at the same time Peter Tummons of Methuen cheerfully and readily agreed to publish the book in association with MCC.

There ensued a number of visits to the South Coast where Hubert and Sue Doggart's wonderful hospitality extended to the point of being totally unfazed at seeing their carpet strewn with copy. Innumerable pieces of paper were sifted and slotted into thematic sections in an attempt to get some sort of order from our rumble through the jumble. The realisation quickly dawned that even without exploring many byways, we were wrestling with over 600 items of verse vying for inclusion. Clearly, it was not going to be a question of where to start, more of where to finish.

Sadly, shortly afterwards, and through totally unforeseen circumstances, Hubert was forced to take a back seat in the progression of the anthology, though not before providing most of the chapter headings.

The intention from the outset was to give a platform for a high percentage of what might be termed, modern cricket verse. In other words, work that had been composed in the last fifty years or so. And there was to be a further emphasis on verse that had not been seen before in mainstream cricket publications. That was not to exclude the favourite warhorses from previous eras – even if they could be ridden elsewhere. Far from it, for the joy of any anthology is to find work juxtaposed from different periods. And it would be wholly self-defeating should any dateline be an overly significant factor at the book's immigration control. But the aim was and indeed is, to surprise the reader with something they perhaps will not have seen anywhere else.

Another aim was to spread the net as widely as possible – to include verse from other cricketing corners of the globe as well as our own. Essentially, it was hoped the book would be fun – almost, in a way, a book of the people.

In presenting an assembly of over 260 pieces of poetry, it would be strange not to find a slightly uneven standard overall. Poets and their poems have different impulses and here we find high art and low doggerel. Both serve their purpose, one does not preclude the other, each has appeal. There also is every kind of offering in-between. Nothing has been omitted on the basis of some esoteric criteria, for this happy mix of career poets and those who write verse solely as a hobby has, I suspect, a common thread. And that is, an affection for the game of cricket.

There remains the pleasant task of recording my gratitude to Lord Alexander for his gracious preface and to Sir Tim Rice for his splendid foreword. I also would like to pass a vote of thanks to the Poet Laureate Andrew Motion for his generous and inventive response to a request for a poem on the game. His was not the only commission. With but a few days at his disposal, Jeff Cloves was undaunted by the challenge of composing a poem on the retirement of the Waugh twins – to him, my grateful thanks.

There has been much goodwill in the making of this anthology and many other individuals who deserve fulsome responses are to be found in the acknowledgement section at the end of the book.

As we begin to flick through the pages, I think we can do no better than remember the words of Dylan Thomas. In his introductory remarks to a reading given at the Massachusetts Institute of Technology one year before his untimely death, he said: 'Poetry is what in a poem makes you laugh, cry, prickle, be silent, makes your toenails twinkle, makes you want to do this or that or nothing, makes you know that you are alone in the unknown world, that your bliss and suffering is forever shared and forever your own.'

Somewhere in this book, I hope you will find poems that make all these things happen . . .

David Rayvern Allen
May 2004

PROLEGOMENON

~

The sole starter (inedible variety) – the dishy Greek section title of which was dreamt up by Hubert Doggart – presents an idyllic view of what for many is surely regarded as *the* match of any season – the Lord's Test. With his final couplet though, John Groves takes us far beyond the geographical boundaries of a pampered field in St John's Wood, and it is here that we rediscover an undeniable truth. It means that wherever the greatest of all games is being played, no one has to take sides . . .

D. R. A.

1   THE GAME

John Groves

A painter's sky over Lord's.
A gentle zephyr, blowing without brace,
The crowd engaged in all that joy affords
And England batting with admired grace.
The sun ablaze, an unforgiving pitch,
A bowler with a patriotic itch,
A ticking scoreboard and a close-run thing,
A resolute gull, high on a drowsy wing.

Though one team triumph, victory's all the same:
The winner is the beauty of the game.

I

THE SEASON'S OPENING

(At the Toss of a Coin)

~

As we metaphorically set about preparing a pitch for our literary encounters, Hubert Doggart flies the flag for the figure who gave his name to the home of cricket.

Colin Shakespeare then provides the result of his self-imposed challenge to associate the game with every month of the year before Daniel Pettiward admits to being captivated by the sounds rather than the sight of cricket. His ending is positively onomatopoeic.

D. R. A.

Hubert Doggart

It is a truth acknowledged by the wise:
Instinctively the English minimise
Their heroes and are rarely atavistic,
Preferring to be subtly euphemistic
About the seminal figures of the past,
And not to fly flags proudly from the mast,
Or pay respects to those whose attitude
And beneficial acts deserve our gratitude.

But when we analyse the Years of Grace,
This view may seem to have another face.
Much praise has been bestowed on W.G.,
Who found a branch and left a mighty tree.
'The one-stringed instrument' I early learned,
'Into a many-chorded lyre he turned'.
And e'en before the 'one-string' there were chords
From Wealden pitches, Hambledon and Lord's.

Much praise, more recently, has been bestowed
On Lord's heroes from whom runs have flowed,
Like Hearne and Hendren – stylish and successful,
Not least when times for Middlesex were stressful.
Between the wars, on days of good or ill,
They plied their trade with true professional skill.
And Verity and Hammond, both with zest,
Imposed himself upon a thirties Test.

And praise attaches, not without good reason,
To those who 'stole' the '47 season,
Edrich and Compton, bound by special ties,
Whom we find testing not to lionise.
Praise too for Warner, Allen, Altham too,
All of whom 'builded better than they knew',
And Secretaries, whose instinct and design
Is progress and tradition to combine.

Is 'Lord be Praised' sufficient for the man
Who sowed the seeds when M.C.C. began
Its sacred trust, and Dorset Field saw cricket,
And Thomas Lord himself prepared each 'wicket' –
Until the time, protected twice by fate,
He moved his turf on to the Eyre estate . . .
And there he made, as history has unfurled,
A ground that is the envy of the world?

About our Founder let no doubts be raised.
Let's fly our flags. Let Lord be justly Praised.

Colin Shakespeare

January, and fresh hopes rise
Like bubbles in champagne,
To head the averages
Or be the team captain.

Boys blow hands to keep warm
It's frosty and snowing,
And soon with practised arm
They are snowball throwing.

Pad up into the March nets
And practise the game indoors,
Though not the same when it's
Played on hard wooden floors.

April, and spring is here
And life's worth living, lads,
Get out your cricket gear
And buckle on your pads.

There's a nip in the air
And some zip off the pitch,
And batsmen suspect there
May be a tricky patch.

The game as it should be
June sunshine the setting,
Crowd and cricketers happy
And runs for the getting.

July scoreboard threatening
Imminent disaster
Finds a hero emerging –
A minnow to master.

This August game can crowd
An hour into a minute,
And silences grow loud
To all the glories in it.

Sponsored knock-out finals
With many fours and threes,
September festivals
With sea air and marquees.

October. With regret
We put away our gear,
We were just getting set
But leaves say autumn's here.

November, with dinners,
Talk, a tankard and toasts:
To the game, its winners;
All visitors and hosts.

December could bring
Books for your stocking,
Giving joy to those of us
Cricket crackers at Christmas.

Daniel Pettiward

Oh, take me to a cricket ground,
To hear the cricket's call,
The soothing sentimental sound
As bat belabours ball,
The thunder of a swelling score,
The rich unearthly rent,
Fuller and fiercer than a four,
Of sixes heaven-bent;
The sudden song as second slip
Concedes a finger nail,
The gentle lapping of a grip,
The brushing of a bail.
How fervently I love the sound
Of pad-enshrouded feet,
Boldly and boisterously bound
For their white-walled retreat.
But more than all I love to hear
The male magnificat,
The joyous paean, thick or clear,
The clarion call, 'HAAAAA-AT?'

II

LAUREATES AND THEIR LIKE

(From Motion back to Wordsworth)

~

Many of our Laureates have had a liking for cricket and many of their like – meaning those poets of a similar stature and renown – have liked it as well. If holders of the post have come to be mostly free of specific poetic duties – and indeed no longer receive an annual 'butt of canary wine' as such – they still tend to respond to royal and national occasions as the spirit moves them.

Therefore, it is with a great sense of gratitude and privilege that we thank the present incumbent for responding to a request to compose a poem especially for this volume. Much of Andrew Motion's work has an autobiographical touch, but usually as a vehicle to universal ideas.

From the present day we tread a backward path to Wordsworth in his pre-Victorian time. The stark realism of Ted Hughes's lines sculpted from his roots around the Mytholmroyd mill and Yorkshire Pennines is counterbalanced by the unmistakeable drollish overtones of John Betjeman as he relives his chequered career as a preparatory school master at Heddon Court, Cockfosters – just as realistic (obviously) in its own way. In 'Cricket Master' two of Betjeman's colleagues are barely disguised: Winters was Walter Summers, a pillar of a previous regime, and Barnstaple was Huxtable, the other new master. The pupil called Rice was Kenric Rice, a protégé of Betjeman's who became a lifelong friend; Vera Spencer-Clarke (Vera Moule) atypical of those dominant sporty young ladies to whom the poet was constantly attracted. In the poem Betjeman chose not to mention several jolly episodes which took place between the leaving of the Cock Inn and the desecretion of the school pitch. For a full account of some successful bets at the Haringay *(spelling at the time)* Greyhound Stadium; J. B. adopting the *persona* of a lino salesman at a pub in Piccadilly; and a stinking kipper, turn to Bevis Hillier's splendid biography, *Young Betjeman.*

Taking a detour around Cecil Day-Lewis, whose tribute to Oxford, Kent and Gloucestershire cricketer Lionel Hedges (who suffered an untimely death from septicaemia) is more concerned with his personality than with the game, we arrive in Masefield country. Masefield was a cricket enthusiast and spent much time searching for details of a match between Eleven Masefields and Eleven Lytteltons which was thought to have taken place in Shropshire sometime in the second half of the nineteenth century.

His epic poem on the Oval Test of 1882 which first appeared in *The Times,* 29 August 1956, was later included in his publication *The Bluebells and other Verse.* Subsequently, it appeared in the periodical *The Cricket Quarterly* and it is this version, which contains several changes from that which appeared in *The Times* and also a further change from the one in the collected volume, which is reproduced here.

G. K. Chesterton, the reactionary 'prince of paradox' was almost certainly too opinionated to be ever seriously considered as a Laureate, even though his views were generally hidden behind a light, energetic and whimsical style. In any case, his verse – much of which when not uproariously comic was frankly partisan and didactic – was not his only preoccupation. Chesterton's tongue-in-cheek 'Lines on a Cricket Match' relate to the visit of Sir John Squires' team 'The Invalids' to play Knotty Green (a village near the poet's Beaconsfield home) in September, 1922. Burke and Waller (named in the fifth verse) had lived in the neighbour-hood.

That lucid historian Eric Midwinter in his engaging *Quill on Willow* tells how A. E. Housman 'found no comfort in cricket, although apparently he favoured a cricket-cap for head-gear'. A solitary figure, Housman keeps an emotional distance through his spare, simple writing and conveys a sobering, pessimistic view of life that was never offset even by the eventual immense popularity of *A Shropshire Lad.* Housman, at least, wrote about cricket, albeit in a deprecating way, which was more, it would seem, than his contemporary Robert Bridges managed to do. Bridges, Poet Laureate from 1913 to 1930, is to be found in *Cricket Country* as one of Edmund Blunden's selections in his Poet's XI, 'in exquisite flannels – one of our main hopes with the bat'.

His predecessor, as a salaried member of the Royal Household, Alfred Austin, was, in the estimation of a writer for *British Authors of the Nineteenth Century*, 'appointed over the heads of abler men because of sins he had not committed'. Austin may not have been in the front ranks of poets, but he was capable of amused detachment as can be seen in his 'Epigram': 'If at cricket a cypher I get to my name, Who then can deny that I've won Oval fame?'

Tennyson's singular anti-feminist fantasia *The Princess*, of 1847, was his first long poem. The two chosen extracts pertain to the Maidstone Mechanics Institute fête held in 1842 in the grounds of Park House, Boxley, which was owned by his brother-in-law, E. L. Lushington, when, according to a local paper, 'several sets of cricketers' occupied the lower part of the ground and the visitors included 'Alfred Tennyson, Esq., the distinguished poet'. Tennyson's reign as Laureate (1850-92) has thus far been unsurpassed.

William Wordsworth composed his 'Sonnet' in the summer of 1802 after he and his sister Dorothy had landed at Dover from a visit to the Continent. The version reproduced is as it first appeared in his two-volume publication of *Poems* (1807) and not a later lection which contained slight revisions. Dorothy Wordsworth noted in her Journal of 1820: 'When within a mile of Dover, saw crowds of people at a cricket match, the numerous combatants dressed in "white-sleeved shirts", and it was in the very same field where, when we "trod the grass of England" once again, twenty years ago we had seen an Assemblage of Youths engaged in the same sport, so very like the present that all might have been the same.' The actual ground was once called Coomb Hole, situated in Buckland Parish just outside the town.

The appointment of Wordsworth as Poet Laureate in 1843 by Queen Victoria signified that the post had become the reward for eminence in poetry and since then the office has not taxed the holder with any designated tasks, more perhaps a distant sense of expectation. Before that date there was a political flavour with a number of the appointments and in some instances, very definite expectations. John Drydon was dismissed following the Revolution of 1688 for refusing the oath of allegiance. His two predecessors, William Davenant and Ben Jonson, with whom the office began in a rather unofficial way, were loosely employed and granted pensions before the laureateship became established. But none of these three literary troubadours, nor indeed their successors Shadwell, Tate, Rowe, Eusden, Cibber, Whitehead, Warton, Pye and Southey, troubled the scorers with cherished cricketing poesy.

We finish our courtly excursion with an aristocratic champion of liberty's cause. When at Harrow, Lord Byron had played cricket for the school in a match against Eton at Lord's in 1805. In a letter at the time, he wrote: 'We have played Eton, and were most confoundedly beat: however, it was of some comfort to me that I got eleven notches in the first innings and seven in the second, which was more than any of our side, except Brockman and Ipswich, could contrive to hit.'

A touch of vocational license is surely allowable (Byron actually scored seven and two) in that his own captain, John Arthur Lloyd, had opposed his selection and was of the opinion that Byron had played 'very badly'. Owing to his lameness (the tendo Achillis *[19th c. usage]* of each foot was so contracted that he could only walk on the balls of the toes) he needed a runner, but the deformity had increased his desire for athletic glory. The proximity of a team-mate called Shakespeare should have persuaded him that his talents lay in another direction. Two years later, when at Trinity College, Cambridge, Byron produced *Hours of Idleness* in which were 'Childish Recollections', a reminiscence of his time at Harrow.

D. R. A.

CRICKET

Andrew Motion

Once upon a time
I'm

A boy dragged off to cricket,
Pinned by heat in ricket–

y deck-chair arms
And safe from harm–

Except for the undone button
And yellow lips of cotton

There
At my mother's breast where,

(*Tell her!*) a glimpse of naked skin
Draws in

The danger–
ous gaze of strangers,

And
On the other hand

More than a little concerned
Having just discerned

My father, sprinting in from long on
Blinded by sun

To snatch
An almost-impossible catch,

But really about to crash
(*Watch out!*) into the equally pass–

ionate fellow haring round
From the shadier side of the ground.

Mine! They shout
When they're about

To collide,
And in that second I wonder: which side

Am I on?
Am I my father's son

Or my mother's?
Whose

Hurt matters most
And will be remembered best?

The open yellow dress, the ball
Falling, and all

My life to come
Balanced while I stayed dumb,

Knowing, whichever I chose,
I was bound to lose.

Ted Hughes

The freedom of Saturday afternoons
Starched to cricket dazzle, nagged at a theorem –
Shaggy valley parapets
Pending like thunder, narrowing the spin-bowler's angle.

The click, disconnected, might have escaped –
A six! And the ball slammed flat!
And the bat in flinders! The heart soaring!
And everybody jumping up and running –

Fleeing after the ball, stampeding
Through the sudden hole in Saturday – but
Already clapped into hands and the trap-shout
The ball jerked back to the stumper on its elastic.

Everything collapsed that bit deeper
Towards Monday.

Misery of the brassy sycamores!
Misery of the swans and the hard ripple!

Then again Yes Yes a wild YES –
The bat flashed round the neck in a tight coil,
The stretched shout snatching for the North Sea –
But it fell far short, even of Midgeley.

And the legs running for dear life, twinkling white
In the cage of wickets
Were cornered again by the ball, pinned to the crease,
Chained to the green and white pavilion.

Cross-eyed, mid-stump, sun-descending headache!
Brains sewn into the ball's hide
Hammering at four corners of abstraction
And caught and flung back, and caught, and again caught

To be bounced on baked earth, to be clubbed
Toward the wage-mirage sparkle of mills
Toward Lord Savile's heather
Toward the veto of the poisonous Calder

Till the eyes, glad of anything, dropped
From the bails
Into the bottom of a teacup,
To sandwich crusts for the canal cygnets.

The bowler had flogged himself to a dishclout.
And the burned batsmen returned, with changed faces,
Like men returned from a far journey,
Under the long glare walls of evening

To the cool sheet and the black slot of home.

John Betjeman

(*An Incident*)

My undergraduate eyes beholding,
   As I climbed your slope, Cat Hill:
Emerald chestnut fans unfolding,
   Symbols of my hope, Cat Hill.
What cared I for past disaster,
Applicant for cricket master,
Nothing much of cricket knowing,
Conscious but of money owing?
   Somehow I would cope, Cat Hill.

'The sort of man we want must be prepared
To take our first eleven. Many boys
From last year's team are with us. You will find
Their bowling's pretty good and they are keen.'
'And so am I, Sir, very keen indeed.'
Oh where's mid-on? And what is silly point?
Do six balls make an over? Help me, God!
'Of course you'll get some first-class cricket too;
The MCC send down an A team here.'
My bluff had worked. I sought the common-room,
Of last term's pipe-smoke faintly redolent.
It waited empty with its worn armchairs
For senior bums to mine, when in there came
A fierce old eagle in whose piercing eye
I saw that instant-registered dislike
Of all unhealthy aesthetes such as me.
'I'm Winters – you're our other new recruit
And here's another new man – Barnstaple.'
He introduced a thick Devonian.
'Let's go and have some practice in the nets.
You'd better go in first.' With but one pad,
No gloves, and knees that knocked in utter fright,
Vainly I tried to fend the hail of balls
Hurled at my head by brutal Barnstaple

And at my shins by Winters. Nasty quiet
Followed my poor performance. When the sun
Had sunk behind the fringe of Hadley Wood
And Barnstaple and I were left alone
Among the ash-trays of the common-room,
He murmured in his soft West-Country tones:
'D'you know what Winters told me, Betjeman?
He didn't think you'd ever held a bat.'
    The trusting boys returned. 'We're jolly glad
You're on our side, Sir, in the trial match.'
'But I'm no good at all.' 'Oh yes, you are.'
When I was out first ball, they said 'Bad luck!
You hadn't got your eye in.' Still I see
Barnstaple's smile of undisguised contempt,
Still feel the sting of Winters' silent sneer.
Disgraced, demoted to the seventh game,
Even the boys had lost their faith in me.
God guard his aesthetes. If by chance these lines
Are read by one who in some common-room
Has had his bluff called, let him now take heart:
In every school there is a sacred place
More holy than the chapel. Ours was yours:
I mean, of course, the first-eleven pitch.
Here in the welcome break from morning work,
The heavier boys, of milk and biscuits full,
Sat on the roller while we others pushed
Its weighty cargo slowly up and down.
We searched the grass for weeds, caressed the turf,
Lay on our stomachs squinting down its length
To see that all was absolutely smooth.
The prize-day neared. And, on the eve before,
We masters hung our college blazers out
In readiness for tomorrow. Matron made
A final survey of the boys' best clothes –
Clean shirts. Clean collars. 'Rice, your jacket's torn.
Bring it to me this instant!' Supper done,
Barnstaple drove his round-nosed Morris out
And he and I and Vera Spencer-Clarke,
Our strong gymnasium mistress, squashed ourselves
Into the front and rattled to The Cock.
    Sweet bean-fields then were scenting Middlesex;
Narrow lanes led between the dairy farms

To ponds reflecting weather-boarded inns.
There on the wooden bench outside The Cock
Sat Barnstaple, Miss Spencer-Clarke and I,
At last forgetful of tomorrow's dread
And gazing into sky-blue Hertfordshire.
Three pints for Barnstaple, three halves for me,
Sherry of course for Vera Spencer-Clarke.

    Pre-prize day nerves? Or too much bitter beer?
What had that evening done to Barnstaple?
I only know that singing we returned;
The more we sang, the faster Barnstaple
Drove his old Morris, swerving down the drive
And in and out the rhododendron clumps,
Over the very playing-field itself,
And then – oh horror! – right across the pitch
Not once, but twice or thrice. The mark of tyres
Next day was noticed at the Parents' Match.
That settled Barnstaple and he was sacked,
While I survived him, lasting three more terms.

    Shops and Villas have invaded
        Your chestnut quiet there, Cat Hill.
    Cricket field and pitch degraded,
        Nothing did they spare, Cat Hill.
    Vera Spencer-Clarke is married
    And the rest are dead and buried;
    I am thirty summers older,
    Richer, wickeder and colder,
        Fuller too of care, Cat Hill.

John Masefield

England's second innings against the Australian Eleven at Kennington Oval on Tuesday, 29 August 1882.

THE AUSTRALIAN ELEVEN	THE ENGLISH ELEVEN
A. C. Bannerman	R. G. Barlow
H. H. Massie	Dr. W. G. Grace
W. L. Murdoch (*Captain*)	G. Ulyett
G. J. Bonnor	A. P. Lucas
T. Horan	Hon. A. Lyttelton
G. Giffen	C. T. Studd
J. McC. Blackham	J. M. Read
T. W. Garrett	W. Barnes
H. F. Boyle	A. G. Steel
S. P. Jones	A. N. Hornby (*Captain*)
F. R. Spofforth	E. Peate

Though wayward Time be changeful as Man's will,
We have the game, we have the Oval still,
And still the Gas-Works mark the Gas-Works End
And still our sun shines and the rains descend.

Speak to me, Muse, and tell me of the game
When Murdoch's great Eleven overcame.
Laurels were tensely lost and hardly won
In that wild afternoon at Kennington,
When more than twenty thousand watchers stared
And cheered, and hoped, and anguished, and despaired.

Tell of the Day, how heavy rain had cleared
To sunshine and mad wind as noon-time neared,
Then showers (sometimes hail) on strong blasts cold,
Making a wicket good for men who bowled.
Such was the Day, when England's side went in
Just before four, with eighty-five to win.

Grace and the Captain (Hornby), led the way,
(Grace to face Spofforth) in beginning play.
Spofforth was bowling from the Gas-Works End,
Garrett across.   The opposites contend.

What was this Spofforth, called The Demon yet,
For men forget, but cannot all forget?
A tall, lean, wiry athlete inly lit
With mind, and saturnine control of it.
Is it not said, that he, with either hand,
Could fling a hen's egg, on to grass or sand,
Clear seventy yards, yet never crack the shell?

Then, when he bowled, he seemed a thing of Hell,
Writhing; grimacing; batsmen, catching breath,
Thought him no mortal man but very Death;
For no man ever knew what ball would come
From that wild whirl, save one from devildom.

Now the sharp fears came tugging at the heart,
As Cunning strove with Care and Skill with Art.

Hornby and Grace, with eighty-five to win,
Watched for some balls, then made the runs begin.

Ten had gone up, when Hornby's wicket went
(His off-stump), from a ball that Spofforth sent.
One, for fifteen; and Barlow took his place.
Barlow, our safest bat, came in with Grace:
Barlow, the wonder, famed in song and story,
The Red Rose county's well-remembered glory.
The first ball Spofforth sent him bowled him clean.
Two gone, of England's surest, for fifteen.

But Grace alone was power manifest,
(Of all men there, he is remembered best)
The great, black-bearded Doctor, watchful-eyed,
Next to our Queen, that vanished England's pride;
Grace was still in; and Ulyett joined him there.

Slowly the scoring mounted from the pair.
To Twenty, Thirty, Forty, and anon
Garrett was taken off and Boyle put on
And Spofforth changed to the Pavilion End.

Thirty odd runs and seven bats to spend,
Surely a task so simple could be done?
Ulyett and Grace seemed settled and at one.

Fifty went up, and then a marvel came,
Still something told by lovers of the game.
Spofforth sent down a ball that Ulyett hit,

No barest chance (it seemed) to mortal wit.
Snicked, high and wide it went, yet with one hand,
Blackham just caught it and dissolved the stand.
Three gone, for fifty-one.

              Lucas joined Grace,
Two partners famed in many a happy case,
But not, alas, for them, for two runs more,
Grace was caught out, at fifty-three for four,
Caught from a ball by Boyle, for Boyle had found
All he could wish in that uncertain ground.

Still thirty-two to win, with six to fall,
Lyttelton joined, and brought delight to all,
Enchanting promise came, for runs were scored,
Lucas and he put sixty on the board.
And then the conflict quieted to grim.

For master-spirits shine when hopes are dim;
Australia's best, all at their best, were there.
Light, wicket, and themselves, all bade beware.
The field were all lithe leopards on the pounce:
Each ball had a new break upon its bounce.

Twelve deadly overs followed without score.
Then came a run, then deadly maidens more.
Then Spofforth shattered Destiny's arrest.
And Lyttelton's mid stump was scattered west.

Five gone, for sixty-six, but Hope, still green,
Felt, the last five would make the last nineteen.
Had we not Steel and Studd, and Maurice Read,
Three superb bats? how could we fail to speed?
Here, Hornby, saving a reserve to win,
Re-made the order of the going-in,
Putting in steel not, Studd, at fifth man gone,
Thinking that Studd might save us later on,
If any later on might need a stay.

A strain and anguish settled on the day,
As Steel came in; but Lucas cut a four;
Not nineteen now but only fifteen more.

Steel hit his first ball back to Spofforth's hand.

Then Maurice Read gave centre and took stand . . .

Read, Surrey's pride, who ever made hope thrill
In doubtful games when things were going ill.
If Read could stay . . .
              But Spofforth's second ball
Made the mid-stump of Surrey's pride fall.
Seven men out, and fifteen still to get.

But William Barnes was never careless yet;
A watchful batsman he, though skilled to smite,
Barnes joined with Lucas in the doubtful fight.

Wild was the cheerless weather, wild the light,
Wild the contesting souls whom Hope had fired.
All the Australian team were men inspired,
Spofforth had said the matter 'could be done',
And all the live eleven were as one
The Hope was theirs, the Hope that ever wins,
The Hope that sways the tossed coin as it spins,
The starry Hope that ever makes man learn
That to the man who Hopes the luck will turn.
The twenty-two at bay were face to face.

The watchers' hearts stood still about the place.

In risk so hateful, hoping so intense,
One English watcher died there, of suspense.

Barnes hit a two; three lucky byes were run;
Ten more to win, what joy to everyone.
All cheered for every run and faces shone,
Then Lucas played a ball of Spofforth's on.
Eight of ten, out, and seventy-five the score.
'Over' was called: the fieldsmen loitered o'er.

They paused in little groups to mutter low
The secret hints the bats were not to know.
Then, watching Studd, they tautened, each in place.
Studd, our reserve, acclaimed a second Grace.

Studd stood at watch by Boyle, the Gas-Works End;
On Boyle and Barnes the minute's issues pend.

The ball had come to Boyle, who paused awhile,
To give it hand-hold in the sawdust-pile,
Then, walked intent, and as he turned to run,
Saw twenty thousand faces blurred to one,
And saw, ahead, a great bat tensely wait
The ball he held, the undelivered Fate.

He ran, he bowled, his length ball took its flight
Down the drear wicket in uncertain light,
It lifted, stuck on Barnes's glove, and leapt
To Murdoch, watching point, who caught, and kept.
Nine gone, for seventy-five, and the last man in.
Just nine more runs to tie, and ten to win.

Peate, Yorkshire's bowler, came in Barnes's place.
The last man in, with three more balls to face.
Could he but stand until Boyle's over ended,
Stand, keeping in, then all might be amended.

The other end would bat, and Studd was there;
Studd, Cambridge Studd, the bright bat debonair.
A prayer to Peate went up from England's sons:
'Keep steady, Yorkshire, Studd will get the runs.
You, who throughout the game have done so much . . .
Now, stand . . .keep in . . .put nothing to the touch.'

Peate took his stand: Boyle bowled his second ball.

A tumult of glad shouting broke from all,
Peate smote it lustily to leg, for two.

The ball returned and Boyle began anew.

Seven to tie, and eight to win the game.

Boyle launched another, subtly not the same;
And half the white-faced watchers, staring tense,
Bit their umbrella handles in suspense.

The third ball came, but like a deedless day
It passed unhit, and ceased to be in play.

An instant's respite: only one more ball
And Studd will play, unless Peate's wicket fall.

Boyle took the ball; he turned; he ran; he bowled,
All England's watching heart was stricken cold.

Peate's whirling bat met nothing in its sweep.
The ball put all his wickets in a heap;
All out, with Studd untried; our star had set,
All England out, with seven runs to get.

The crowd sat stunned an instant at the blow,
Then cheered (and none had heared men cheering so),
Cheered the great cricket that had won the game.

In flood on to the pitch the watchers came,
Spofforth and Boyle were lifted shoulder high.

Brief, brief, the glow, even of Victory.
Man's memory is but a moment green.
Chronicle now the actors in the scene,
Unmentioned yet, as Massie, who had made
Life-giving runs, with Bannerman to aid:
Jones, Giffen, Bonnor, Horan, all who shared
Those deadly hours when disaster stared.

Quickly the crowd dispersed to life's routine
Of Life and Death and wonder what they mean.

A thunder muttered and a shower fell
As twilight came with star and Vesper-bell.
Over the Oval, stamped where Spofforth bowled,
Reviving grass-blades lifted from the mould.

G. K. Chesterton

How was my spirit torn in twain
When on the field arrayed
My neighbours with my comrades strove
My town against my trade

And are the penmen players all?
Did Shakespeare shine at cricket?
And in what hour did Bunyan wait
Like Christian at the wicket?

When did domestic Dickens stand
A fireside willow wielding?
And playing cricket – on the hearth,
And where was Henry Fielding?

Is Kipling, as a flannelled fool,
Or Belloc, bowling guns,
The name that he who runs may read
By reading of his runs?

Come all; our land hath laurels too,
While round our beech-tree grows
The Shamrock of the exiled Burke
Or Waller's lovely rose.

Who ever win or lose, our flags
Of fun and honour furled,
The glory of the game shall stand
Stonewalling all the world,

While those historic types survive
For England to admire,
Twin pillars of the storied past,
The Burgess and the Squire.

A. E. Housman

XVII

Twice a week the winter thorough
   Here stood I to keep the goal:
Football then was fighting sorrow
   For the young man's soul.

Now in Maytime to the wicket
   Out I march with bat and pad:
See the son of grief at cricket
   Trying to be glad.

Try I will; no harm in trying:
   Wonder 'tis how little mirth
Keep the bones of man from lying
   On the bed of earth.

Alfred Austin

Away ye dull months! which no pleasure can yield
To the heart whose delight is the bat and the ball;
Restore me once more to the tent-covered field
And the shouts which rise high at each wicket's dread fall
Come, Health-giving pleasure! and light up the cheek
With roses which spring not from pastimes more weak.

Why mourn you the age of bright chivalry fled
While each knight of the bat has a fair one to win?
Why deem we that courage an honour of dead,
While cricket ennobles the young heart within?
Then, warriors prepare! For beauty's soft power
Your guerdon shall be in stern victory's hour.

One thought to the friends who are far on the brine
By the stout British oak born to regions of gold
May prosperity on them all smilingly shine,
And their feats in old England full often be told.
That though borne by the oak o'er the dark restless billow
They ne'er may forget its soft sister, the willow!

from THE PRINCESS (A MEDLEY)
PROLOGUE

Alfred, Lord Tennyson

Two Extracts:

. . . And there thro' twenty posts of telegraph
They flash'd saucy message to and fro
Between the mimic stations; so that sport
Went hand in hand with Science; otherwhere
Pure sport: a herd of boys with clamour bowl'd
And stump the wicket; babies roll'd about
Like tumbled fruit in grass; and men and maids
Arranged a country dance, and flew thro' light
And shadow, while the twangling violin
Struck up with Soldier-laddie and overhead
The broad ambrosial aisles of lofty lime
Made noise with bees and breeze end to end . . .

. . . Petulant she spoke, and at herself she laugh'd
A rosebud set with little wilful thorns,
And sweet as English air could make her, she:
But Walter hail'd a score of names upon her,
And "petty Ogress" and "ungrateful Puss,"
And swore he long'd at college, only long'd,
All else was well, for she-society.
They boated and they cricketed; they talk'd
At wine, in clubs, of art, of politics;
They lost their weeks; they vext the souls of deans;
They rode; they betted; made a hundred friends,
And caught the blossom of the flying terms,
But miss'd the mignonette of Vivian-place,
The little hearth-flower Lilia . . .

William Wordsworth

Dear fellow Traveller! here we are once more.
The cock that crows, the smoke that curls, that sound
Of Bells, those boys that in yon meadow ground
In white-sleev'd shirts are playing by the score,
And even this little River's gentle roar,
All, all are English. Oft I have looked round
With joy in Kent's green vales; but never found
Myself so satisfied in heart before.
Europe is yet in bounds; but let that pass,
Thought for another moment. Thou art free,
My Country! And 'tis joy enough and pride
For one hour's perfect bliss, to tread the grass
Of England once again, and hear and see,
With such a dear Companion at my side.

Lord Byron

(from 'Childish Recollections')

High, through those elms, with hoary branches crown'd,
Fair Ida's bower adorns the landscape round;
There Science, from her favour'd seat, surveys
The vale where rural Nature claims her praise;
To her awhile resigns her youthful train,
Who move in joy, and dance along the plain;
In scatter'd groups each favour'd haunt pursue:
Repeat old pastimes and discover new;
Flush'd with his rays, beneath the noontide sun,
In rival bands, between the wickets run,
Drive o'er the sward the ball with active force,
Or chase with nimble feet its rapid course.

Alonzo! best and dearest of my friends . . .

. . . when confinement's lingering hour was done,
Our sport, our studies, and our souls were one:
Together we impell'd the flying ball;
Together waited in our tutor's hall;
Together join'd in cricket's 'manly' toil.

III

CRICKET'S APPEAL

(How's This? How's That?)

~

Cricket's appeal is infinite and, it would appear, can be seen in every living form.

R. C. Scriven's joyful flight of fancy as he likens elements of the game to the natural movement of a tree and furry and feline friends is matched by the aerial navigations of a swallow and insects which distract Robert Gray from a match in which he is a player. The pastoral theme is continued by Gerald Bullett and Denis Griffiths who extol the essential timelessness of cricket before George Rostrevor Hamilton casts a cloud over the idyllic scene with an epigrammatic interruption from an urban backwater.

A. A. Milne then addresses an inanimate object – in this case, his old bat, reliving past deeds and hoping for future glory. In the aftermath of World War One, Thomas Hutchinson defends those who had preferred to play cricket rather than involve themselves in military training, pointing out that the 'flannelled fools' responded when needed and, because of disciplines learned on the field, were better equipped to cope with the demands of the task. The game can be interpreted meta-phorically as a battlefield of life inherent in growing up in 'Boy at a Cricket Match' by Hugo Williams. Whereas Williams's youngster is reluctant to surrender maternal protection, Norman Gale's 'lad' adopts a paternal pose towards his 'dad'.

The section concludes with three grumpy old men. The first in 'Ninth Wicket' by A. P. Herbert continually bemoans his fate and we are reminded of the character 'in a dreadful funk' of the *Punch* cartoons. Whatever his mental state, though, he 'can't' be *kept* from 'this game'.

Crusoe's (Robertson-Glasgow) 'One-Way Critic' is to be found in any group of spectators. What a pity that not all such ingrates are accosted similarly. Finally, John Bunting castigates the invasion of modern-day technology and media practice in 'Can we know too much?' Answer, if you must . . .

D. R. A.

R. C. Scriven

Light
as the flight
of a bird on the wing
my feet skim the grass
and my heart seems to sing:
'How green is the wicket.
It's cricket.
It's spring.'
Maybe the swallow
high in the air
knows what I feel
when I bowl fast and follow
the ball's twist and bounce.
Maybe the cat
knows what I feel like, holding my bat
and ready to pounce.
Maybe the tree
so supple and yielding
to the wind's sway
then swinging back, gay,
might know the way
I feel when I'm fielding.

Oh, the bird, the cat and the tree:
they're cricket, they're me.

Robert Gray

Once, playing cricket, beneath a toast-dry hill,
I heard the bat crack, but watched a moment longer
a swallow, racing lightly, just above the ground, I was
impressed by the way
the bird skimmed, fast as a cricket ball.
It was decided for me within that instant
where my interests lay.

And the trajectories at dusk of random moths and loud
decisive swallow
will often still preoccupy me, until dew occludes the air.

Gerald Bullett

Flowing together by devious channels
From farm and brickyard, forest and dene,
Thirteen men in glittering flannels
Move to their stations out on the green.

Long-limbed Waggoner, stern, unbudging,
Stands like a rock behind the bails,
Dairyman umpire, gravely judging,
Spares no thought for his milking-pails.

Two to the boundary, a four and a six,
Put the spectators in fear of their lives:
Shepherd the slogger is up to his tricks,
Blithely unwary of weans and wives.

Lord of the manor makes thirty-four,
Parson contributes, smooth and trim,
A cautious twelve to the mounting score:
Leg-before-wicket disposes of him.

Patient, dramatic, serious, genial,
From over to over the game goes on,
Weaving a pattern of hardy perennial
Civilization under the sun.

Denis Griffiths

This cricket is leisurely continuing
The summer heritage of English fields,
The batsman's artistry, the bowler's guile.

Telegraph please: someone changes the numbers,
Somnambulists assimilate the score
As cricket is leisurely continuing.

A large-limbed bowler with a lumbering pace
Jumps at the wicket and whirls a brawny arm:
The batsman leans deflecting ball to space

With perfect elegance and practised charm
Accompanied by lazy clapping from distant chairs
Circling the cricket leisurely continuing.

Tea at a hundred and twenty for six:
The home side faces the dazzling dipping sun:
The batsman opening pulls his blue-ringed cap

And wristily cuts the medium pacer through
The crouching slips and runs are briskly run
As cricket leisurely continues with
The batsman's cunning and the bowler's guile.

George Rostrevor Hamilton

Where else, you ask, can England's game be seen
Rooted so deep as on the village green?
Here, in the slum, where doubtful sunlight falls
To gild three stumps chalked on decaying walls.

A. A. Milne

When Vesper trails her gown of grey
   Across the lawn at six or seven
The diligent observer may
   (Or may not) see, athwart the heaven,
An aimless rodent on the wing. Well, that
   Is (probably) a Bat . . .
In any case I shall not sing of that.

O Willow, in our hours of ease
   (That is to say, throughout the Winter),
I take you sometimes on my knees,
   And careless of the frequent splinter,
Caress you tenderly, and sigh, and say,
   "Ye Gods, how long till May?"

And so as soon as April's here
   I do not sob for Spring to show its
Pale daffodils and all the dear
   Old flowers that keep the minor poets;
I sing it just because a month (about)
   Will find *you* fairly out.

Revered, beloved, O you whose job
   Is but to serve throughout the season
To make, if so it be, the Blob,
   And not (thank heaven!) to ask the reason –
To stand, like Mrs. Hemans' little friend,
   Undoubting to the end.

Old Willow, what a tale to tell –
   Our steady rise, from small beginnings,
Ab ovo usque-usque-well,
   To eighty-four, our highest innings;
(Ah, me, that crowded hour of glorious lives –
   Ten of them, all from drives!)

Once only have you let me in,
    Through all the knocks we've had together;
That time, when wanting four to win,
    I fairly tried to tonk the leather–
And lo! a full-faced welt, without the least
    Warning went S.S.E.

A painful scene. In point of fact
    I'm doubtful if I ought to hymn it;
Enough to say you went and cracked,
    And left me thinking things like "Dimmit"
(And not like "Dimmit"), as I heard slip call
    "Mine!" and he pouched the ball.

Do you remember, too, the game
    One August somewhere down in Dorset
When, being told to force the same,
    We straightway started in to force it . . .
For half an hour or so we saw it through,
    And scratched a priceless two;

Or how the prayer to play for keeps
    And hang the runs, we didn't need 'em,
So stirred us, we collected heaps
    With rather more than usual freedom;
Fifty in fourteen minutes – till a catch
    Abruptly closed the match?

Well, well – the coming years (if fine)
    Shall see us going even stronger;
So pouring out the oil and wine,
    Let's sit and drink a little longer;
Here's to a decent average of ten!
    (Yours is the oil. Say when . . .)

When Morning on the heels of Night
    Picks up her shroud at five and after,
The diffident observer might
    (or might not) see, beneath a rafter,
A pensive rodent upside down. Well, that
    Is (possibly) a Bat . . .
In any case I have not sung of that.

Thomas Hutchinson

A poet once, of so great fame
That the whole Empire knew his name,
In angry terms denounced the game –
    Our English game of cricket;
And in defiance of the rules
Of loyalty taught in the schools,
Them stigmatised as "flannelled fools,"
    Who loved bat, ball, and wicket.

He thought, in sooth, that every one,
As soon as his day's task was done,
With sword or rifle, lance or gun,
    Should drill-drill-drill till nightfall,
Rather than wing the hours away
In what – to him – was childish play,
For war was sure to come some day,
    And then right would to might fall.

And war did come, without a doubt,
And fleet and army hurried out;
Alas! they failed the foe to rout,
    And volunteers were needed.
Then cast aside were bat and ball,
And "flannelled fools," both great and small,
Responded to their country's call,
    And many a gallant deed did.

The game demands a watchful eye,
A cleanly life and courage high,
A fearlessness of dangers nigh,
    A discipline, a training.
And thus the men who it had played,
On forlorn hopes sped unafraid,
Not e'en by death itself dismayed,
    Though shot and shell were raining.

In war as peace, in peace as war,
Such the ideals of cricket are,
To mankind it's a guiding star,
    And pessimism cureth;
Of pastimes the unchallenged king
To all it dauntless health doth bring,
And so, despite satiric sting,
Loud and more loud its praise we'll sing,
    As long as life endureth.

Hugo Williams

Holding his hands like strange ivy,
He twines them round his mother's broad shadow;
She is his tree, only with her he grows.
For him she keeps her leaves, her first love,
All the year round. He does not know.

(The sun coming through the branches, green,
And leaves, like warm water unseen.)

Turning horizon-smiling eyes around,
He sees the sky aghast with light
Between the trees, oppressive boughs, and sees
The bowler flex his arms like wings
And knows a real need for flight.

Norman Gale

When I was small
  My Father began,
With the help of a ball,
  To make me a man.

When I was tall
  And broad I was glad,
With the help of a ball,
  To keep him a lad.

A. P. Herbert

The bowling looks exceptionally sound,
The wicket seems unusually worn,
The balls fly up or run along the ground;
I rather wish that I had not been born.
I have been sitting here since two o'clock;
My pads are both inelegant and hot;
I do not want what people call my 'knock',
And this pavilion is a sultry spot.
I shall not win one clap or word of praise,
I know that I shall bat like a baboon;
And I can think of many better ways
In which to spend a summer afternoon.
I might be swimming in a crystal pool;
I might be wooing some delicious dame;
I might be drinking something long and cool –
I can't imagine why I play this game.

Why is the wicket seven miles away,
And why have I to walk to it alone?
I hope my borrowed bat will drive today –
I ought to buy a weapon of my own.
I wonder if this walk will ever cease;
They should provide a motor-car or crane
To drop the batsman on the popping-crease
And, when he's out, convey him back again.
Is it a dream? Can this be truly me,
Alone and friendless in a waste of grass?
The fielding side are sniggering, I see,
And long-leg sort of shudders as I pass.
How very small and funny I must look!
I only hope that no one knows my name,
I might be in a hammock with a book –
I can't imagine why I play this game.

Well, here we are. We're feeling rather ill.
What is this pedant of an umpire at?
Middle and off, or centre – what you will!
It cannot matter where I park the bat.
I look around me in a knowing way
To show that I am not to be cajoled;
I shall play forward gracefully and pray . . .
I *have* played forward and I am not bowled!
I do not like the wicket-keeper's face,
And why are all the fielders crowding round?
The bowler makes an imbecile grimace,
And mid-off makes a silly whistling sound.
These innuendoes I could do without;
They mean to say the ball defied the bat,
They indicate that I was nearly out . . .
Well darn their impudence, I know all that.
Why am I standing in this comic pose,
Hemmed in by men that I should like to maim?
I might be lying in a punt with Rose –
I can't imagine why I play this game.

And there are people sitting over there
Who fondly hope that I shall make a run;
They cannot guess how blinding is the glare;
They do not know the ball is like a bun.
But courage, heart! We have survived a ball;
I pat the pitch to show that it is bad;
We are not such a rabbit after all;
Now we shall show them what is what, my lad!
The second ball is very, very swift;
It breaks and stands steeply in the air;
It looks at me, and I could swear it sniffed;
I gesture at it – but it is not there!
Ah, what a ball! Mind you, I do not say
That Bradman, Hobbs, and Ranji in his prime,
Rolled into one, and that one on his day,
Might not have got a bat to it in time . . .
But long-stop's looking for my middle stump,
And I am walking in a world of shame;
My captain has addressed me as a chump!
I can't imagine why I play this game.

R. C. Robertson-Glasgow

Upon the groaning bench he took his seat –
Sunlight and shadow on the dew-blessed grass –
He spread the *Daily Moan* beneath his feet,
Hitched to his eye an astigmatic glass,
Then, like a corn-crake calling to an owl
That knows no answer, he began to curse,
Remarking, with an unattractive scowl,
'The state of cricket goes from bad to worse;
Where are the bowlers of my boyhood's prime?
Where are the batsmen of the pristine years?
Where are the fieldsmen of the former time?'
And, as he spoke, my eyelids filled with tears;
For I perhaps alone, knew they were dead,
Mynn an old myth, and Hambledon a name,
And it occurred to me that I had read
(In classroom) 'All things always are the same';
So, comfort drawing from this maxim, turned
To the myopic moaner on the seat;
A flame of rage, not pity, in me burned,
Yet I replied in accents clear and sweet -
'There *were* no bowlers in your boyhood's prime,
There *were* no batsmen in the pristine years,
There *were* no fieldsmen in that former time' –
My voice grew firm, my eyes were dry of tears -
'*Your* fathers cursed the bowlers you adored,
Your fathers damned the batsmen of your choice,
Your fine, ecstatic rapture they deplored,
There was the *One-Way Critic's* ageless voice,
And their immortal curse is yours today,
The croak which kills all airy Cricket Dryads,
Withers the light on tree and grass and spray,
The strangling fugue of senile jeremiads.'

I ceas'd; and turn'd to Larwood's bounding run,
And Woolley's rapier flashing in the sun.

John Bunting

Part of our national summer game's appeal
    lies in its mysteries that tease and tax
the intellect, so stern resolved defence
    intrigues as much as lusty, bold attacks
and this starts when white forms cascade down steps
    onto the grass, for we should know each face
without a spooky voice to tell who bowls
    with left arm guile or pounding right arm pace
while batsmen too should have mysterious airs
    that test those well kept score cards, while good eyes
should know who scored and from the umpire's signs
    sort out the fours and singles from the byes.

We do not need the irritant of sound
    as some oaf's radio blasts ball by ball
the Blofeld wisdom, Martin-Jenkins's thoughts
    on who should score and who should just stonewall
and when two teams in gaudy jazzed up strip
    compete in games when overs are curtailed,
it is quite obvious who took which catch
    and who is bowling and which batsman failed;
and why on salad days have needless haste
    to have the first team's overs bowled before
some preset time, since people paid to see
    which fifty overs yields the highest score?

I well remember mornings when I strained
    to hear McGilvray from the Melbourne Test
describe the struggle of the England team
    against the pace of Lindwall at his best,
and listened with a boy's devoted ear
    as cricket's legends cracked through the haze
so in my mind I saw a Hammond drive
    conjured from words spun in a Cardus phrase;
on misty photographs in black and grey,
    taken when action made the tension climb,
left there forever in dramatic pose
    were sporting rivals in suspended time.

Soon came the season when the spirits rose
     fresh as the moment that saw Winter pass
and earth felt warmth from Spring's weak welcome rays
     that wakened hedgerows and the sleeping grass;
I searched the papers for late April games,
     cold days of fielding with the fingers numb,
this was a price that cricket players paid
     staking a claim on languid days to come;
then real excitement as the tourists docked,
     who were the bowlers and the ones who'd score
on English pitches that they'd never seen
     apart from those who had toured here before.

Some would soon join those mystics of the game,
     the magic legends who adorn their age
with spells that last a lifetime and beyond
     the day when even famous leave the stage;
but these are frantic times and series played
     will fade soon after tawdry cups are won
so will our grandsons' thoughts rush down the years
     to live again those fond days in the sun?
or will his mind be tarnished since he knows
     that famed top scorer was caught out first ball
for as he raised his bat to thank the crowd
     the umpire's blunder was displayed to all.

But do we need to know about these gaffs
     that aren't reversed despite repeated plays
they undermine the umpire as the law
     and so encourage players' rude displays.
but then, perhaps, most television thrives
     on some dissent to give the game more bite,
for all we know when play is seen as dull
     the network longs for streakers or a fight!
as stripes appear in blue right up the pitch
     so all but umpires see where each ball lands,
then stumps are faded in as pads fade out
     to fuel a hot debate high in the stands.

Unless some laptop image can be seen
   by umpires long before they must decide,
the replay after serves no useful role
   and on the ground it's use should be denied;
if more high tech takes over at the crease
   then let the umpire merely count the balls,
while magic eyes and Cyclops runs the game
   they'd put back bails each time the wicket falls;
but this is surely not the way ahead
   for our great game deserves to keep its soul,
return to roots, let virtuosos weave
   their batting magic as the craftsmen bowl.

IV

TIME REMEMBERED

(The Broad Sweep)

~

The time capsule first goes back to 1706 when a graduate of King's College, Cambridge, proficient in Latin, persuaded a London publisher to produce a collection entitled *Musae Juveniles,* in which was the earliest full description, yet found, of a cricket match. 'In Certamen Pilae' by William Goldwin has attracted at least two English translations and the one reproduced here, which first appeared in 1923, is by H. P.-T. (Percy Thomas), or to use his own nickname, 'Hippo-Pott-Thomas'. Thomas's interpretation is more literally based than the often-seen artistic translation by Harold Perry which came out in the previous year.

Staying in the eighteenth century, albeit with a look through the telescope of twentieth-century scholar, Edmund Blunden, we then view an exercise in period script based at Merchant Taylors' School. Published in *The Gentleman's Magazine* at St John's Gate, Clerkenwell, London, in 1756, 'The Game of Cricket' draws parallels between the element of chance in what happens on the field of play and the vicissitudes of life. Percy Thomas, mentioned above, thought that this anonymous offering was possibly a retouched early work of James Love (Dance) of 'Cricket: an heroic poem' fame.

Richard Stilgoe then injects some welcome levity with his prehistoric-sounding 'It all began at Hambledon', though, of course, he knows that it didn't and what's more he knows that we know that it didn't and furthermore we ... Enough! There follow verses on four matches or occasions at local level that reached wider readership through the columns of national newspapers or magazines which, in turn, precede a rhyme from 'Century', the pseudonym of a young lady, who adopts a journalistic role in 'Choosing an All-England XI in 1896'.

Then come two sets of rarely-seen verses from Albert Craig, the Yorkshire-born 'Surrey Poet', who made an income by declaiming and selling his rhythmic wares for a penny a time on the county grounds of southern England and mostly at Kennington Oval. Craig was known for his sparkling repartee, but not for the quality of his typical and cheerful versifying. And yet, maybe he has been done an injustice, for these two examples reveal a depth of feeling and sensitivity that is foreign to generally accepted opinion. Craig's 'Notts v Surrey' is fundamentally imaginary. (Incidentally, when the poem was written each side had either finished top or equal top of the County XIs for the past nine seasons.) Nevertheless, seemingly one can hear embroidered echoes of his own early experiences mixed together with every man's fantasy. This is particularly noticeable in the adopted role of the boy berated by the parson who eventually triumphs in his chosen profession. The simple, moralistic and indeed timely Victorian device was used frequently by Craig in his verses and one wonders whether it was some kind of subconscious act of self-atonement for youthful misdemeanours. Perhaps it is better though not to try and look under too many stones and instead just enjoy the gatherings from the surface.

An uncomplicated reminiscence of youth comes from the pen of Thomas Moult before the sight, in a London shop window, of Yorkshire and England opening batsman John Brown's bat, with which he made his only Test hundred in Australia during the tour of 1894/95, which similarly encouraged Alfred Cochrane to brush the dust off his Latin primer with 'Arma Virumque' (Arms and the Man).

Henry Newbolt again uses Latin for his crusading 'Vitai Lampada', which is probably his most famous poem, although 'Drake's Drum' is a close contender. The sentiments expressed by Newbolt are unfashionable today, even abhorrent to some. However, Newbolt, a member of the establishment and a friend of the influential, was no hearty, bluff, or overtly patriotic figure; rather he was a gentle, courteous intellectual. For him, 'Vitai Lampada' quickly dimmed. On a lecture tour in Canada in 1923, his clarion call became, what he called 'a Frankenstein monster'. 'I created [it] thirty years ago and I find it falling on my neck at every street corner. In vain do I explain what is poetry; they roar for "play up!": they put it on their flags, and on their war memorials and tombstones: it's their National Anthem.' One is reminded of Newbolt's contemporary, Sir Edward Elgar and his 'March: Pomp and Circumstance No. 1'. The composer found that there were not really enough proper circumstances to warrant all that pomp and very soon wearied of the endless repetition of 'Land of Hope and Glory', and of his identification solely with what he referred to as 'that bloody tune'.

Albatrosses and nationalistic fervour aside, war provokes more sombre messages. For us, they arrive through the words of Arnold Wall, Ralph Westwood Moore and someone who, in literary terms, has been an unknown soldier. The authorship of 'The Cricketers of Flanders' more than once has been described as 'anonymous' and is, in fact, now known to be the hand of Royal Fusilier, James Norman Hall.

Back on the field of play, Humphrey Clucas's 'History' gives a true perspective of time as does Anthony Greenstreet in 'The Old Boys' Match' and in between C. A. Alington recalls two close encounters – by way of the result and in proximity – at Lord's in 1928. On the 'Wednesday evening' of 11 July, during the University Match, the last Oxford pair, C. K. Hill-Wood, whose ginger hair was described as 'head of carrots', and E. T. Benson, stayed together for half an hour to save the game. Two days later, Eton were struggling against Harrow. Having had a deficit of over a hundred runs at the end of their first innings, they lost two quick wickets when going in again. By dint of a great recovery, however, they set a target of 308 in three and a half hours and eventually emerged victorious by 28 runs.

For modern-era poets, Dannie Abse, John Whitworth and Gavin Ewart, inspiration came from specific events in cricket's first-class arenas: Abse cherishing Glamorgan's Cyril Smart smiting 32 runs off one over from Gerald Hill of Hampshire at Cardiff in 1935; Whitworth's seventeenth-century style homage to David Gower on the occasion of his first Test century against New Zealand at the Oval in 1978; and Ewart's classic pindaric ode in honour of England's epic victory over Australia in the third Test at Headingley in 1981.

'Cricket' by Chris Bendon might be described as post-modernist and is an affectionate satire of a British upbringing. The poet is lying semi-comatosed on a grassy mound beyond the boundary. Images flit in and out of his consciousness as he plays with puns: the clock of the willow as time is suspended, the air wobbling in the heat as remnants of Empire slither away; from the Indian sub-continent looking upwards to the Northern Hemisphere where a boyish Heaven still exists; the ungainly coffin-like instruments of the musicians in the bandstand redolent of an Edwardian era and the throes of World War One; political propaganda and the destruction of thousands of lives until the final checkmate. The moon can be seen before the sun has set. The focus is blurred. Has it all been a Greek tragedy?

'The Railings' by Roger McGough was motivated by memories of his father's distant spectating when he was playing cricket at Crosby Grammar School in Liverpool. Apparently his dad, who worked in the Docks, felt he had no place within the school precincts standing by the pavilion with all those other 'posh' parents watching their sons play and miss, and so he remained outside the railings where he happened to be 'just passing'. The poem is succinct and infinitely touching.

Mention of infinity paradoxically leads to a conclusion. 'Time Remembered' can only apply to 'Futuristic Cricket' if space travel overtakes the clock. In this age of Martian exploration who can say whether that is too fanciful a notion?

D. R. A.

William Goldwin

Springtime anew, with mild and limpid air
Smiling, with kindness coaxes earth to bear,
And active feet to sport where fields spread wide;
A team of youths, with crooked bats supplied,
By cunning hand trimm'd fitly for their game,
Thither troop gaily down: I sing whose fame.
　　This one can swiftly throw across the ground,
Watches alertly, quickly scours around
And turns about: Far with the zephyrs throws
This one the ball, or yet against rude blows;
A third has skill that no one else exceeds,
Along the pitch the ball his poised hand speeds
To spill before the stroke its flight can beat.
　　The coming rival side with glee these greet
And fall to parley, – presently to wage
A little squabble; artful, they'd engage
Each by own laws. An old grey-headed chap
Is there to quell the wrangle, by good hap;
He joins the throng, lends an impartial ear
To judge, and, – though he's laid by cricket gear,
So lov'd, long since, he minds its institute, –
Lays down the Law and settles the dispute.

The pitch then's chosen, where the meadows start
More flat. Each end, the proper length apart
And opposite, twin uprights, cleft atop,
With little interval between, upcrop,
Thrust in the ground; a clean bail caps their ends,
A bar on the contest's fate depends,
And well it needs detending: Leather Sphere
May force its downfall; if by chance severe
She's straightly aimed, and strikes the wicket's stay,
It falls, and its shamed guardian slinks away.
　　Two umpires stand, each in convenient place,
Resting on bats, to see one touch the crease
As law directs, else running is in vain.

And more aloof, where they have vision plain,
Two trusted friends squat on the rising floor
To notch, with knives on sticks, the mounting score.
    The teams and 'pointed captains, intermixt,
Sort out, and one a coin, casts up betwixt
To settle which the opening hands shall get,
This side or that. Not in position yet
The striplings wait around; till one well-tried
Selects the bowlers and for t'other side
A stopper who is sure with either hand
To take and hold. The rest bide his command.
And with what care they're placed! Though mighty smart
To watch, throw, sprint, these youths, when once they start,
They quiver now while they await the game
With thudding hearts, yet all athirst for fame.
    The jolly game is set. By meed of birth
Two gentlemen go in; both bats of worth.
Play called, the lively ball, propelled with strength,
From bowler's end flies down the wicket's length,
Scouring a passage swift. The striker's limbs
Flex as he marks the course the missile skims
And, as it bounds, with an unfailing slash
His lusty arms descend, afar to crash
The sounding sphere. Up through the air it heaves
And, whizzing on, the vault of heaven cleaves.
    But, eyes upturned, a seeker all intent,
With outspread hands awaits the ball's descent,
Joyously grasps and deftly throws it in,
To boist'rous plaudits. Cover'd with chagrin
The striker's silent comrades sit deprest.
Bad start! But one man out daunts not the rest.
Keen to avenge the accident, a friend,
With vaunts of that intention takes his end.
Still fortune mocks, and barely three or four
Deliveries he meets: three stops, no more,
When one he makes a rash attempt to thump
Evades his menace and disturbs a stump.

He with vex'd looks throws down his implement,
Denouncing Fate and stars malevolent.
Meanwhile a neighbour stubborn effort makes
Their drooping fortunes, for their common sakes,
To yet repair; but he as well is soon
In the game's drift, for, trying twice to run,
In turning on his track he slides his toes.
Unhappy work; He o'er the wicket goes
Flat, and the quaking earth beneath him groans.
Huge hulk! The yokels roar in mirthful tones.
The rest take hands to keep possession still
Prevents their object, and they all go back
With hopeless visages and hearts grown slack.

But better fortune smile upon the foe's
Going in. They flog the ball with constant blows.
Hot work! They sweat profusely at their deeds
Till, by and by, as the stern game proceeds
Propitiously, one stroke divides the scores.
A forceful blow: the ball up heavenward soars,
Fetches the needed mark, and crowning brings.
Long worked for Victory spreads her strident wing,
And with far-echoing shouts the welkin rings.

Translated by H. P.-T.

COUPLETS FOR LEARNERS
AS THEY MIGHT HAVE BEEN WRITTEN
IN 1753

Edmund Blunden

'Tis not alone the Notches that accrue,
My Son, in Cricket's noble Game, to you,
Nor tale of Wickets by your Art bowl'd down
Which shall your Name among your Fellows crown.
Success, I grant, is much, and vig'rous Play
With Cunning mixt must mark a Conqu'ror's Way;
For who can doubt, the farther drivn' the Ball,
The more the Runs? but Totals are not all.
It must be still our Aim to beat the Bat
When our Opponents take their Turns with that,
And yet our Victory will be dearly gain'd
Were nothing of more lasting Worth attain'd.
Be this your Counsel then: Succeed with Grace,
And should you fail, fail with a gen'rous Face;
Inquire what more that Runs your Bat may give,
For when the Runs are past, the Style may live;
Express a happy Chance in ev'ry Stroke,
Nor like some Spinster at the small Coals poke;
Be fair in Bowling, just to Life and Limb,
The Batsman's Knuckles still belong to him,
And all admire his Downfall caus'd by Thought
Rather than Terror by fast Bumpers wrought.
When fielding out, although the Task be dry,
Still watch the Game with sharp yet loving Eye;
Pursue the fleeting Orb as Hounds the Hare,
And when the fierce Hit flies into the Air
With merry manner risk your Fingers there.
Deny no Praise even if 'tis at your Cost,
A Match that makes for Friendship is well lost,
And Consolation to th'unlucky speak,
Which you yourself may wish another Week.
E'en lend your Bat, and if it come back chipped,
Betray no slightest Hint of being hipp'd.

And thus in all observe that Cricket grows
Not out of mere Results as some suppose
But from sweet Temper, equable Address,
Friendship with Fortune, handy Willingness;
As when the Gods on bright Olympus met.

Anon

(*The Gentleman's Magazine*, 1756)

Peace and her arts, we sing – her genial pow'r
Can give the breast, the tho't to tow'r,
The' guiltless not inglorious souls inspires,
And boasts less savage, not less noble fires,
Such is her sway, when Cricket calls her train,
The sons of labour, to the accustom'd plain,
With all the hero's passion and desire,
They swell, they glow, they envy and admire:
Despair and resolution reign by turns;
Suspense torments, and emulation burns,
See! in due rank dispos'd, intent they stand,
In act to start – the eye, the foot, the hand,
Still active, eager, seem conjoin'd in one;
Tho fixt, all moving, and while present gone.
In ancient combat, from the Partheon steed,
Not more unerring slew the barbed reed
Then rolls the ball, with vary'd vigour play'd,
Now levell'd, whizzing o'er the springing blade,
Now tofst to rise more fatal from the ground,
Exact and faithful to th'appointed bound,
Yet vain its speed, yet vain its certain aim;
The wary batsman watches o'er the game;
Before his stroke the leathern circle flies,
Now wheels oblique, now mounting threats the skies,
Nor yet less the wary batsman's blow,
Is intercepted by the circling foe,
Too soon the nimble arm retorts the ball,

Or ready fingers catch it in its fall:
Thus various art with vary'd fortune strives,
And with each changing chance the sport revives.
Emblem of many-colour'd life — the state
By Cricket-rules discriminates the great:
The outward side, who place and profit want,
Watch to surprize, and labour to supplant:
While those who taste the sweets of present winnings,
Labour as heartily to keep their innings,
On either side the whole great game is play'd,
Untry'd no shift is left, unsought no aid:
Skill vies with skill, & pow'r contends with pow'r,
And squint-eyed prejudice computes the score,
In private life, like single-handed play'rs,
We get less notches, but we meet less cares.
Full many a lusty effort, which at court
Would fix the doubtful issue of the sport,
Wide of its mark, or impotent to rise,
Ruins the rash, and disappoints the wise,
Yet all in public, and in private, thrive
To keep the ball of action still alive,
And just to all, when each his ground has run,
Death tips the wicket, and the game is done.

Richard Stilgoe

Written for an edition of Highway *with Brian Johnston.*

At Hambledon, upon this spot, high up on Hampshire's chalk,
A million, trillion years ago, the dinosaurs did walk.
The great Gattingosauruses – short-legged, with thick necks.
That fearsome giant carnivore, Bothamosaurus Rex.
Across this very turf they strode – one short and fat, one tall –
And came across an ancient pub they call the Bat & Ball.
Declared Gattingosaurus – "There's a field and a pub,
It's the Ice Age and it's raining – we should start a cricket club!"

So it all began at Hambledon, a billion years ago –
Brian Johnston saw it, and Brian ought to know.

Bothamosaurus Rex then found a Pterodactyl's egg,
And rubbed it on his scaly tail, so it would swing to leg.
He went and pulled three trees up from a nearby Hampshire thicket –
And cried, "Look, Gatt – the wheel!" Gatt said "Rubbish – that's a wicket".
And then Gattingosaurus found a club of slate so vast,
So long and wide from side to side that no ball could get past.
Bothamosaurus Rex then took the obvious revenge,
And made the wickets bigger – which is how we got Stonehenge.

Yes it all took place at Hambledon, as the world began to wake,
And Brian Johnston watched while eating prehistoric cake.

They batted through the Stone Age, the scores became colossal
Boycottodon was in so long he turned into a fossil.
They said, "If only we had Hickthyosaurus in the side –
But he hasn't been here long enough, and isn't qualified".

Eventually the dinosaurs of Hambledon got sent
A letter postmarked London (which was forwarded from Kent).
"The Mammoth Cricket Club (that is the M.C.C. to you)
Is happy to inform you that your membership's come through".
And so the dinosaurs marched off to London in their hordes –
They're not extinct at all – they're all alive and well at Lord's.
They sleep in the pavilion, dreaming neolithic dreams
And evr'y now and then wake up, and pick the England teams –

But it all began at Hambledon – it did – I do declare –
Brian Johnston told me, and he knows, 'cos he was there.

31 ON THE SECOND CRICKET MATCH BETWEEN MITCHAM AND COULSDON, PLAYED AT SMITHAM BOTTOM, SEPTEMBER 21ST AND 22ND, 1791

Anon

Mitcham! well done, my boys, a second time,
Thy glory now must still extend my rhyme.
Now Coulsdon is by Mitcham beat once more,
And now she glories as she did before,
Your triumph, neighbours, now it is complete,
Coulsdon was fairly by eight wickets beat.

Tho' Coulsdon first got five times ten,
It was exceeded by the Mitcham men,
Lads of Mitcham, the most gallant 'leven,
Fairly headed them by five times seven.
The Coulsdon next they just got forty-four,
And all the 'leven they could get no more.

The Mitcham men they little had to do,
The work was fairly done in wickets two;
Four Mitcham lads advanced upon the plain,
And wielded not the cricket bat in vain;
Tho' forty-four Coulsdon had gained complete,
Soon Mitcham gained forty-five to beat.

Sanders, the Tipstaff, Hinckley, all gained fame,
And as for Mitcham lads they closed the game,
'Twas Hinckley's lot to strike the final blow,
To gain the notch that proved their overthrow;
They fairly showed how Mitcham men could play,
And gallantly they early closed the day.

Anon

Among the other demonstrations of loyalty displayed in Glasgow in honour of the Coronation, were those of the truly loyal and patriotic King William IV Cricket Club (a blue printed chemise, bearing the impress of our Gracious Sovereign's head, a crown, anchor and W. R. IV) assembled on the Green in the morning, having their 'field' streaming with various flags etc. After enjoying the 'noble game' for a couple of hours, these true blues 'adjourned the diet' till evening, when they met in Easton's 'Royal Tavern', to celebrate His Majesty's Coronation in a Crown bowl, and drank a hearty and loyal bumper to the health and happiness of our beloved Monarch and his consort, the Queen. During the evening, (borrowing two hours from the morning) which was spent with much glee and harmony, the following verses, composed for the occasion by a Member of the club were recited, and obtained a hearty reception:

Come, Fielders, round the table *pop*,

A health to our good King to *tip*;
Be every one, though strange, *long stop*,
But do not take to *leg* or *slip*.

Grim care has often held the bat,
And boasted of her doleful *winnings*;
But we will *run her out* of that,
And jovial mirth shall have his *innings*.

Should fortune dare to take the *ball* up,
Resolv'd to *knock our wickets down*,
We'll *keep our ground*, nor fancy all up,
But smile and laugh at Fortune's frown.

Though fiends themselves should be her *fielders*,
And use all cunning *out to catch us* –
We'll show them we are good *bat* wielders,
And how unfit they are to *match* us.

Then come, my boys, your glasses fill –
Let none at liquor take the dumps;
But drink regardless of *the Bill*,
As long as he can keep his *stumps*.

Here's then a health to good King William,
Long may he live to grace the Crown;
Let us a flowing *Crown* bowl fill him,
And in it all but loyalty drown.

If foes or traitors dare approach
May William prove a *striker* stout;
And, ere the knaves can *score a notch,*
Bowl every rascal of them out.

A Single Dorset

Haste, gentle Muse, O hither haste,
   And lend me your assistance;
Or how can I presume to sing
   While you are at a distance;
No humble theme inspires my pen,
   No childish play my story;
For Cricket is the game I sing,
   And in that game I glory.

Near where Stonehenge uprears its head,
   In antiquated grandeur,
A cricket ground's been lately made,
   Which to the scene adds splendour;
And on this ground, the other day,
   There was a match decided;
Which many persons went to see,
   As Mr. L. – and I did.

The Stonehenge 'gainst the Anglesea,
   Or Wiltshire versus Dorset;
Good fellows as you'd wish to meet,
   On both sides – standing or sat; –
The ground's mark'd out – the wickets' pitch'd –
   The Stonehenge have the inning;
The point -the slip – each man's in place,
And now the game's beginning.

The Anglesea are in the field,
   And Floyer bowls the over;
Well bowl'd – well play'd – aye well done all,
From long stop to points cover!
Now Marsh hits out, the ball being wide,
   See there it goes *"a fourer;"*
Right over leg long field it flies,
   "To Marsh four" – writes the scorer –

And now the *over being o'er*,
    The ball is held by Bower;
"*A Lady's Bower?*" it may be so,
    Although I do not know her:
"Take care who's in, or through the game
Your bat you will not carry;"
Down go the stumps, and all the field
    Sing out "*well bowl'd by Harry!*"

"*Another and a better man*" –
    "'Tis Poulter" – where's a fitter?
See how the field's extended now,
He's such a devilish hitter!
"Look to the leg," aye there it goes,
    One -two -three -how they're running!
"Well thrown by Huddlestone." – "How's that?"
    "Run out," now "*Cease your funning.*"

"That Bracher's bat's too wide by half,
    For all the stumps it covers;
When out he scores a score of runs,
    In twice as many overs:
And Barker hits so very hard,
    And Baker plays so steady,
I wish sincerely from my soul
    They'd call out 'Dinner's ready!'"

But dinner is not ready yet,
    And so the game must go on;
Now Barker's bowl'd out -Baker caught –
    Yet, still they seem to flow on.
"What, not all out?" No – on my life –
    "Nay – do not think I'm humming;"
Or if I am - 'tis but a tune –
    "*The Eyre – The Campbells coming!*"

"*And still they come,*" was yet the cry,
    Till Wickets ten were lower'd;
And then "the question" was to know,
    "How many runs they scored?"
The dinner's spread within the tent,
    While with each pick'd eleven;
Members and visitors – in all
    We sat down forty-seven –

Now all the witty, good things said,
   When round the table seated;
My memory will not serve to tell –
   Nor shall they be repeated: –
Let his suffice - *from gen'rous Port* –
   No more could be desired;
And more such "spirits, light as Eyre,"
   Are very seldom tired.

"Now turn out Stonehenge, in your turn,"
   And go in Blunt and Floyer;
"Keep up your spirits and your stumps,
   In Terminer and Oyer:"
An equitable court, no doubt,
   Like that where some old grudges,
Between old friends are made "all right,"
   By Umpires alias Judges.

The play is call'd, and Poulter bowls
   A regular off twister;
While Blunt tries at a slashing hit,
   By all that's good he's miss'd her!
The second over Baker gives,
   A good length *"slow and aisy"*
Not even Floyer gets a run,
   "Well bowl'd says Mr. Casey!"

Against such bowling who could stand?
   Pool, Eyre, and Windham fielding;
Biggs, Campbell, Hetley, Bracher, Marsh –
   (No wonder at their yielding)
And Barker famous any where –
   Thus when the runs were reckoned,
The first match Dorset won – *"at home"* –
   So Stonehenge won the second.

In spite of all that Medlicott,
   Or Port or Lagden, could do;
Though Bower and Farquharson tried,
   Yet no manoeuvre would do:
Still Digby, Simpson, Huddlestone,
   All struggled in the race, sir;
And beaten men made "lots of fun",
   At Cricket, that's in place, sir!

My Muse now flags, or I would tell
  What ladies on that morning,
Came to the down, our match to view,
  Thus more the scene adorning!
But did she not, without the kind
  Assistance of the Graces;
How could I e'er hope to describe
  Their lovely shapes and faces!

Than I myself, none more admires
  A pretty female's features;
And I'd do aught I could to please
  The "dear bewitching creatures!"
But oft *instead of cricket ball,*
  A lady's eye one catches;
His thoughts, who plays, should be confin'd
  To none but *"cricket matches!"*

"But who the devil can refrain,
  With youth and beauty round him,
From looking where he should not look;
  Two things at once confound him:
For when a hit comes near his ground,
  Amid his mate's loud laughter,
In thought *he's dancing at a ball,*
  Instead of dancing after!"

Let honours due to both be given,
  Nor any interfering;
One with the other be allow'd,
  To me they're both endearing! –
This I advise – and my advice
  By no means should be slighted;
That cricket balls be Lords by day,
  And ladies balls be-nighted!

Now "game and game" at present stands,
  The match between the parties;
And ere the conquering one comes on,
  The time I know but short is;
At Stallbridge, on their own fine ground,
  The Anglesea men play it;
And Stonehenge may be beat again,
  'Tis five to four, *"who'll lay it?"*

"Not I," – I seldom bet at all,
    And very low my purse is;
Yet I will venture half a crown
    That this makes twenty verses;
"Farewell," – we'll drink "prosperity
    Unto a thing that green is,"
A Cricket Ground should ever be,
    And so your Magazine is!

W. Puttock

At a meeting of Dorking CC, Bulls Head Inn, for the presentation of a bat to John Boxall, 'Little John' on 9th August 1847.

Dear Little John, or otherwise John Boxall,
Accept his bat, – 'twas made by Page, near Vauxhall.
At cricket you're as famous as a Box,
And give the ball some very pretty knocks;
May this, the promised bat, keep up your wicket;
And ever prove a friend to you at cricket;
And when the bowler Death trolls up his ball,
May it be batted well by John Boxall,
And many years elapse before your bales (*sic*)
Are lowered by that ball of coffin nails.

'Century'

You need not ask concerning Grace,
Of course he has a certain place,
Jackson, too, will help us win,
Can hit and bowl, so put him in.
The Indian Prince has earnt his post,
And he deserves it more than most,
Although a deal of fuss was made
About an Indian being played.
But Stoddart! Now I'm in a storm,
He cannot play on present form,
To leave him out would cause much pain,
So we will try him once again.
Three more we have – a bowler one –
Abel and Richardson and Gunn.
The trundler, J. T. Hearne, we'll try,
For he can make the wickets fly,
Young Hayward Surrey will produce,
Who proves himself to be of use.
Lilley behind the stumps shall stay
To stop the balls that come that way,
The final place I really feel
Is truly earned by Bobby Peel.

36 DEDICATED TO THE FAMOUS NOTTS AND SURREY ELEVENS

Albert Craig

Written in 1892 and sold at the August Bank Holiday match at Kennington Oval.

When I was a bit of a youngster, I cared for nothing at all;
I've gone without food a hundred times for an hour with bat and ball;
Age didn't improve me either, if anything, I grew worse,
I may say our village parson vowed cricket would be my curse.

He dubbed me most awfully stupid, I didn't care what he said,
When he offered me books as prizes, I yearned for wickets instead.
He declared my deep love for cricket would be my besetting sin,
But in trying to knock it out of me, he hammered it further in.

He got in a terrible temper, created an awful shine,
When I told him to mind his own business and I would attend to mine;
So I thought the affair was ended, each went his separate way.
He hurried away to his preaching, and I hurried off to my play.

And just gave my mind to the business, to prove it was no idle dream,
And bless you, I soon was acknowledged and placed in the County's team;
And I never disgraced 'em either, so long as I wielded the bat,
I was honest in all my actions, I always feel proud of that.

My mother taught me lessons, and I managed to learn them well
Ah! bless her, in duty's pathway she prayed that I might excel.
Ah! Lads, it's a downright pity when we live to grow ashamed,
Ashamed of our dear old parents whenever we hear them named.

In one Notts and Surrey encounter, a regular and grand affair,
Thirty thousand lined the ropes that day, all the world and his wife were
    there;
Our five best batsmen had fallen most lucklessly in the fray,
And our score was a modest thirty, not man had made a stay.

I was seventh to take up the willow, but wasn't a bit depress'd,
A score of admirers whispered – take courage and do thy best;
I felt nerved while the grand assembly were cheering me all the while,
Until I ran up my century grandly in fine and brilliant style.

I was carried to the pavilion and heartily feted there,
For we lowered their colours nobly, with fifty-five runs to spare.
The crowd gathered round the entrance, from every point they came,
And there wasn't a man amongst them but said that I'd won the game.

In front of me stood a veteran with white and silvery hair,
Accompanied by his daughter, a lady young and fair;
My friend, he exclaimed, forgive me since I was so harsh to you
I've learnt that a lover of cricket may be a true gentleman too.

'Twas the parson I knew in my childhood, he stood there as real as life,
since then we're akin – through marriage, his daughter is now my wife.
One word of advice and I've finished for I've taken a lengthy spell,
Guard your wickets and watch the ball lads, but guard your actions as well.

Albert Craig

Written in 1893. This year Surrey finished fifth in the County Championship.

I sat myself down on the Oval.
    Got buried in quiet thought,
Thinking of old dear byegones,
Learning the lessons they taught.
Methought I saw old Surrey –
    Saw her in all her pride,
I fancied I sang the same old song,
    The song of the winning side.
I saw grand old Jupp at the wicket,
    I heard the people cheer,
Although I knew he was far away,
He seem'd to be so near.
There stood kind-hearted Bowden,
    Of Surreyites – one of the best,
Then I thought there must be some mistake
    For I knew he was laid to rest.
I saw the pride of our county,
    Who never knew how to yield,
The only perfect fielder,
    That ever yet graced a field.
The essence of pluck and daring,
    Whose courage could never wane –
I fancied our monarch, Lohmann,
    Was back with his mates again.
I imagin'd the sun was shining,
    No sign of a cloud could I see;
That I heard loud shouts of victory,
    Just as it used to be.
But a friendly tap on the shoulder
    My quiet reverie broke –
    "What makes you so calm and thoughtful?",
    It was good old Apted who spoke.

I explain'd to him my musings,
   Said he, 'tis but a dream;
In the pleasant world of fancy
   Things are far from what they seem.
Thus I found to my bitter sorrow
   There still was an absent face;
A gang of pain came o'er me,
   On viewing the vacant place.
I know in my heart that Surrey
   At present are under a cloud;
That the grief of committee and players
   Is shared by the Oval crowd.
But Surrey will rise from her ashes,
And struggle against the fates,
When Lohmann, our pride and glory,
   Is number'd amongst his mates.

Thomas Moult

There's music in the names I used to know,
And magic when I heard them, long ago.
'Is Tyldesley batting?' Ah, the wonder still!
   . . . The school clock crawled, but cricket-thoughts would fill
The last slow lesson-hour deliciously.
(Drone on, O teacher: you can't trouble me.)
'Kent will be out by now.' . . . (Well, if you choose
To keep us here while cricket's in the air,
You must expect our minds to wander loose
Along the roads to Leicester, Lord's and Leeds,
Old Trafford and the Oval, and the Taunton meads . . .)

And then, at last, we'd raid the laneway where
A man might pass, perchance with latest news.
Grey-grown and grave, yet he would smile to hear
Our thirsty questions as we crowded near.
Greedily from the quenching page we'd drink –
How its white sun-glare made our young eyes wink!
'Yes, Tyldesley's batting still. He's ninety-four.
Barlow and Mold play well. Notts win once more.
Glo'ster (with Grace) have lost to Somerset –
Easy: ten wickets: Woods and Palairet . . .'
So worked the magic in that summer lane.
The stranger beamed. Maybe he felt again
As I feel now to tell the linked names
Jewelling the loveliest of our English games.
Abel and Albert Trott, Lilley, Lillywhite,
Hirst, Hearne, and Tunnicliffe – they catch the light –
Lord Hawke and Hornby, Jessop, A. O. Jones –
Surely the glow they held was the high sun's!

Or did a young boy's worship think it so,
And is it but his heart that's aching now?

Alfred Cochrane

The Bat with which J. T. Brown made his first great score against Australia was exhibited in a London shop window.

Against the window young and old
    Pressed eager noses flat,
Thousands all anxious to behold
    The justly famous bat.

The youth of London, well content,
    The future Peels and Gunns,
Stared at the magic implement
    That made so many runs.

And some of those who came to stare
    Admired it through the pane,
Enlarging with the expert's air
    Upon its blade and grain.

But one poor player, who had made
    More noughts than runs, maybe,
Wondered why here should be displayed
    A slice of willow tree.

'It won the rubber,' murmured he,
    'Why, that was very good,
Yet, after all, it seems to me
    A common piece of wood.

'Show us your pencil, if you will
    With which Sir Joshua drew,
The inkpot Scott was wont to fill,
    And Roberts' billiard cue.

'Arms and the man! It is not that
    Which purchases renowns,
For many men can buy a bat,
    But very few be Brown's.

Henry Newbolt

There's a breathless hush in the Close to-night –
  Ten to make and the match to win –
A bumping pitch and a blinding light,
  An hour to play and the last man in.
And it's not for the sake of a ribboned coat,
  Or the selfish hope of a season's fame,
But his Captain's hand on his shoulder smote -
  'Play up! play up! and play the game!'

The sand of the desert is sodden red,
  Red with the wreck of a square that broke; –
The Gatling's jammed and the Colonel dead,
  And the regiment blind with dust and smoke.
The river of death has brimmed his banks,
  And England's far, and Honour a name,
But the voice of a schoolboy rallies in the ranks:
  'Play up! play up! and play the game!'

This is the word that year by year,
  While in her place the school is set,
Every one of her sons must hear,
  And none that hears it dare forget.
This they all with a joyful mind
  Bear through like a torch in flame,
And falling fling to the host behind –
  'Play up! play up! and play the game!'

Arnold Wall

A time will come, a time will come,
    (Though the world will never be quite the same)
When the people sit in the summer sun,
    Watching, watching the beautiful game.

A time will come, a time will come,
    With fifteen stars in a green heaven,
Two will be batting, and two to judge,
And round about them the fair Eleven.

A time will come, a time will come,
    When the people sit with a peaceful heart,
Watching the beautiful, beautiful game,
    This is battle and service and sport and art.

A time will come, a time will come,
    When the crowds will gaze on the game and the green,
Soberly watching the beautiful game,
    Orderly, decent, calm, serene.

A time will come, a time will come,
    The click of the bat sounds clear and well,
And over the studying, critical crowds
    Cricket will cast her witching spell.

Yet a time will come, a time will come,
    Come to us all as we watch and seem
To be heart and soul in the beautiful game,
When we shall remember and wistfully dream –

Dream of the boys who never were here,
    Born in the days of evil chance,
Who never knew sport or easy days,
    But played their game in the fields of France.

James Norman Hall

The first to climb the parapet
With 'cricket-ball' in either hand;
The first to vanish in the smoke
Of God-forsaken No-Man's land.
First at the wire and soonest through,
First at those re-mouthed hounds of hell
The Maxims, and the first to fall, –
They do their bit, and do it well.

Fully sixty yards I've seen them throw
With all that nicety of aim
They learned on British cricket-fields.
Ah! Bombing is a Briton's game!
Shell-hole, trench to trench,
'Lobbing them over'. With an eye
As true as though it *were* a game,
And friends were having tea close by.

Pull down some art-offending thing
Of carven stone, and in its stead
Let splendid bronze commemorate
These men, the living and the dead.
No figure in heroic size
Towering skyward like a god;
But just a lad who might have stepped
From any British bombing squad.

His shrapnel helmet set a-tilt,
His bombing waistcoat sagging low,
His rifle slung across his back:
Poised in the very act to throw.
And let some raven legend tell
Of those weird battles in the West
Wherein he put old skill to use
And played old games with sterner zest.

Thus should he stand, reminding those
In less believing days, perchance,
How Britain's fighting cricketers
Helped bomb the Germans out of France.
And other eyes than ours would see;
And other hearts than ours would thrill,
And others say, as we have said:
'A sportsman and a soldier still!'

R. W. Moore

The air is hushed; but thoughts that keep
Patrol above the aerodrome,
Circling the treadmill toils of sleep,
Lying on the cricket-ground at home.

I seek out the ordered square,
The outfield seared in August heat
And where the measured turf shows bare
Scarred by the plunging bowlers' feet.

And see the flashing wand awake
The flickering forms that start and run
And catch the rumbling taunts that take
The pleasured air when play is done.

But all is altered; ragwort reigns
Unchallenged in the tarnished maze;
The nets lie rotting in the rains,
The benches gone to make a blaze.

And in the littered dressing-room
A boy stares through the broken door,
Like one who breaks a royal tomb.
At bats and pads strewn on the floor.

And all the players where are they?
Earthwide they wander quick and slain,
And those who shall return to play
Shall scan the scorebook all in vain.

Humphrey Clucas

Of course it's all
Decline and Fall;
The Snows of yesteryear
Increase the thirst
For Rhodes and Hirst,
And older, rarer beer.

So here's to Peel,
And Studd and Steel;
Turn off the TV Test,
And let the page
Improve with age:
Whatever was, was best.

LORD'S, 1928

C. A. Alington

Lord's – Lord's on Wednesday evening!
Cambridge fieldsmen crowding round,
Oxford's hardly a chance of saving it –
Hardly a chance, but still you found
   Elderly cricketers gnawing their sticks,
   Blameless Bishops, forgetful of Jix,
   Publicly praying at half-past six,
And prayers and curses arise from the Mound
   On that head of carrots (or possibly gold)
   On that watchful eye on each ball that's bowled –
And a deadly silence around the ground.

Lord's -Lord's on Friday evening!
Two men out and an hour to play –
Lose another, and that's the end of it,
Why not call it a harrowing day?
   Harrow's lips are at last on the cup,
   Harrow's tail unmistakably up,
   And Eton! Eton can only pray
For a captain's heart in a captain's breast,
   And some decent batting among the rest,
   And sit and shiver and hope for the best –
If those fellows can only stay!

Stay they did – can we ever forget it? –
Till those who had bidden us all despair
Lit their pipes with a new assurance,
Toyed instead with the word 'declare'
   Harrow's glorious hours begin,
   Harrow's batsmen hurrying in,
   One and all with the will to win,
Cheers and counter-cheers rend the air!
   Harrow's down with her colours flying
   Great in doing and great in dying,
Eton's home with a head to spare!

Anthony Greenstreet

Across the turf two swallows race and twist
And batsman cuts again the stroke he missed
Off the last ball. Dark copper in the sun
Glows the vast beech: the bowler starts his run.
Who planted this great tree stamped in the brain
What their past youth would mean to future men.
White figures shift on field of vivid green;
The scoreboard whirs and clacks behind the screen;
Red brick, grey slate, massed under pompous towers
And solemn hum of bees in lime tree flowers.
With elegant and parabolic curve
The spinner loops the ball to test the nerve
Of forward-prodding batsman. With like loop
The wagtail curves down to the grass to swoop
On insect prey with sudden daring run,
As square leg races round to cut off one.
From the high blue the sickle-whirling swift
Drops his thin scream, and round the boundary drift
Some who remember still their score
In this same match – but forty years before.

Dannie Abse

1935, I watched Glamorgan play
especially Slogger Smart, free
from the disgrace of fame, unrenowned,
but the biggest hit with me.

A three-spring flash of willow
and, suddenly, the sound of summer
as the thumped ball, alive, would leave
the applauding ground.

Once, hell for leather, it curled
over the workman's crane
in Westgate Street
to crash, they said, through a discreet
Angel Hotel windowpane

But I, a pre-war boy,
(or someone with my name)
wanted it, that Eden day,
to scoot around the turning world,
to mock physics and gravity,
to rainbow-arch the posh hotel
higher, deranged, on and on, allegro,
(the Taff a gleam of mercury below)
going, going, gone
towards the Caerphilly mountain range.

Vanishings! The years, too, gone like change.
But the travelling Taff seems the same.
It's late. I peer at the failing sky
over Westgate Street
and wait. I smell cut grass.
I shine an apple on my thigh.

Chris Bendon

A runner rubs the ball which becomes an apple.
That chock is of a backward clock
taking one back to that hot hot summer
before the jelly of empire set, before
the jolly flags came down: it's half past
India, dinner's in the heaven
which actually is Hampshire but the Hemisphere's right.
White linen and candles and this band make
negative undertakers stroking odd shaped coffins,
or it is chess with both sides ivory,
or a vigil with long tapers.

A thwack awakes me from all this nonsense.
A man jumps, joins the Fallen in long grass
by a willowy stream which seems to pause . . .
The run goes into the brain's dark continent.
Heroism's white lie is covered by applause.

After, the moon is caught, silly mid off.
The poet's stumped.
Someone snogs with a *Spectator.*
A bat hovers darkly above.

John Whitworth

Written in seventeenth-century style, on the occasion of David Gower's first Test century against New Zealand at the Oval in July 1978.

We honour him because
He is young, and all he does
Partakes of youthfulness,
Simplicity and grace.
In the old time, they say
Venus kept away
From Hades' iron rede
Pretty Ganymede
Who measured wine to Jove
And touched the Queen of Love
With human sorrow, long
Ago when the Earth was young.

Roger McGough

You came to watch me playing cricket once.
Quite a few of the fathers did.
At ease, outside the pavilion
they would while away a Saturday afternoon.
Joke with the masters, urge on
their flannelled offspring. But not you.

Fielding deep near the boundary
I saw you through the railings.
You were embarrassed when I waved
and moved out of sight down the road.
When it was my turn to bowl though
I knew you'd still be watching.

Third ball, a wicket, and three more followed.
When we came in at the end of the innings
the other dads applauded and joined us for tea.
Of course, you had gone by then. Later,
you said you'd found yourself there by accident.
Just passing. Spotted me through the railings.

*   *   *

Speech-days • Prize-givings • School-plays •
The Twentyfirst • The Wedding • The Christening •
You would find yourself there by accident.
Just passing. Spotted me through the railings.

51 A PINDARIC ODE ON THE OCCASION OF THE THIRD TEST BETWEEN ENGLAND AND AUSTRALIA, PLAYED AT HEADINGLEY, 16TH–21ST JULY, 1981

Gavin Ewart

Well, GATTING was batting and YALLOP came in at a
gallop to save a single . . . we could mix and mingle
with the loud crowd, on our telescreens we saw the
best match ever to be called a Test Match . . .

Don't be abrupt, don't interrupt,
just keep quiet, don't riot, sit still and listen,
hear the Umpires' bell – I'm ready to tell
a story of glory and the unfading laurel crowns
    that glisten . . .

THURSDAY
Australia went in first, they were soon grinding
    away on a day
when England were finding it hard. I tell you, mate,
the English bowlers didn't bowl very straight,
it was like watching a coffee-grinder or standing
behind a cement-mixer, as those batsmen went
through the motions, they knew they had oceans of
    time. Their slowness was a crime
and didn't produce standing ovations – but justified,
buildings don't stand up without foundations . . .

FRIDAY
203 for 3, and a catch dropped by GOWER, the power
and the glory seemed as though it had really
    deserted BREARLEY.
OLD bowled quite well; but all this day
the Australians seemed well on their way.
DYSON didn't charge at the ball like a bison;
but he made 102 and 102s. like 89 made by HUGHES,
and YALLOP's 58, meant a good score – and a lot
    more. Confidence.

They declared at 9 for 401 – for England not much fun.
though BOTHAM bowled straight and moved the ball
    both early and late.
the one ray of light in the gloom (6 for 95). Still,
    England's doom
could be seen to loom. BOTHAM seemed to prove it –
if he could swing it, the Australians too would
    certainly move it,
by seam and flight.
But no untoward fright. No English wicket fell
    that night.

SATURDAY
Yet England didn't rise again on the third day.
GOOCH out for 2. The thing to do seemed to be to
mooch around, BOYCOTT 12, BREARLEY 10, even
GOWER only very briefly came into flower.
24. Again some light from BOTHAM – where others
    were thrifty
he was prodigal, with a well-struck 50.
LILLEE, ALDERMAN, LAWSON bowled well – at the stumps.
Far better than the English bowlers. A bad night,
    with grinding molars
and all England's supporters down in the dumps.

MONDAY
England 174 all out and following on,
GOOCH, with the score at Zero, had already gone.
The radio mentioned odds of 500 to 1
for an England win. But this wasn't the Oval, there
    weren't any LAKERS,
and, with regard to these odds, there can't have been
    many takers.
Would Australia even have to bat again?
The most sensible thing seemed to be pray
    for rain.
227 to avoid the innings defeat.
BOYCOTT played straight, calm and unflappable (46),
some of WILLEY'S more aggressive strokes (33) were
    very clappable.
But 4 down for 41! Even 5 for 105,
there didn't seem to be much to keep our hopes alive.

It was like the tide inexorably flooding in over
    the sand,
seven wickets had gone for 135. No sign of a stand,
like King Canute, nobody could send me the sea back
    with a cricket boot.
92 runs still needed for Australia to bat again, the
    steep hill of the follow-on
and only three wickets left,
any English laugh must have been a hollow one!

But BOTHAM, looking like a lion on a British egg,
seemed to have a brief, glorious thrash,
pulling, driving, cutting and sweeping to leg,
with (once) something not much different from a
    tennis overhead smash . . .

and, slowly but surely, we realised that he knew
    what he was doing
and although it was very clear that he was riding
    his luck
the ball met the meat of the bat, this wasn't just
    cause for booing
or irresponsible (like the slogger who's out for
    a duck).

The next day's papers compared him to
that six-hitting fabulous Croucher. Jessop –
and indeed he jumped down the pitch like a gressop
(the Old English for what James Joyce with his Irish
    voice called a gracehoper
and most ordinary people call a grasshopper).
One particular six, a tremendous one, parabola-tall,
made one feel pretty sorry for the ball.

DILLEY, too, turned aggressive. 56 runs, and all made
    with style.
Someone shouted 'Why didn't you bowl like that?'
He was out at 252. A century partnership.
The Australian bowlers, even LILLEE, began to
    look ordinary.
BOTHAM'S hundred. BREARLEY gave him the *stay there!*
    signal, very clearly.
From then on he shielded OLD, running singles at the
    ends of overs

and scoring in fours for 29, a good innings.
Then it was WILLIS. 351 for nine
at close of play. Fine. A commentator was heard
    to say:
'They need a hundred runs to bowl at!' These
    they had.
It still looked hopeless, but not quite so bad.

TUESDAY
BOTHAM hit one more four, ALDERMAN got WILLIS.
356 all out.When they went in
Australia needed only 130 to win.
It all went quietly ahead, though BOTHAM got WOOD
    for ten.
DYSON and CHAPPELL looked as firm as rocks,
    and then
DILLEY went off to have a boot repaired. WILLIS
    took over –
and from then on the Australian batsmen were never
    in clover.
That wild Goose flew in like a bat out of Hell –
3 wickets in 11 balls, without a run being scored!
Surely the batsmen to come must have prayed to
    the Lord!
CHAPPELL, HUGHES and YALLOP – the names say it all.

This was the kind of bowling you can't play at all!
OLD had BORDER for a duck. MARSH didn't have
    BOTHAM'S luck
and DILLEY boundary-caught him at fine leg, one of
    the hardest blows struck.
Before that DYSON went. 68 for 6. Soon just 75 for 8.
Only LILLEE at the end, with BRIGHT, showed any
    kind of flight.
BRIGHT 19, LILLEE 17 (DYSON made 34
and this was very easily the top score).
55 runs needed. Two wickets to fall.
WILLIS had LILLEE caught by GATTING, a mishit hook
    off a less straight ball.

BREARLEY said afterwards, in a sort of magnificat,
'I didn't think WILLIS could still bowl like that.'

BOTHAM came back. OLD dropped ALDERMAN twice
    in an over.
If it had been FLETCHER
that Yorkshire chauvinist crowd would have made a
    meal of it, you betcher
life, as one of the commentators said.
Still, though everyone was tense, under his beard
    OLD'S face must have been a bit red . . .

Finally, though, WILLIS knocked out BRIGHT'S
    middle stump,
and everyone jumped for joy, a really
    unbelievable jump!
111 all out. They'd done it by 18 runs . . .
and this is an ode to Cricket and its white–
    robed sons!
Like the bounce of a rugger ball, you can't tell which
    way it'll go
it's totally unpredictable, if it's like anything at all
it's truly like a game of soccer played with a
    rugger ball!
But of course you must praise WILLIS (8 for 43)
and BOTHAM'S magnificent innings – 149 not out.
Goose and Guy the Gorilla
were the two favourite flavours, like (say)
    Strawberry and Vanilla –
but MIKE BREARLEY also deserves praise,
as a first-class Captain in a good many
    different ways.

This tribute that mangles the epic and the lyric,
this rough populist Pindaric panegyric,
this dithyrambic doggerel is here to make the claim
that since STODDART did it in Sydney in 1894
no other test side in history has ever followed on
    and still won the game!

Anon

It was whispered in the heavens that the Martians were due,
But their pitch was always turfless, and the rules they had were new,
For the wickets that they wanted were between the Earth and Sun,
In the diaphanous ether, where the batsmen couldn't run.

Now 'W. G.' was captain and he ruminated then
How, with all his dead and buried, he could crush the Martian men;
For the ball was made of lightning, and it flashed from stump to stump,
And the batsmen tapped and flicked it with a weightless camel's hump.

To-day the match is being played and the fielders can't discern
The ball upon the Milky Way or Mars from vague Saturn;
And the bowler's mostly dying ere the ball he bowled is played,
And several scorers wither ere they see the ball waylaid.

After years of listless floating as of old the team runs in
And reports a shower of comets to the batsmen drifting in;
Then from aeon until aeon they'll smugly take their ease,
In the comfy old pavilion, just behind the Pleiades.

V

THE POWER OF PLACE AND PROTEST

(Points of View)

~

This chapter might well have coined the title 'Look Back in Anger' had all the backward glances been seen through a red mist. That is not the case, however, for some of the looks into the past positively glow with affection and nostalgia, and in fact there are other introspections which occupy a sort of in-between state of concern and regret, as if written with a resigned shrug.

We start on a positive note with the places, which is not to infer that protest is anything but positive. And indeed there are some poems which intertwine the two aspects in such a way that they cannot be disentangled.

A geographical line traced southwards from the beautiful Cumbrian grounds at Keswick and Millom, lingers first at Barnsley in Yorkshire and then at the departed Bramall Lane where Irving Rosenwater complements a sad farewell to the ground in 1973 with another offering, a 'Reverie' that intersperses childhood memories with the inspiration drawn from a favourite environ.

American Sandy Solomon was motivated to write a poem on the Thrumpton Cricket Ground in Nottinghamshire while watching her English husband take part in the annual game first organised by members of the local Seymour and Cust families. A magnificent Jacobean mansion and grazing animals nearby conjure up an idyllic scene.

South once more to Brentwood, another vanished first-class venue; to Brighton and the mixed emotions of Alan Ross; westwards for a short stay with Clifford Bax at his Wiltshire home at Broughton-Gifford, and then to Swansea where John Arlott used to sit on the top of the pavilion with his friend Dylan Thomas, who was busy scribbling cricket poems on old envelopes which may now lie unrecognised in the archive of an American university.

A flight to 'Adelaide and its Oval', once more with Rosenwater, and his new invention given impulse by the old architecture . . . Suddenly, we are faced with conflict: the protests of outrage and despair:

That old monster, bodyline bowling; the intrusion of cricket into the parks; the incursion of the concrete jungle on to the playing fields; rampant materialism; the loss of a loved landmark through unacceptable behaviour: Gerald Howat's note to his poem 'Metamorphoses' reads, 'When Middlesex played Kent in the National Westminster Bank Final at Lord's in 1984 the authorities decided to close the Tavern Bar and build a temporary stand. This was in response to criticism of the conduct of some supporters in past years which had "brought into disrepute" the cricket atmosphere at the game's headquarters. Opinions were divided. The immediate consequence of the change was a cathedral-like atmosphere throughout most of the day only broken when Middlesex won a cliff-hanger on the final ball.'

The deprecations continue with a touch of political egocentricity, selectorial omissions, and, particularly disturbing, the agonised cry for help in a mental institution where corruscatingly clear perception is linked to a smothered mind. There is also a savage indictment of those who took the blood-splattered coin on the rebel tour to South Africa followed by a sardonic appraisal of those who chose to remain at home.

It is important to highlight a few of the other poems. Aboriginal Rikki Shields' commentary on his fellow-countryman King Cole who in 1868 during the first Aboriginal cricket tour of Britain, lay dead and disregarded in a London hospital, is deeply affecting. Shields commemorates also the unveiling of a plaque in his memory in 1996.

David Phillips felt compelled to compose when confronted by a vast and ugly brick building during a visit to the stately Quex House in Birchington. He thought it was a folly, but it turned out to be a mausoleum dedicated to the Powell-Cotton family, owners of Quex House for many generations. 'I immediately saw that the death and mortality would make a profound and important meditation for a book of poems' observed Phillips, 'but when I returned home I found myself writing about a worn-out county cricketer ruefully commenting on the game as he approaches the end of his career – the two subjects are not as dissimilar as I first thought'. '14th April' comes from the resulting booklet, *Man in the Long Grass*.

'Four' by Martin Booth reflects a moment at Lord's suspended in time. 'In the middle of a cricket ground, in the middle of a city, in the middle of an over, in the middle of a session, in the middle of a day, in the middle of a week, in the middle of a season, in the middle of the year, a bowler bowls and a batter bats. It's timeless.

People are there, watching. Writers, pensioners. But there are others: civil servants, accountants, solicitors. All sneaking an hour or a day out of the office to sit and simply refresh in the presence of cricket. And they are all wearing suits. They are all suspended in time, just for a while. Ageless. It's always been this way, always will be. Victorians, Edwardians, New Elizabethans . . .'

Booth likes the word 'skimjingle': leaves can skimjingle, so can birds. So, too, can cricket . . .

D. R. A.

William Perfect

Scarce potent Sol's meridian lustre o'er,
When from the village throngs promiscuous pour
In blended group around the level dale,
While CRICKET does obstreperously prevail.
Mindless of toil, and of the sultry ray,
The eager youth the admiring crowds survey,
Commence the game, when some their vigour lend,
To bowl velocious, and the wicket rend;
Some strike the ball, and all the gazers please.
Those watch the wicket and the field keep these.
Some catch the ball and gather instant fame,
And all the dale resounds with loud acclaim.
Some mark the strokes upon the shaven spray,
And others umpires stand whom all obey.
But now slow-setting sinks the western sun;
The toil is ended, and the game is done.
Then all return, and o'er the goblet tell
How far one struck, another bowl'd how well –
How all performed, till Morpheus seize the tale,
And spread his pinions o'er the weary vale.

54 'OUR CONSTITUTION IS THE POST TRUE BATSMEN WILL DEFEND' (DIBDIN)

Christopher Kemp

The cricketing cracks of the year '89,
Felt a sociable tour of fair France would be fine;
But no English bowler delivered an over,
Since his Grace turned them back when he met them at Dover.

What gallant, what elegant, games might have been
In front of the château, where, perched by the green
The Count and the Countess would welcome the sport
Far from the cliques and corruptions of court!

Who knows? The curé might have stopped at the spot
And stood at square leg to say whether, or not,
Some rustical swiper was stumped or run out
When 'Comment est celà?' was the questioning shout.

In the sweet shades of the flower-bedecked tent
The thirsty contestants from Yorkshire and Kent
Would not have disdained the cool cup of Vouvray
Or Entre-deux-mers, brought round on a tray.

Such stylish French hundreds, immaculate knocks,
Applauded, perhaps, by the brown Charles James Fox,
Across for the cricket, the chat and the fizz
And suave strolls by the Loire with his own dearest Liz.

Our breakfasting gentry, taking their toast
With steaming French coffee, the Times and the Post
Might have checked on the rumour which proved to be true
That Provence were 600 for 3, v. Anjou.

But as our trim cricketers roved to the pub
The Frenchmen turned in to their Jacobin club,
Where they picked up their Rights, put their cricket bags down
And paraded in tricolour all round the town.

Danton, the demon, then summoned his strength,
(Wide, wild and furious; no hint of good length)
With a hop, skip and jump he hurled into the ring
The guillotined head of the last Capet King.

'This is simply too much' thought Prime Minister Pitt,
'Our line is cricket, and claret, and wit',
While Brissot and Buzot in Anglophobe oaths
Bawled at Britannia to fit some new clothes.

Before they had given the form a good look
They started a Test, which was not in the book,
In a game for La Gloire, a French pastime, in which
Twenty-two miles is the length of the pitch.

King George was delighted, and every French jerk,
Has already been no-balled by vigilant Burke,
SO JACK AND HORATIO STOOD TO THEIR WICKET
TO PROVE THAT EQUALITY JUST WASN'T CRICKET.

Rikki Shields

In memory of King Cole, Aboriginal cricketer who died on 24 June 1868.

Your Aboriginal dreamtime home. Wish you peace. Nyuntu Anangu
  Tjukapa Wiltja Nga Palya Nga.

Legend of the Southern Cross Stars that light the night-sky over Australia.
Seven Aboriginal Women fetch the wood at sundown. Then they fly into the
  sky
and make seven campfires, while they wait eternally for the lost warriors to
  return home.

1866 was a Stormy night as the women watched the wooden ship sailing
from Botany Bay, inside the ship were twelve gallant warriors
They went as Ambassadors in Games and Humanity, To play this strange
      sport . . . . . .Cricket.
Behind their land was ravaged and claimed in the name of fair play

Loyoranna the Wind, blew the ship, across mountainous Seas
Then finally to the River Snake . . .Thames.

London Town where Clay People dwell, Who rule by class, Stone hearts,
Darkness, No Fire in the Sky.

The Cricket warriors knew the dangers if they failed on this Mission
Wondrous people did they meet, the old, Young, but not Politicians.

then tragedy struck off spinner bowler, Sugar, Died where-abouts unknown.
Chief King Cole passed away in white-fella death house at St Guy's
No Sacred Ceremony, No Weeping Women, to help their bones and spirit
    return
to their beginning time

Did the evil Clayface Doctor swap Kings bones for their own?
Does he sit in a Shoe Box or glass jar in Royal College of Surgeons
in central London Town . . . We'll never know.

Yet the seven Aboriginal Women night fire shines brightly
The Women still Weeping, still hoping.

There is humanity in this hostile jungle city of London
The People of Tower Hamlets, Erected a stone for the Journey
and memory of Our Dusky Warrior of Cricket
Ambassador King Cole . . .

The names of other members in team were: SUGAR, NEDDY, JELLICO
 COUSINS,
MULLAGH, BULLOCKY, TARPOT, SUNDOWN, OFFICER, PETER and
 CAPTAIN.

E. V. Lucas

Lines suggested by the new entrance at Lord's, erected in memory of W. G. Grace and issued on the occasion of the Eton v Harrow match at Lord's, 14 and 15 July 1922.

If every ball you have to play
Is dealt with in the finest way:
Or hit for four or placed for one,
But almost always yields a run;
If every ball you bowl is meant
To cause the batsmen discontent,
And fog their brain with sterile doubt
Until they blunder and are out;
If every ball that comes to you
Is fielded clean and flung back true;
If every moment of the game
Your keenness in it's just the same,

No matter though good fortune dogs
The other fellows' wildest slogs,
And in your comrades' buttered fingers
The simplest sitter never lingers;
If every hour that's lost through wet
Fills you with anguish and regret,
And every interval for tea
With scorn, disgust and misery;
If every – but enough! Why then,
If such you be, some where, some when,
Another pair of gates may rise,
Your glory to immortalise.

Bob Horne

On summer Saturdays they weave motifs across Fitz park
between the River Greta and the pavilion boundary
where the ground swells to become Skiddaw.

Light on the wind and the eye,
in their mayblossom whiteness they seem like a newsreel
of something their grandfathers did in the Thirties,
talking at tea of Larwood and Bradman, Verity and Voce,
or sitting beneath black drizzling crags waiting for play.

Norsemen came here, cleared the land of rocks
the last Ice Age had left behind
so that cattle could be kept, cricket can be played.
They passed the spot where Wordsworth would be born,
heard the water's ceaseless music,
settled where Coleridge couldn't.

Cricketers look up at close of day to see the same relief:
Latrigg; Lonscale; Carl Side; Dodd.
The sun loops through their lives in a faultless flight
over Derwentwater and Grisedale Pike
pitching, somewhere out of sight, on to the Solway.

They will wait all afternoon, weeks of weekends,
for the chance to become their quintessence.
The diving catch at deep extra cover,
the desperate second run to short fine-leg which wins the match
is their vindication, perfection in a perfect world,
as nothing else between birth and death can ever be.

Norman Nicholson

Millom, Cumberland

Let me first describe the field:
Its size, a double acre; walled
Along the north by a schoolyard,
West by a hedge and orchards; tarred
Wood railings on the east to fence
The grass from the station shunting lines,
That crook like a defensive ditch
Below the ramparts of the church;
And south, the butter meadows, yellow
As fat and bumpy as a pillow,
Rumpling down the mile or more
That slopes to the wide Cumbrian shore,
With not a brick to lift a ban
Between the eye and the Isle of Man.
A common sort of field you'll say:
You'd find a dozen any day
In any northern town, a sour
Flat landscape shaped with weed and wire,
And nettle clump and ragwort thicket –
But this field is put by for cricket.
Here among the grass and plantains
Molehills matter more than mountains,
And generations watch the score
Closer than toss of peace or war.
Here, in matches won and lost,
The town hoards an heroic past,
And legendary bowlers tie
The child's dream in the father's lie.
This is no Wisden pitch; no place
For classic cuts and Newbolt's verse,
But the luck of the league, stiff and stark
With animosity of dark
In-grown village and mining town,
When evening smoke-light drizzles down,

And the fist is tight in the trouser pocket,
And the heart turns black for the want of a wicket.
Or knock-out cricket, brisk as a bird,
Twenty overs and league men barred –
Heels in the popping crease, crouch and clout,
And the crowd half-codding the batsmen out.
Over the thorn and elder hedge
The sunlight floods, but leaves a ledge
Of shadow where the old men sit,
Dozing their pipes out. Frays of light
Seam a blue-serge suit; gnats swarm,
And swallows dip round the bowler's arm.
Here in a small-town game is seen
The long-linked dance of the village green:
Wishing well and maypole ring,
Mumming and ritual of spring.

Donald Davie

Now the heat comes, I am demoralized.
Important letters lie unanswered, dry
Shreds of tobacco spike the typewriter,
No undertaking but is ill-advised.

Unanswerable even the shortest missive,
Replies not sealed, or sealed without conviction.
Thumb-marks dry out, leaving the paper pouchy,
Tousled with effort, desperate, inconclusive.

'A thing worth doing is worth doing well,'
Says Shaw Lane Cricket Ground
Between the showers of a July evening,
As the catch is held and staid hand-clappings swell.

This almost vertical sun, this blur of heat,
All stinging furze and snagged unravelling,
Denies the axiom which has kept
My father's summers shadowy and sweet.

Remembering many times when he has laughed
Softly, and slapped his thigh, because the trap
So suavely set was consummately sprung,
I wish, to all I love, his love of craft.

Hard to instruct myself, and then my son,
That things which would be natural are done
After a style less consummate; that an art's
More noble office is to leave half-done.

How soon the shadows fall, how soon and long!
The score-board stretches to a grandson's feet.
This layabout July in another climate
Ought not to prove firm turf, well-tended, wrong.

Irving Rosenwater

No trees, no picnic lunches on the grass:
Just chimneys, row on row on row.
No social graces for a special class,
But honour done alike to friend and foe.

Sounds that no aesthete would salute:
Just noises – a loud factory hoot,
And tramcars on their routine clatter
Adding grist to local chatter.

Bombs did not still the game at Bramall Lane:
Just two-day wins brought temporary halt.
Now pungent memories alone remain.
With Bramall Lane *we* found no fault.

Irving Rosenwater

What are the average boy's reactions
To decimal points and vulgar fractions?
In matters arithmetical, I think,
From such dislikes he'd rather shrink.
But put before him cricket scores
And you'll earn at once his real applause,
For Fletcher's batting at Valentine's Park
Is *infinitely* better than a master's bark.
The opening stand at Leeds today
Has passed the hundred, I've heard them say:
If only maths I could ignore
And attend instead to Boycott's score.

By three p.m. my fancy roams
And leaves behind those wretched tomes
Packed full of dull atomic weights
And silly sums on interest rates.
Instead my fancy's spreading me
Beside the turf at Headingley.
The Yorkshire score moves on serene
(All thoughts of school now taste obscene).
Will Boycott's cover-drive unfold,
To leave a mark of joy untold?
Not once, not twice, but many times –
And all the while the total climbs.
Fielders run and bowlers sweat,
But little sympathy they get
As Yorkshire's captain hits a four
To bring his score to ninety-four.
Deliberations are to no avail:
Surely Boycott *cannot* fail?
A single now, another one.
The score creeps slowly, run by run.
But suddenly, oh dear – a catch?
This will completely spoil my match.

"He's out!" I cry. "IS HE, MY BOY?"
This scholarly voice I *don't* enjoy.
So, sad-faced, I turn from my summer abstractions
To the doubtful rewards of vulgar fractions.

ANNUAL GAME,
THRUMPTON CRICKET GROUND

Sandy Solomon

Game today at the Thrumpton Cricket Ground,
its trimmed grass barely claimed from fields
where sheep and cattle graze. We luff our blanket
in a patch clear of droppings, then settle to the dance
around the pitch: the bowler's sprint and arc,
batsman's twisting thwack, fielder's lunge –
missed catch – as the ball skitters for the rough.

Sun harrows down and a stiff breeze flips
the half-read page while we chat and watch, sometimes,
and clap. The sense of timelessness expands.
We might be lounging, out for a daylong sail –
the water changing but unchanged as it slaps by –
so much do the white figures hypnotise
as they switch from side to side, together and apart.

Soon they break for lunch – players sprawl,
gentry and village, circles apart, to eat
with parents, wives, and kids, while the toddler weaves,
clutching a soggy sweet, among the clusters.
Soon we take our tea at Thrumpton Hall
with its jumble of Jacobean rooms, its priest's hole,
its pool. But, throughout, the game defines us all.

Like the chorus to a song it keeps coming up,
not just today, but every June for years –
one day when son, now father, waits out rain
or takes the field as his father did and plays,
and the old order reigns, briefly, out of time.
But stumps must be drawn; we mind the current hour
near an emptied field. Sheep pink the hill beyond.

D. A. Williams

Do you remember Brentwood
Where Essex used to play
On a sporting wicket
Every year in May?

Do you remember Silcock
And Round, and Green, and Pickett?
When Essex first played cricket
At Brentwood, years ago?
Players there were gentlemen
Except for one or two.
They whiled away the golden hours
Those Parsons, not a few
And soldiers, lawyers and the lucky ones
From Public Schools. Filling in their time
Until a generation of their sons
Fell victims of the Flanders guns,
And Shenfield Road was filled with trucks
On the way to Warley Barracks.

I remember Brentwood later
A pleasant tree-lined ground
Where we smoked our pipes
In peace, and sat around the boundary rope
And watched the first Cudmore and Pope,
Then Avery and Dodds
Open the innings.
Then Bailey with his forward prods
Saved matches all against the odds.
Massive scores and weary feet
For bowlers when the pitch played true.
With Michael Bear from "up the road"
And Gordon Barker small and neat
Essex fortunes ebbed and flowed.
Then the ghost of Kortright, buried near
Must have often shed a tear
And whispered to the ghost of Fane
"Essex have just lost again."

They do not play at Brentwood now.
The umpires in their long white coats, and players
All have gone.
Uneconomic, so they cried
Much too small . . .
. . . So Brentwood died.

Alan Ross

At night the Front like coloured barley-sugar; but now
Soft blue, all soda, the air goes flat over flower-beds,
Blue railings and beaches; below, half-painted boats, bow
Up, settle in sand, names like Moss-Rose and Dolphin
Drying in a breeze that flicks at the ribs of the ride.
The chalk coastline folds up its wings of Beachy Head
And Worthing, fluttering white over water like brides.
Regency Squares, the Pavilion, oyster and mussels and gin.

Piers like wading confectionery, esplanades of striped tulip,
Cricket began here yesterday, the air heavy, suitable
For medium-paced bowlers; but deck-chairs mostly were vacant,
Faces white over startling green. Later, trains will decant
People with baskets, litter and opinions, the seaside's staple
Ingredients. Today Langridge pushes the ball for unfussed
Singles; ladies clap from check rugs, talk to retired colonels;
On tomato-red verandas the scoring rate is discussed.

Sussex v Lancashire, the air birded and fresh after rain,
Dew on syringa and cherry. Seaward the water
Is satin, pale emerald, fretted with lace at the edges,
The whole sky rinsed easy like nerves after pain.
May here is childhood, lost somewhere between and never
Recovered, but again moved nearer like a lever
Turned on the pier flickers the Past into pictures.
A time of immediacy, optimism, without stricture.

Post-cards and bathing machines and old prints.
Something comes back, the inkling and momentary hint
Of what we had wanted to be, though differently now
For the conditions are different, and what we had wanted
We wanted as we were then, without conscience, unhaunted,
And given the chance must refuse to want it again.
Only, occasionally, we escape, we return where we were:
Watching cricket at Brighton, Cornford bowling through sea-scented air.

Clifford Bax

When life was budding and I new-married, I made my home in a house that
stood
Grey in the green of the Wiltshire meadows – a hoary dwelling of stone and
beam;
And there, when summer had burst the poppy and skies were brazen,
the men I loved –
Letting the world go by – would gather for days of cricket in field or park.

Days of delight! For delight unmeasured it was to fare through the morning
lanes,
And hour by hour, as the sun went over, to strive for victory, friend with
friend;
Or, jogging home as the twilight settled on ancient village or farm, to see
The curtained windows, the candles lighted, the supper spread and the cider
drawn.

Beautiful too were the nights that followed when, strolling forth in a glad
fatigue
And lazing long where the starlight glimmered on ghostlike lilies that fringed
the lawn,
We shared our thought or our laughter, forging a love between us that years
of change
Have left but stronger, alike responsive to this man's learning or that man's
wit.

I knew, indeed, as the days went by, how none of all that were yet to be
Could bring delight that was more unclouded. I did not know that with every
hour
We stored a joy that would last forever – like Arab merchants that fill their
gourds
With crystal water from some white city and then set forth to the desert sand.

John Arlott

Glamorgan in the Field

From the top of the hill-top pavilion,
The sea is a cheat to the eye,
Where it secretly seeps into coastline
Or fades in the yellow grey sky;
But the crease-marks are sharp on the green
As the axe's first taste of the tree,
And keen is the Welshmen's assault
As the freshening fret from the sea.
The ball is a withering weapon,
Fraught with a strong-fingered spin
And the fieldsmen, with fingers prehensile,
Arc the arms of attack moving in.
In the field of a new Cymric mission,
With outcricket cruel as a cat
They pounce on the perilous snick
As it breaks from the spin-harried bat.

On this turf, the remembered of rugby –
'The Invincibles' – came by their name,
And now, in the calm of the clubhouse,
Frown down from their old-fashioned frame.
Their might has outlived their moustaches,
For photos fade faster than fame;
And this cricket rekindles the temper
Of their high-tramping, scrummaging game:
As intense as an Eisteddfod anthem
It burns down the day like a flame.

Irving Rosenwater

Architecture most august, Victorian survivals,
Alike a joy to ancient hands as well as fresh arrivals:
The streets so planned with apt foresight,
The lasting dower of Colonel Light.
The long proud ground that we now attend,
The stately spires at the northern end,
Gums and pines around the grass,
A scene not easy to surpass.
A sky so spacious in its blueness,
A well-nursed turf famed for its trueness.
The heat that shimmers on the distant hills
Strives to sap a player's skills –
Gruelling heat, remorseless heat,
Whence men and teams can scarce retreat.
Here once did Giffen, Darling, Hill
Each season faithful watchers thrill:
Two Richardsons and 'Nip' Pellew,
And Clarrie Grimmett long on view;
The mighty Bradman, Chappells three,
Sobers, Hawke – what pedigree!

Oh Adelaide, oh Adelaide . . .
You have no need us to persuade:
Your city and not least your ground
In promise, charm and deed abound.

Anon

The Brisbane Courier, 23 January 1933

This is not the game you taught us!
Is it cricket?
It has lost the charm it brought us!
Is it cricket?
On the dear old village green,
Where the vicar and the dean
Kept the bowling "all serene":
That was cricket!
If you're "short weight" in the mart
It's not "cricket"!
If your business deals are "smart" –
That's not "cricket"!
Hanki panki is for fools,
It's not taught you in your schools
So expunge it from your Rules:
It's not cricket.
Age-long query of the Saxon!
Is it cricket?
See the bruises, there, our backs on:
Is it cricket?
No, this new fangled bumping
That has set Australia "jumping"
And our batsmen's hearts a-thumping –
Isn't cricket.

Lewis Carroll

Amidst thy bowers the tyrant's hand is seen,
The rude pavilions sadden all thy green;
One selfish pastime grasps the whole domain,
And half a faction swallows up the plain;
Adown thy glades, all sacrificed to cricket,
The hollow-sounding bat now guards the wicket.
Sunk are thy mounds in shapeless level all,
Lest aught impede the swiftly rolling ball;
And trembling, shrinking from the fatal blow,
Far, far away thy hapless children go.

The man of wealth and pride
Takes up a space that many poor supplied;
Space for the game, and all its instruments,
Space for pavilions and for scorers' tents;
The ball, that raps his shins in padding cased,
Has wore the verdure to an arid waste;
His Park, where these exclusive sports are seen,
Indignant spurns the rustic from the green;
While through the plain, consigned to silence all,
In barren splendour flits the russet ball.

R. D. Lancaster

Their refuse tip increased. One day
A lorry shot down flattened tins,
The next half an old house. But play
Continues. Oil drums pitched, coin spins.
The skippers thumb the wicket, glance
Up at the sky, decide. All field,
Except the two men in, whose stance
Means business. Play. Wait, haven't peeled
Off yet (to quote the Gem), not stripped
Our jackets off. Bats dig their graves.
Dust, more dust, as more clinker's tipped
Before the first man swipes. He saves
His strength for bowling. Caught. He pouts,
Then bowls at both ends he's so big,
Bounces down like rubble bricks, shouts
To warn a nipper whose smart jig
Is chasing butterflies across
Cloud shadows, rushes, halts, hops, leaps –
What? Googly, yorker, wide, full toss?
Swinging, the bat flings dust up, heaps
Chalk white clouds. No one sees at first
The ball soaring away, sun high,
So close in line it seems to burst
Poles scaffolding a cold glass eye
(The new Tube station) in lark skies,
Then drops inside the refuse tip.
Lost ball. Fetch it. Six and out. Cries
The nipper, haven't batted. Slip
Across and ask. You. But the big
Star bat and bowler stirs and dust.
You go, you're fielding. And all dig
Toes harder in. You go. You. Trust
Him not to. Batsman fetches. Fists –
But ten a.m.'s too soon and hot
And he's too big to fight, his writs
Hair covered. A fresh lorry's shot

Sticks, beams. Whose ball? It's buried now.
Not worth a tanner. Bob. Say please.
Who hit it? Who bowled? Hold your row.
A mutiny subdues to bees,
This endless August sun above,
That asphalt road, the cars close by,
Tipped water bottles fitting glove
Tight to red lips, and guzzled sigh
In nettles and tall thistles and
Unwanted hay. A driver yells
This yours? And throws it, huge paw hand
A friendly wave. The big boy tells
All he knew where to find it, but
Prefers to laze while play goes on.
Next year sign-board, contractors' hut;
Sand, barrows, mixers, Hayfields gone.

Louis Herzberg

Pillars, incandescent, concrete,
Towering vultures
Token to mammon – flare out
Pure light to seduce money
To bring youth and ignorance unaware of
white purity.
Glances and cuts unknown, worshipping
brute force, hatred, aggro.
Ball hit high to heavens, yet beyond vulture's
reach,
And still high enough to destroy the gods
of light.
So farewell skill, grace, beauty and elegant
willow eloquence.
Fading away in bedlam, pollution,
    People pollution
    Paper pollution
    Cardboard pollution
    Culture pollution
    Cash pollution
A Hill entombed in debris –
A civilisation enshrouded in waste,
A wasting civilisation.
Wasting away to Roman hordes
Battering tin, tin, tintabulation
A ringing round, a crescendo of folly
XXXced, hate, noise – noise, noise
A tumult to greet great Caesar
As he strikes the coin.

Gerald Howat

The closure of the Tavern Bar and the building of a temporary stand.

Before

Too much litter,
Pints of bitter,
Spoiled Lord's.

Horns and whistles,
Explicit epistles,
Shocked Lord's.

Pitch intrusion,
Police invasion,
Angered Lord's.

Boisterous crowd,
Singing loud,
Jarred Lord's.

Finally
The crowd came alive,
At a quarter to five,
Awoke Lord's.

Kent's two-three-two
was deemed just too few,
Speculated Lord's.

Supporters cheered gladly,
As Downton and Radley,
Dominated Lord's.

Kent's prospects were holding,
With Underwood bowling,
Agreed Lord's.

Last ball of the day,
And all to Play,
Thrilled Lord's.

Then

A day to remember,
in sunny September,
Appealed to Lord's.

The Tavern closed,
Spectators dozed,
Changed Lord's.

Polite clapping,
Like waves lapping,
Engulfed Lord's.

Respectability reigned,
Bad manners refrained,
Thought Lord's.

But at twenty to eight,
Kent met their fate,
Summed up Lord's.

Explosions of noise,
Excited small boys,
Tolerated Lord's.

Then away from the scene,
On the tube to Wood Green,
Dispatched from Lord's.

Or to houses in Dover,
For the season is over,
Concluded Lord's.

Men from NatWest,
Dressed in their best,
Invited to Lord's.

*The A B of C,
Seen having his tea,
Impressed Lord's . . .

. . . This supporter of Kent,
Heaven-sent,
Sanctified Lord's.

But "Middlesex for Winner",
Purred a punter from Pinner,
Paraded at Lord's.

*Dr. Robert Runcie, Archbishop of Canterbury

Simon Rae

By the party conference season in 1989 the SDP had split from its Alliance partners, the Liberals, and was reduced to a tiny rump dominated by its leader, who spent part of the Sunday preceding the conference playing cricket.

Dr. David Owen
Opened with himself –
There was really no one else;
The rest were on the shelf.

And like another doctor,
Renowned throughout the world,
He struck the ball a mighty blow:
Into the sky it curled.

Then Dr. David Owen
Put off his gloves and pads
And confidently strolled into
The covers with the lads.

The ball soared high above him.
Then dropped, of course it did.
The captain of the team was calm.
He neither slipped nor slid.

So Dr. David Owen
Caught Dr. David Owen.
Bowled – you might have known it –
By Dr. David Owen.

Back to the crease he sauntered,
And nobody would dare
To question his continuing:
He never turned a hair.

Eventually his colleagues
Escaped him one by one.
And all alone, in failing light,
He scored the winning run.

Simon Rae

Controversy surrounded the omission of David Gower from the winter tour of India in 1992/93. England lost the first Test in Calcutta by 8 wickets. It was Graham Gooch's 100th Test Match, but not one he is likely to want to remember, even though he was presented with a copy of Rabindrinath Tagore's poems.

Down by the banks of the Hooghly River
Wanders a man with a face full of woe;
Down by the ghats where the vultures hover,
On he wanders with footsteps slow.

Veteran now of his hundredth Test match,
A hundred Tests, so he knows the score,
He leaves Calcutta with a dented record
And a book of poems by a man called Tagore.

Down by the banks of the Hooghly River
He sees a ghost who shouldn't be there,
A not particularly old ghost either,
Handsome, willowy, debonair.

Hello, old ghost, he calls out softly,
Hello, old ghost, just passing through?
Where were you at Eden Gardens?
Where were you when we needed you?

Where were you when the wickets tumbled?
When the fire-crackers roared and they had us on toast?
Where were you when the crowds exploded?
Where were you when we needed you most?

The ghost just smiled and shrugged his shoulders,
Flicked his wrists as though to say:
Here I am, and here I will be,
Whenever, wherever, you'd like me to play.

Kit Wright

Dr. Tyerley practised in a Victorian mental hospital and believed in the psycho-therapeutic value of cricket.

1 A Player to the Luncheon Guests

I was a bowler for Dr.Tyerley's team
    That played another of this name
Lately, on the Doctor's grounds. You came,
    You remember, by the privet gate
        To the field's edge that day
        To see the madmen play –
And the Doctor's Burgundy and haunch of pork
Slurred in your bellies as rich talk
    Of Hunt and Steam and State
    Gave, down the orchard, way
        To the white gleam
Of us odd fellows dancing the Doctor's dream.

But I was a bowler for Dr. Tyerley's side
    Against another – his men too –
And the first trick of all was mine to do:
    Bowl the first ball, begin the game.
        I tell you this is so:
        I could not let it go.
I ran up to the stumps. Then shied. Stopped.
Three times I tried. And stuck. So I was dropped
    From the Doctor's side. The shame
    Killed me when I came
        To the tree where he tied
My arms and legs and left me. I'm a wide.

2 A Player to the Doctor

Fat Dr. Tyerley
  Sweatily scrabbled:
Played the game hard.
Charged round the yard
Like a bull in a ring,
Booming us on
For the game was the thing
To make a man well:

Dear Dr. Tyerley,
How could you tell?

Fat Dr. Tyerley
  Grovelled and grappled:
Hurled the burst ball
At the stump-painted wall,
Cranked the chipped bat
That was gone in the spring,
Thundered *How's that?*
At a wicket laid low:

Sweet Dr. Tyerley,
How should we know?

Fat Dr. Tyerley
  Mightily struggled:
Rearing and clouting,
Praising and shouting
Over the scrum
In the exercise yard
Of the wailing and dumb
Advice and abuse:

Kind Dr. Tyerley,
What was the use?

Much, Dr. Tyerley.
  Sadly we straggled:
I and the rest.
Players long past our best,
Kept, mortally, error.
That lay beyond games,
But who, from locked terror,
First gave me the key?

You, Dr. Tyerley,
Playing for me.

Kit Wright

Meat smell of blood in locked rooms I cannot smell it,
Screams of the brave in torture loges I never heard nor heard of
Apartheid I wouldn't know how to spell it,
None of these things am I paid to believe a word of
For I am a stranger to cant and contumely.
I am a professional cricketer.
My only consideration is my family.

I get my head down nothing to me or mine
Blood is geysering now from ear, from mouth, from eye,
How they take a fresh guard after breaking the spine,
I must play wherever I like or die
So spare me your news your views spare me your homily.
I am a professional cricketer.
My only consideration is my family.

Electrodes wired to their brains they should have had helmets,
Balls wired up they should have been wearing a box,
The danger was the game would turn into a stalemate,
Skin of their feet burnt off I like thick woollen socks
With buckskin boots that accommodate them roomily
For I am a professional cricketer.
My only consideration is my family.

They keep falling out of the window they must be clumsy
And unprofessional not that anyone told me,
Spare me your wittering spare me your whimsy,
Sixty thousand pounds is what they sold me
And I have no brain. I am an anomaly.
I am a professional cricketer.
My only consideration is my family.

Richard Congreve

We're purer than this winter's driven snow
And just about as thin upon the ground
For we are cricketers who have said 'no'
To Afric's sun – where colleagues do abound.
We are the hopefuls who'll accept low pay
For staying at home and never playing the Boer
T'await the magic of that golden day
When we are asked to join a Test Match tour.
The teams we play against may be comprised
Of scoundrels, rogues and every sort of cad,
But in litany (as now revised)
'Tis only Southern Africans who're bad!
Thus England's team stand chaste before the wicket
To win with God but not, alas, at cricket.

14TH APRIL

David Phillips

Counted on the fingers of three hands
a crowd wrapped up for winter in the stands
applaud us into summer as we're blown
by gusting April winds which bite the bone.

And daffodils wave by the betting tent,
an outstayed welcome in this endless lent;
horse-chestnut buds keep resolutely sealed
as fifteen men stand shivering in a field.

Until at last it's lunchtime; chapped with cold
we stagger up the steps and lunch is doled
by ladies who think cricket meals a breeze:
cold ham salad, ice cream, iced tea, hard cheese.

Martin Booth

Taxis hacking by.
Exhaust fumes cocoon the gatemen
around the round-edged rectangle,
walled in like Wormwood Scrubs.
Within, it is library quiet.
Old, like its oldest member,
the ancient orange edifice,
the couched, dozing Mandarin,
contemplative,
wears a sun-induced smile.

White watery flicks of an artist's brush
eddy with each ball bowled.
While two of them, importantly,
rebound between the wickets,
over the scuffed, tufted concrete landing strip.

Peaked caps, agitated.
Pointing like noses.
Fox-faced gentlemen
plot escape routes for the ball.

Crook'd elbows jutting, jab.
Skittering across the grass,
round red fish on invisible hook,
leaps up at the boundary rope in spasm.
Then slaps against the hoarding and,
as if in surprise at its own violence
squirms to a stop.

The empty tiers, flaking white, grey cemented,
crowned by looming peaks of hard white icing.
Silence broken by patterned claps,
like the snap snap snapping of briefcases.

And the inscrutable pavilion
smiles benignly.

Mo Muir

A bell across the cornfield
tolls
telling
gloved
and muddy moles
beneath the surface
ready rolled
and ringing wet
to rise;

As
Over the border
Of day and night
a crack of blue
a snatch of light
Warns
the game
the carnivore
(the match
of talon, fang and claw
with sinews) of a night
once more

that's
over.

Something scatters
something growls
Something through the wicket
prowls
The vanishing badger
the fading owls
see the village windows lit
through yellow
hungry
narrowing slits
reflect
on the day
and the breakfast dish
of cat and dog
think
better of it

And the Fox
slips . . .

cont'd

deep
into extra cover.

The sun, up
from Australia
bursts,
beaming,
bloody
Brilliant shot
pavilion windows
blaze,
But not
half
high enough
to pierce
the field
yet
picks the spot
the mouse played in.
And mist
hangs
steaming in the gulley ringed

with flashing
flying, singing sparks
hovering sunlit
piping larks
upon a perfect pitch;

The bell rings
Ring the bell again!
For all is well
in the world of men
But . . .wait!
upon the hallowed turf
– movement!
spinning
bits of earth
Right through the groundsman's pride
– a paw!
The Mole!
with sharpened tooth and claw
and pushing up with all his strength
bangslap upon the line and length
has built his ruddy door!

VI

CHARACTER RECAPTURED

(Straight Drive or Square Cut)

~

The chapter title really says all that needs to be said. Here are forty studies in verse of characters legendary and fictional. To mention but a few.

Jeff Cloves's magnificent freshly-minted response to a last-minute commission to reflect the retirement of the Waugh twins rightly opens the batting. Coming in at number three is Arthur Conan Doyle with his rapturous reminiscence of his lone first-class wicket – that of W. G. Grace. Understandably perhaps, there is no mention of the fact that Grace had made a hundred before he was dismissed. Then immediately following are two short poems from Gerard Martineau, the first, specially composed for the Trent Bridge Centenary in 1938, 'To the Shade of William Clarke', and secondly, 'Recollections of Ranji'.

Fictional figures are represented by two stonewallers – that carved by Hubert Phillips reckons 'An Englishman's crease is 'is Castle' and that lyricised by John Arlott blocks 'and never has a crack'. 'Stonewall Jack' was set to the music of that well-known group from Dorset called 'The Yetties'. When at school Arlott was called Jack by his friends and for a time he had a theory that if he planted his bat directly in front of the wicket and never moved it he could not be bowled. The theory did not survive for long.

A trio of tributes after the death of the immortal Don Bradman come first from Felix Dennis, the one-time co-editor of *Oz*, then from John Stuart in Australia, and finally from the erudite pen of the Don's biographer, Irving Rosenwater. Rosenwater also provides a tribute to another Australian, that elegant batsman, Greg Chappell, which was composed 'on a steamy day in Sydney in 1982'. It was one of those rare joyful occasions for any writer when thoughts were transmitted directly on to the page without need of alteration or chiselling into place.

There are also half-a-dozen evocative cameos from Colin Shakespeare, Tim Rice's specially written lyrics to music from *The Mikado* which were sung by Richard Suart and the Choir at the Service of Thanksgiving at Westminster Abbey for the life of Colin Cowdrey; and individual salutations to three of the greatest batsmen in the history of cricket.

D. R. A.

Jeff Cloves

Mark Waugh retired from Test Cricket in 2003. Steve Waugh retired from Test Cricket and as Captain of Australia in 2004.

First one then the other
so how to tell Steve from Mark
brother from brother
highflyer from lark?
Once all twins were Bedsers
then came these marvellous boys
whey-faced ground-standing grudgers
who flogged our dogged bowlers with disdain
until the Death of English Cricket
was once again proclaimed:
dust to dust hot ashes to ashes
our sorely tested teams
all cindered in the sun:
like the ozone layer – bombarded
like the Van Allen Belt – undone

Collars up sleeves down they wore
those twice-damned faded baggy caps
batted bowled caught smouldered swore
forever masked with sunblocker
smiles rarer than failure
success as constant as every season
victory expected with cocky reason

Once a boy bereft saw brave England fall
once he supposed all captains began with 'B'
once Brown F. R. and Bradman arranged the day
once English gent and Colonial pro held sway
once fielding fast bowlers fell in behind the ball
once they ushered it politely to the welcome fence
once Bradman doffed his cap at centuries
once his opponents applauded without offence
once helmets were only worn by coppers

once a boy sat on the grass at Lord's
once he queued six hours for his ticket
once he saw sun-burned Bradman lose his wicket

So did The Don ever bowl and bowl moreover like Mark
did Mark ever strive to drive like Steve
how well did Bradman bat swear field and catch
against the peerless pugnacious Waughs
can we know now how he would match?
Ah to hell with green baggies and classic straight bats
take a look at the twins' so similar stats
whatever the toss their gain was our loss
but now they've declared
there's a glimmer of hope
the Nation breathes a sigh of relief
beyond the boundary rope.

Oscar Lloyd

I saw the 'Old Man' once
When he was old as I
Was young. He did not score,
So far as I recall, a heap of runs,
Nor even hit a four.
But still he lives before my schoolboy eye
A giant among pygmies. In his hand
The bat looked like a toy. I saw him stand
Firm set on legs as massive as the piers
Of the Norman nave at Gloucester; and the cheers
Which greeted him on the 'Spa' were heard
As far as the Cathedral. When he stirred
The ground shook, and the crazy old
Pavilion creaked and groaned. I saw him field
– At point. When 'Father' Roberts bowled
And the batsman, now forgotten, from the group
Around the wicket cut a fast one square
Along the ground, the Doctor saw it there
A moment ere it was concealed
By his great bulk. He did not deign to stoop,
But let it pass. He bowled a few
Himself, slow lumbering to the crease. The batsmen knew
By then his simple bluff, and did not care.

Upon the Spa no county players pace;
The great ones of to-day it does not know.
I deem it better so,
Leaving the elm-girt field its dreams of Grace.

Arthur Conan Doyle

Once in my heyday of cricket,
  Oh day I shall ever recall!
I captured that glorious wicket,
  The greatest, the grandest of all.

Before me he stands like a vision,
  Bearded and burly and brown,
A smile of good-humoured derision
  As he waits for the first to come down.

A statue from Thebes or from Cnossus,
  A Hercules shrouded in white,
Assyrian bull-like Colossus,
  He stands in his might.

With the beard of a Goth or a Vandal,
  His bat hanging ready and free,
His great hairy hands on the handle,
  And his menacing eyes upon me.

And I – I had tricks for the rabbits,
  The feeble of mind or of eye,
I could see all the duffer's bad habits
  And guess where his ruin might lie.

The capture of such might elate one,
  But it seemed like some horrible jest
That I should serve tosh to the great one,
  Who had broken the hearts of the best.

Well, here goes! Good Lord, what a rotter!
  Such a sitter as never was dreamt;
It was clay in the hands of the potter,
But he tapped it with quiet contempt.

The second was better – a leetle;
  It was low, but was nearly long-hop;
As the housemaid comes down on the beetle
  So down came the bat with a chop.

He was sizing me up with some wonder,
    My broken-kneed action and ways;
I could see the grim menace from under
    The striped peak that shaded his gaze.

The third was a gift or it looked it –
    A foot off the wicket or so;
His huge figure swooped as he hooked it,
    His great body swung to the blow.

Still when my dreams are night-marish,
    I picture that terrible smite,
It was meant for a neighbouring parish,
    Or any old place out of sight.

But – yes there's a but to the story –
    The blade swished a trifle too low;
Oh wonder, and vision of glory!
    It was up like a shaft from a bow.

Up, up, like a towering game-bird,
    Up, up to a speck in the blue,
And then coming down like the same bird,
    Dead straight on the line that it flew.

Good Lord, it was mine! Such a soarer
    Would call for a safe pair of hands;
None safer than Derbyshire Storer
    And there, face uplifted, he stands.

Wicket-keep Storer, the knowing,
    Wary and steady of nerve,
Watching it falling and growing
    Marking the pace and the curve.

I stood with my two eyes fixed on it,
    Paralysed, helpless, inert;
There was 'plunk' as the gloves shut upon it,
    And he cuddled it up to his shirt.

Out – beyond question or wrangle!
    Homeward he lurched to his lunch!
His bat was tucked up at an angle,
    His great shoulders curved into a hunch.

Walking he rumbled and grumbled,
　　Scolding himself and not me;
One glove was off, and he fumbled,
　　Twisting the other one free.

Did I give Storer the credit
　　The thanks he so splendidly earned?
It was mere empty talk if I said it,
　　For Grace was already returned.

G. D. Martineau

On The First Test at Trent Bridge in 1938. Inn-keeper/entrepreneur William Clarke opened Trent Bridge in 1838.

Poem especially composed for this historic Anniversary, given by its Author, G. D. Martineau, to Mr A. W. Shelton. Printed from the MSS for Mr Shelton, and presented with his compliments and kind regards.

Look how they muster. William, can you see?
    Here's where you fared along o' Pitch and Mynn.
Could you have dreamed that such as this would be
    When first you met with Mary at the inn?

Here is all England, gathered for the bout,
    All England watching, while All England plays:
Your own team, William – could you bow them out
    As promptly as you did in those old days?

The same green meads, yet somehow not the same,
    Stretch out, inviting, for the hosts engaged.
A smoother carpet bears the modern game,
    And maybe you would find it oddly waged.

Do you smile grimly, William, from the shades
    To mark the filing throng, their earnest mien,
The buffets hard dispending lemonades,
    And think of beer and benches on the green?

'Tis all changed, William – matches four days long.
    Still there are sights and sounds to bridge the years,
The deep ring thrilling to the same old song,
    The stir, the roar, the burst of rolling cheers.

G. D. Martineau

An hour of Ranji . . . I can close these eyes
   And watch again those moments charmed away;
Applause rolls out, as from the surge of surf,
   A form is moving with a supple stride,
Who, that has seen it, does not love the glide,
   The pliant work of wrists in sympathy,
The lightning turn, that flicks the ball aside,
   And bids us taste the game's sweet luxury?

'Century'

Since this season has begun,
Many a wonder has been done,
By the famous William Gunn,

In averages a 'rising star',
And from the top he is not far,
Stoddart and Peel below him are.

And if he plays his very best,
I say, and mean it, not in jest,
He'll soon be leading all the rest.

'Tis very fine to watch him bat
(Though slow at times, I must say that)
When he begins the ball to pat.

But he can hit, and what is more,
He's often shown us how to score,
And drive across the grassy floor.

He stands just six feet four in height,
And for his wicket he can fight,
And out the many 'fields' to flight.

For Notts he's been of service great,
Because he learnt to watch and wait,
And take his chance ere 'twas too late.

For England several times he's played,
And many a useful score has made,
And his most perfect form displayed.

And now I'll end my lengthy praise,
I wish him many lengthy 'stays',
And luck throughout his cricket days.

Francis Thompson

It is little I repair to the matches of the Southron folk,
　　Though my own red roses there may blow;
It is little I repair to the matches of the Southron folk,
　　Though the red roses crest the caps, I know.
For the field is full of shades as I near the shadowy coast,
And a ghostly batsman plays to the bowling of a ghost,
And I look through my tears on a soundless-clapping host
　　As the run-stealers flicker to and fro,
　　　　To and fro:
　　Oh my Hornby and my Barlow long ago!

It is Glo'ster coming North, the irresistible,
　　The Shire of Graces, long ago!
It is Gloucestershire up North, the irresistible,
　　And new-risen Lancashire the foe!
A Shire so young that has scarce impressed its traces,
Ah, how shall it stand before all-resistless Graces?
Oh little red rose, their bats are as maces
　　To beat thee down, this summer long ago!

This day of seventy-eight they are come up North against thee,
　　This day of seventy-eight, long ago!
The champion of the centuries, he cometh up against thee,
　　With his brethren, every one a famous foe!
The long-whiskered Doctor, that laugheth rules to scorn,
While the bowler, pitched against him, bans the day that he was born;
And G.F. with his science makes the fairest length forlorn;
　　They are come from the West to work thee woe!

It is little I repair to the matches of the Southron folk,
　　Though my own red roses there may blow;
It is little I repair to the matches of the Southron folk,
　　Though the red roses crest the caps, I know.
For the field is full of shades as I near the shadowy coast,
And a ghostly batsman plays to the bowling of a ghost,
And I look through my tears on a soundless-clapping host,
　　As the run-stealers flicker to and fro,
　　　　To and fro:
　　Oh my Hornby and my Barlow long ago!

Anon

V ictor he in name and deed, pride of Austral seas,
I n a blaze of glory such as few recall.
C linking strokes that blind us, dazzle and remind us,
T rumper, Victor Trumper, is the peer of all;
O nward still where'er he be, England or Australia,
R eeling out his hundreds while the crowds acclaim.

T iming driving, glancing, hooking that's entrancing,
R ushing up the pathway to the Hall of Fame;
U nder all this triumph what do we discern –
M odesty, refreshing as a desert rain,
P ride, well-curbed and glowing,
E arnest and straight-going
R ound his brow the victor's wreath will long remain.

W. A. B.

On reports that Clem Hill was considering retirement

O Clement, Clement, this is hard
    To bear. We cannot bear it.
Your name must be upon the card
    In future 'tests'. We swear it.

What will your colleague, Victor, say
    (You two were boys together)
If you with him no longer play
    At punishing the leather?

Must the Australians take the field
    While you sit in pavilions?
Must they to every foeman yield,
    And sadden waiting millions,

Because they can no more rely
    On you to paste a swerver?
Oh Clement, Clement, go and buy
    An *Adelaide Observer*.

And see what pretty things it says
    About your plucky cricket;
Then think about the bygone days
    Before you leave the wicket.

J. A. Gibney

Bats off to C. V. Grimmett,
   The wizard of the ball,
Who routed England's champions,
   Hobbs, Sandham, Hearne, and all.
Who in his opening test match
   Displayed such magic skill.
Australia sought a bowler
   And Grimmett filled the bill.

Hats off to C. V. Grimmett,
   We're justly proud to-day
Of South Australia's champion,
   Who quickly forced his way
Through England's grim endeavours
   To guard her polished sticks.
Success attend his efforts
   In nineteen twenty six.

Frank Quarterman

I remember well the day I sat enthralled
To watch the ball fair skimming across
The Oval Lawn,
And though with him you never could be sure
If it would be upon the turf or high up in
The air,
He'd made three hundred plus and yet was out
Ere stumps were drawn.

Nowadays the whole eleven would bat through
To make two-fifty –
Few more than this would be expected
In a Test.

Sometime we may have a joust of Ian Botham
Or of Viv Richards stroking far and wide
When at his best,
But for all the heavy-bat sloggin' and all
The text-book play
Nothing could be so exciting or enthusiast –
Inviting as to see the flashing bat of Frank
Woolley on his day.

While Denis Compton played a game
To please spectators one and all
And in the field Pat Hendren cracked
A joke with them,
Many brilliant bowlers and great fielders –
And Frank himself could field and spin with most
– Many other white-clad sportsmen of the green
Will bear remembering.

I'm not so ancient that
I can remember Doctor Grace;
C. B. Fry and Barnes and Jessop flourished
Well before my time and place;
But ever that flashing bat held in that
Left-hand stance,
Orthodox or unorthodox, the essence grace,
Performing drive and pull and cut and
Sometimes as a change the neatest glance
Will remain a perfect picture
In my memory.

M. J. C. Allom and M. J. L. Turnbull

I hold it better to have seen Frank's swing
And let its fragile beauty magnify
My own poor discord, joyous graceful thing,
Than to have reaped all Painting's harmony.

93 TO JOHN BERRY HOBBS ON HIS
SEVENTIETH BIRTHDAY,
16TH DECEMBER 1952

John Arlott

There falls across this one December day
The light remembered from those suns of June
That you reflected, in the summer play
Of perfect strokes across the afternoon.

No yeoman ever walked his household land
More sure of step or more secure of lease
Than you, accustomed and unhurried, trod
Your small, yet mighty, manor of the crease.

The game the Wealdon rustics handed down
Through growing skill became, in you, a part
Of sense; and ripened to a style that showed
Their country sport matured to balanced art.

There was a wisdom so informed your bat
To understanding of the bowler's trade
That each resource of strength or skill he used
Seemed but the context of the stroke you played.

The Master: records prove the title good:
Yet figures fail you, for they cannot say
How many men whose names you never knew
Are proud to tell their sons they saw you play.

They share the sunlight of your summer day
Of thirty years; and they, with you, recall
How, through those well-wrought centuries, your hand
Reshaped the history of bat and ball.

Edmund Blunden

Since our most beautiful and subtle game
First grew from England's leas and levels green,
In turn its champions in their genius came –
Men who had but to walk into the scene
To be its masters; in each magic name,
A generation felt the whole serene
Enchantment of this play, this art, this test
Of character and skill a thousand ways expressed.

The observed of all observers long ago,
The models of young hearts dreaming of glory,
Great in all lights that fell upon the show
And tournament of cricket, leave the story
To greater still; its scope and problem grow
Beyond their use, nor would their ghosts be sorry
Perhaps that company of kings of cricket
Have means of watching well their followers at the wicket.

Ourselves have watched the classics of our days
With little fear of past or future boasts;
In our own sunshine we have men to praise
Above the lordliest Hambledonian ghost;
Round the wide world the bright pavilions blaze
With modern honours – where to honour most
In Bradman's era is our question; then,
Hammond is taking guard. There stands our man of men.

Not to have seen Hammond in such an hour
Is not to know the stature of true sport,
The quiet instancy of natural power,
Completeness, fluent action in each sort
Of cricket's needs; how this command will tower
Above the skilful rest all minds report;
Not to have seen him leave us unaware
What cricket swiftness, judgement, foresight truly are.

So comes he to the field, and of his sway
And sceptre is by how much more assured
That dynasties in fields where nations play
With danger; call his kingdom Bon Accord,
And mark the entire master to this day,
Still studious of the least thing unexplored,
True to first principles, approving ever
Modesty's patient eye for other men's endeavour.

Cricket's Sir Christopher! His trophies rise
Above the skyline of so many a year
As Wren's clear steeples blazon London skies,
And in their eminence not once appear
Envious of it; their architect decries
The personal sign, content if his career
Interprets what once charmed him as a boy –
The game's delight, the infinite art, event and joy.

Drummond Allison

The ruth and truth you taught have come full circle
On that fell island all whose history lies,
Far now from Bramall Lane and far from Scarborough
You recollect how foolish are the wise.

On this great ground more marvellous than Lord's
– Time takes more spin than nineteen thirty-four –
You face at last that vast that Bradman-shaming
Batsman whose cuts obey no natural law.

Run up again, as gravely smile as ever
Veer without fear your left unlucky arm
In His so dark direction, but no length
However lovely can disturb the harm
That is His style, defer the winning drive
Or shake the crowd from their uproarious calm.

But most when his playing came to a close
That childish Orpheus-tale seemed true,
When handkerchiefs tossed and startled pigeons flew,
And like a forest uprooted the crowd rose,
Followed and danced and stormed with clap and shout,
Wondering if such a wizard could ever be out;
And not till the pavilion sealed from view
His magic, did the swirl of colour recede
Into a staid and whitely sprinkled mead.

Alan Ross

Parks takes ten off two successive balls from Wright,
A cut to the rhododendrons and a hook for six.
And memory begins suddenly to play its tricks:
I see his father batting, as, if here, he might.

Now Tunbridge Wells, 1951; the hair far lighter,
The body boyish, flesh strung across thin bone,
And arms sinewy as the wrists are thrown
At the spinning ball, the stance much straighter.

Now it is June full of heaped petals
The day steamy, tropical; rain glistens
On the pavilion, shining on corrugated metal.
The closeness has an air it listens.

Then it was Eastbourne, 1935; a date
Phrased like a vintage, sea-fret on the windscreen.
And Parks, rubicund and squat, busily sedate,
Pushing Verity square, moving his score to nineteen.

Images of Then, so neatly parcelled and tied
By ribbons of war – but now through a chance
Resemblance re-opened; a son's stance
At the wicket opens the closed years wide.

And it is no good resisting the interior
Assessment, the fusion of memory and hope
That comes flooding to impose on inferior
Attainment – yesterday, today, twisted like a rope.

Parks drives Wright under dripping green trees,
The images compare and a father waves away
Applause, pale sea like a rug over the knees,
Covering him, the son burying his day

With charmed strokes. And abstractly watching,
Drowning, I struggle to shake off the Past
Whose arms clasp like a mother, catching
Up with me, summer at half-mast.

The silent inquisitors subside. The crowd,
Curiously unreal in this regency spa, clap,
A confectionery line under bushes heavily bowed
In the damp. Then Parks pierces Wright's leg-trap.

And we come through, back to the present.
Sussex 300 for 2. Moss roses on the hill.
A dry taste in the mouth, but the moment
Sufficient, being what we are, ourselves still.

ON A GREAT BATSMAN

John Arlott

Suggested by an innings of Denis Compton

As the gull conceals in easeful glide
The inborn gift to curb and ride
The gale – merging the sea wind's force
With lovely movement on a chosen course –
So, in timed swoop, he moves to charm
The ball down-swirling from the bowler's arm
Along some glissade of his own creation,
Beyond the figure's black and white rotation.
    Recorded centuries leave no trace
    On memory of that timeless grace.

Hubert Phillips

I've been standin' 'ere at this wicket since yesterday, just arter tea;
My tally to date is eleven and the total's an 'undred an' three;
The crowd 'as been booin' an' bawlin'; it's booed and it's bawled itself 'oarse,
But barrackin', bawlin' an' booin' I takes as a matter of course.

'Oo am I to be put off my stroke, Mum, becos a few 'ooligans boos?
An Englishman's crease is 'is castle; I shall stay 'ere as long as I choose.

It's not when the wicket's plumb easy that a feller can give of 'is best;
It's not 'ittin' out like a blacksmith that wins any sort of a Test.
The crowd, they knows nuthink about it; they wants us to swipe at the ball;
But the feller 'oo does what the crowd wants, I reckon 'e's no use at all.

'Oo am I to be put off my stroke, Mum, becos a few 'ooligans boos?
An Englishman's crease is 'is castle; I shall stay 'ere as long as I choose.

John Arlott

I am a blocking batsman, me
I blocks and never has a crack
Now John S. Tonewall is my name
But people calls me Stonewall Jack.

I block and never has a crack
And people calls me Stonewall Jack.

Now I am not a pretty bat
But certain as the ace of trumps
The one thing I makes sure to see –
Is no damned bowler gets me out.

I block and never has a crack
And people calls me Stonewall Jack.

I makes it sure I shan't be bowled
By pushin' down the line quite straight.
No light between my bat and pad
They can't get through: there ain't no gate.

I block and never has a crack
And people calls me Stonewall Jack.

I hates them bowlers, so I do;
I hates that horrid ruddy ball
I won't lift up, I won't reach out
I swear I won't be bowled at all.

I block and never has a crack
And people calls me Stonewall Jack.

I covers up with both my pads
I always have, I always will;
Why ain't I ell-be-double-you?
The umpire is my Uncle Bill.

I block and never has a crack
And people calls me Stonewall Jack.

I swears they shall not catch me out;
I will not lift a single stroke;
I will not drive, or hook, or pull;
But nudge and push and dab and poke.

I block and never has a crack
And people calls me Stonewall Jack.

I know I never shall be stumped;
No bowler makes me leave my crease;
No flight, nor spin, nor pace, nor guile
Can e'er disturb my batting peace.

I block and never has a crack
And people calls me Stonewall Jack.

I never would obstruct the field
Nor hit ball twice if once would do;
Nor handle ball with bat in hand;
And who can hit my wicket, who?

I block and never has a crack
And people calls me Stonewall Jack.

The batsman has not yet been born
Can run me out while I am me.
If his first shout ain't same as mine,
Then he's run out I'll guarantee.

I block and never has a crack
And people calls me Stonewall Jack.

I don't retire and don't give up:
You may be certain sure o' that
The only way to end my day
Is when I've carried out my bat.

I block and never has a crack
And people calls me Stonewall Jack.

Now always hate the bowling man;
Don't ask the benefit of doubt;
Oh never let the bowler win,
No, never let him get you out.

I block and never has a crack
And people calls me Stonewall Jack.

Alfred Cochrane

Rustic Cricket in Derbyshire

It were long years back, in t' blacksmith's croft,
   As Jim an' I played cricket
Wi' a bat an' a ball atwixt us both,
   An' a tree as stood for wicket.
We'd never a penny to toss for choice,
   So we'd chuck up t' bat, would we,
     "'Ump!" says Jim,
     "'Oller" says I,
   An' "'Ump it is," says 'e.

We was Test-match men, we was Durby-*shire*,
   An' wouldn't there come a shout,
When Chaterton made a 'it for three,
   Or Docker were bowled for nowt.
When Jim were Spofforth, or summat o' that,
   An' I were W.G.
     "'Ump!" says 'e,
     "'Oller" says I,
   An' "'Oller it is," says 'e.

Eh! But that were a while ago,
   An' there's plenty I've learned sin' that,
But wherever you are, an' whatever you do,
   There's a deal in chuck o' the bat.
For you may call right, an' you may call wrong,
   As 'ud 'appen to Jim an' me,
     "'Ump!" says you,
     "'Oller!" says I,
   An' it canna be both, you see.

Kit Wright

I liked the Captain, all the seams
He fell apart at, going mad

Because he thought the shivered elms
Would fall upon his ashen head

And swifts would peck his eyes. Bad dreams
Can't take the quickness that he had

Who flighted slow leg-breaks that swung
In from the off, then looped away,

Or, lolled on August vapours, hung
And came through flat and how was that?

I liked the Captain, all his schemes
For harassing the right hand bat.

I liked the Captain, all his themes
And each strange learned word he said

Who read solely Victoriana
And had by heart half *Silas Marner*

Along with odd tunes in his head:
He thought the swifts would peck his eyes.

They shall not cut him down to size
Nor seek to break his flighted mind

In institutions. Nothing dead
But he shall be restored again.

Elms shall respect unshaven brain
And birds his wisdom. World needs him.

Come all, come any revolution,
The Captain is the man for spin.

Felix Dennis

In Memoriam Sir Donald George Bradman 1908 – 2001.

The Ump's pulled stumps,
The Don has gone
And now we tally up the score;
Though it was vastly more, my son,
Than ninety-nine point ninety-four.

Howzat! That bat
Would sweep to reap
A double century or more;
And bowlers on their knees would weep
At ninety-nine point ninety-four.

Ah, sure he played
A devilish blade,
As on their feet crowds stood in awe;
For gentlemen aren't born, they're made,
Like ninety-nine point ninety-four.

[*Author's note: 99.94 was The Don's incredible run average in Test cricket.
Prophecy is a dangerous vice, but such an average is unlikely to be repeated.*]

John Stuart

The Don is Dead.
The images,
of authority and power,
an individual of character,
striding assertively to the crease,
pounding the attack,
accepting his fate
uncomplainingly.
From a more gracious era,
the passing away
of the greatest Australian.
Immortality.

'He's just a cricketer,'
his sister once said,
wondering about all the fuss,
and cricket is only a game,
after all,
played by kids in backyards
and bush paddocks,
and adults, more formally,
on manicured ovals,
with some achieving fame,
but in the final innings,
it is just a game.
Rather strange though,
all that dressing-up and preparation,
and for what?
Batsmen going in and getting out,
nothing much happens,
then yell and shout!

And the recording?
Everything is written down,
names, dates and times,
wins and losses,
the eternal question of the tosses,

measuring the meaningless and mundane,
the trivialities of the insane,
still going,
contrasts and comparisons,
more balls bowled, most runs scored,
figures forever, I am bored.
Enough!
What's really going on here?
Well, in this game between two teams,
nothing is as doth seem.

Life and living,
we struggle to survive
and compete to win,
cricket is our nature,
without the sin.
Instinct,
aggression,
controlled violence,
a cult of the primitive
in a modern form . . .
and Bradman,
the finest exponent,
his test average,
99.94,
a glance, a whisper,
from perfection.

The Don is Dead.
He was a man, merely mortal,
But more than a name.
Don Bradman.
Say the words slowly,
with dignity,
strongly stressing each syllable.
Feel these sounds sounding forth,
sounding and resounding,
resonating,
affirming now what is he,
always you and always me,
all that we aspire to be,
all there is, for all is we.

Irving Rosenwater

Written in February 2001, on the death of Sir Donald Bradman.

The spell alas is over now:
A sea of silence lies.
Great things were conqueringly done
That illumined the skies.

Minds cannot justly comprehend
The prizes that were gained –
Mind and muscle finely tuned:
But not to be explained.

The memory of a soaring hour,
Of wrists and eye so vivid yet,
Which could remove men from their squalor
And in its place a fortune set.

A fortune not of wealth or riches
But of sky-blue faultlessness,
Through skill and power – and centuries –
Put forth with ripened peerlessness.

The volcano, awesome in its might, is stilled,
The present from the past unties.
The spell alas is over now:
A sea of silence lies.

Colin Shakespeare

On a small ground, in a small town
In Lancashire, a small man,
Ramadhin, is bowling: his arm comes over
Making disbelievers believe in magic.

Time was he could make cities move,
Crowds converged, with applause ringed him;
Magic enough, his shirt sleeve flapping,
England, no wicket could read him.

Hutton said, 'Treat him like a great man,
Play him down the line.'
Play him down the line into
The passages of time.

Colin Shakespeare

There was no violence in him, rather
The quiet mathematician
Given over to geometrics
And the study of angles,
Arcs,
Perimeters and perpendiculars,
Curves and dividing lines,
But rarely, rarely
The parabola.

And the mystery of it all
Was the mastery of it all.

Jeff Cloves

*'To be a great fast bowler you need a big heart and a big arse' – Fred Trueman of
Yorkshire and England, interviewed by Michael Parkinson.*

bow legger
toe pigeoner
hard hander
quiff flicker
lick finger
shine saver

shirt sailor
hitch trouser
sleeve furler
black scowler
foot fleeter
charge downer

chest heaver
arm wrestler
heart beater
body liner
dip shoulder
maiden over

bump hurler
full tosser
top spinner
swing seamer
late dipper
sweet yorker

bat breaker
hair parter
bail lifter
leg hitter
slip catcher
stump wheeler

appealer
sky pleader
heaven helper
tyke oather
loud mouther
fire eater

Colin Shakespeare

There was no need to time him
Either by stopwatch
Or electronically,
Evans and the slips took steps farther back,
For the batsmen in the pavilion
The message spread like a bushfire,
The Hill went silent;
This was speed
And a speed seldom seen,
Tyson bowling
And fully in possession of himself.

Nurtured
In Middleton,
The raw recruit rapped
Hutton on the pads at Redcar,
The hurt mapped in the mind
A letter to higher authority
Saying a fast bowler was thundering;
The lightning struck at Sydney.

Back home,
Rubbed in the dust
At Northampton,
The pitch with a sign,
NOT WANTED. RESERVED
MOSTLY FOR SPINNERS:
The pulse for the quick fast fading,
He went like Larwood before him
To live and work where the fire was,
Down Under.

Colin Shakespeare

Not the loud fanfare of trumpets
That leads to the boxing ring,
But the long, slow, quiet walk
To the square for cricketing,
But in the make-up of the man
There was the selfsame thing.

To give an inch? Flinch from line?
Or throw the towel in?
With firmness of jaw
Right hand or southpaw
He'd lose his teeth before withdraw,
Which is the cardinal sin.

For in the make-up of the man
The square was a boxing ring.

Alan Ross

Leg-spinners pose problems much like love,
Requiring commitment, the taking of a chance.
Half-way decludes; the bold advance.

Right back, there's time to watch
Developments, though maybe too late.
It's not spectacular, but can conciliate.

Instinctively romantics move towards
Preventing complexities by their embrace,
Batsman and lover embarked as overlords.

Tony Turner

Watching two great fast bowlers at their work
it's like it must have been
to be there at the Coliseum games
when Nero ruled.
The crowd's on fire
lions paw the grass
the emperor settles in his box
and out they come
two gladiators armed with clubs.

A lion makes to charge.
Some of the crowd are crazed
baying for blood as he approaches.

The speed with which his claws rip air
astonishes.
The gladiator, dicing with death,
contorts to miss that fatal touch.
There's blood on the grass
as down he goes
and then another.

And that was how I saw it, years ago,
When Hall and Griffith ruled
at Lord's and England quaked.
Our openers were savaged in this style
when down the pavilion steps
he came as if he owned the place
Lord Ted,
his head held high,
dark eyes, patrician nose
disdainful of the company he kept.

We held our breath
as haughtily he turned to face
big Charlie, whose malevolent eye
could turn a man to stone.

A sickening ball came down
aimed for his head.
He never flinched.
White willow flashed
and ball was gone
crashing the boundary fence.

There was a pause.
For just a moment disbelief
took charge, then wild applause.

I'll never know an hour like that again
or see such strokes, such slaughter,
feel so proud
to see so many lions dead
on such green grass.

Morgan Dockrell

When we first start to follow cricket many of us latch on to great players of the day whom we adopt as 'heroes' and whose careers we follow with particular devotion. My first 'hero' was the South African captain, Dudley Nourse (1910-1981), one of the small band who have averaged over 50 for both Tests and all first class cricket. When I read of his death in The Daily Telegraph in August 1981, I briefly reverted to being a twelve-year-old, seeing Nourse through the eyes of a hero-hungry schoolboy. Nourse bestrode the cricketing world like a Colossus from 1935 to 1951, heading his country's batting averages for five successive series, a feat not managed by Bradman or Hammond. Nourse was the only player to have scored a double century against the formidable Australian spin combination of Grimmett and O'Reilly. He scored an heroic 208 in the Nottingham Test in 1951, batting with a broken thumb, frequently one-handed, for nearly ten hours. This injury refused to heal, forcing Nourse into retirement at the end of a series in which he was plainly unfit to play. Dudley Nourse sacrificed the end of his career for his country. A cricketer of true hero status. I indeed chose my hero well.

M. D.

"NOURSE DIES AT 70" : This headline bleak
Arrested my bored eyes which idly scanned
The Cricket Page. Nourse, lion-heart unique,
My hero thirty years ago, whose hand,
Injured beyond repair, defied the field.
The years roll back. I see him as he stood,
Churchillian, scorning fierce calls to yield.
It seemed he smote with battle-axe of wood.
Unbowed by lost campaigns his massive back
Bore burdens he seemed Atlas-like to hold;
Resolute in defence, swift in attack.
My hero-hungry fancy saw unfold
   A Paladin, a 'very perfect knight'.
   The boy of thirty years ago was right.

Tim Rice

Sung in Westminster Abbey at the Thanksgiving Service for the life of Lord Cowdrey of Tonbridge to the tunes of 'Behold! The Lord High Executioner' and 'I've Got a Little List' from Gilbert and Sullivan's The Mikado.

CHORUS:
> BEHOLD a cricketer most suitable
> As personage with noble rank and title
> Whose sportsmanship was indisputable
> Which on and off the field is simply vital
> Defer, defer
> To a model English cricketer!
> Defer, defer
> To a cricketer, to a cricketer!
> To a model English cricketer!

COLIN:
> TAKING GUARD IN Bangalore
> By a set of curious chances
> I progressed to England's shore
> To the Tonbridge green expanses
>
> Where I fashioned many a score
> That attracted Kentish glances
> And by nineteen fifty-four
> I was taking up my stances
>
> To the sound of Melbourne's roar
> Leading to some great advances
> After forty years or more
> To most noble circumstances
>
> Taking guard in Bangalore
> By a set of curious chances
> After forty years or more
> I had fashioned quite a score

CHORUS:
   Defer, defer
   To a model English cricketer!
   Defer, defer
   To a cricketer, to a cricketer!
   To a model English cricketer!

COLIN:
   As some day it may happen that a victim must
      be found
   I've got a little list – I've got a little list
   Of some cricketing offenders I would banish
      from the ground
   And who never would be missed who never
      would be missed!
   Such as coaches who would rather run ten miles
      than hold a net
   And chaps whose innings end because some
      blighter placed a bet
   I used to think that sledging was a sport that
      needed snow
   But now I know it's something else – it really
      has to go
   And how can stretch pyjama cricket trousers
      still exist?
   They'll none of 'em be missed
   They'll none of 'em be missed!

CHORUS:
   He's got 'em on his list he's got 'em on his list
   and they'll none of 'em be missed –
   They'll none of 'em be missed!

COLIN:
   There's the deadly spin of Ramadhin,
      the blazing speed of Wes
   So tricky to resist I've got them on the list!
   There's running with Sir Geoffrey and no
      matter what he says
   He's going on the list – young Boycs is on
      my list!
   And then there are selectors who decide the
      thing to do

Is make you face some blinding pace when you
    are forty two
Or send you out in fading light in plaster
    head to toe
And EGM's at MCC – I bid them cheerio!
And the off-the-field sensation-seeking tabloid
    journalist
I don't think he'll be missed
I'm sure he won't be missed!

CHORUS:
    He's got 'em on his list he's got 'em on his list
    And they'll none of 'em be missed –
    They'll none of 'em be missed!

COLIN:
    And then there is the batsman who will never
        walk, alas
    I'd slap him on the wrist – I've got him
        on the list!
    Unless at least three stumps have been
        uprooted from the grass
    I think you get the gist – I've got him on the list!
    And sons who think the mid-wicket is the only
        place to aim
    But then perhaps I'm lucky that they loved the
        greatest game
    And my sweet loquacious daughter who'll be
        talking even now
    But always made me chuckle so I think
        I shall allow
    My nearest and my dearest to escape
        my little list
    It's a gesture nepotist – I think they would
        be missed!

CHORUS:
    It's a gesture nepotist – I think they would
        be missed
    Kate, Robert, Jamie, Julius, Fabian, Charlie
    Lucy, Lara, Michael . . .
    He thinks they would be missed!

114 A FLORAL TRIBUTE TO THE FAST AND FURIOUS AUSTRALIAN BOWLER, DENNIS LILLEE

Jeff Cloves

belladonna (bot.) deadly nightshade; plant allied to lily.
(Oxford dictionary)

O Lillee of the valley of the shadow
O shade of the vale of tears and fears
Wizard of Oz – O raging prima donna
accept this bunch of humble belladonna
from the ranks of stricken batsmen – and
with this testimonial and valediction
mark the venomed blackness of the berry
scent the sullen purple flower
clasp them to your lilied bosom – my
how they complement your glower

Colin Shakespeare

In the field, unfussy,
Not a loud, slap-on-the-back man,
He would be just as much at home
Wearing cap and gown,
Crossing quadrangles
To quiet rooms,
Pondering on variables, options,
As he is here, now, on this cricket field,
Quick and alert
Behind the calm exterior,
The slight gesture for a field change,
A raised eyebrow even,
Experience shows like his grey hair,
The whole orchestra aware of his conducting presence.

Not, as a batsman, of the highest class,
But the first to wear a head-protector;
A wise move that for a wise head,
For as captain, players pulled for him
And many a match, seemingly lost
Cost the opposition dearly;
As Rodney Hogg said,
You have a Degree in People, Mike Brearley.

ENGLAND V AUSTRALIA,
HEADINGLEY, JULY 20TH, 1981,
TRIBUTE TO IAN BOTHAM

Colin Shakespeare

Back from zero
To a hero;
Six-wicket-taker,
Fifty-maker,
England, following on
And the match nearly gone,
Mighty Ian Botham
Strides towards the crisis,
Peppers fours to applause –
Keeps as cool as ice is,
Along with Graham Dilley
Lifts the whole of Headingley,
Nineteen fours and a six
Add to his century mix,
Taken all in eighty-seven balls
Oh the rises and the falls,
As the score goes up and up
Some recall the famous Jessop.

Back from zero
To a hero,
Mighty Ian Botham.

Irving Rosenwater

Of those who unleash bat on ball,
Who is most graceful of them all?
With surest eye and nimblest feet,
And bat as broad as King William Street?
Extolled by gamin and Q.C.,   .
With the sweetness of touch of Debussy.
A caress through point or through the covers
Is pabulum for cricket lovers,
Who, in Perth or on the Hill,
Understand a rare-sent skill.
So, be upstanding, raise a cheer
To the lordliest player in the hemisphere.

John Whitworth

There's Aggers and Blaggers and Johnners and Blowers,
There's Fred and old Trevor (who's awfully clever),
There's the Beard and the Nose and a cake from Dundee
Baked by Mary MacPherson (or some other person)
And Zimbabwe are 7 for 3.

They're 7 for 3 and they're following on.
But the covers are out, both the umpires are gone
And there's been no play
Today,
There's been no play
As yet,
And it's wet. It's very wet.

So it's back to the chat again, will England bat again?
7 for 3
That's bad.
The wicket's quite sticky (the cake's pretty icky).
Zimbabwe are plucky and jolly unlucky.
It's sad for Zimbabwe, it's sad.

But it has to be said (says Aggers to Fred)
That their timing's awry and they can't bat for toffee,
Old Cadders, old Goughy, they'll finish them off, eh?
Eh, Fred?
Eh, Fred?

Fred replies at some length on the relative strength
Of his England Eleven and one up in Heaven
That Fred can remember for 1907
When he was a lad.

Oh they knew how to play in those days, yes they did.
They'd be bowling all day for a couple of quid,
An a pint and a packet of fags.

They'd be up from the pits and they'd sluice off the nits,
Then they'd chuck all their togs in their bags
And off to the Test where they'd give of their best,
Where they'd give it a go.

Is that so?
Says Aggers to Fred. Is that so?

Says Fred, yes they would, they were all bloody good,
They were right on the button, were Hammond and Hutton
And Hendren and Hobbs. And they'd play for the nobs
With lots of initials and not many jobs,
Yes they'd play, how they'd play

For A. P. F Chapman and P. B. H May,
For who did you say? Says Aggers to Fred,

For P. G. H. Fender, R. W. V. Robins, R. E. S. Wyatt, J. W. H. T. Douglas,
H. D. G. Leveson-Gower, A. E .R. Gilligan, A. H. H. Gilligan, The Hon. F. S. G.
    Calthorpe,
Old Uncle Plum Warner and all, old Uncle Plum Warner and all.

A marvellous crew, oh yes I'm telling you
They're a marvellous crew but they're dead.

Oh yes that's how it was in the old days,
The bold days, the gold days of yore
When England was England and gave them what-for.
If it came to the crunch and how.

But now?
It's a different ball game now.

Fred shakes his head, takes the cake's last lusciousest slice.
Aaaaah that's nice. A ruminative munch.

It's a different ball game now,
And how.
It's a different ball game now.

Zimbabwe are 7 for 3
And there's been no play since lunch.
But I think it's stopped raining,
Says Aggers.
Says Fred
Oh I'm not complaining,
Not I
You never say die,
No you never say die,
No you *never* say die
Till you're dead.

So there's Cheggers and Duggers and Chuckers and Staggers,
There's Armpit and Buttock and Old Father Time.
There's a bottle of Bells on my knee.

Zimbabwe are 7 for 3.
And there's Mary MacPherson (there *is* such a person)
There's Mary MacPherson and me.

Ian McDonald

Viv in a good mood today, you only have to watch,
See the jaw grinding, he stabbing the pitch, back-lift big.
Look how he look down the wicket, a thunder shock.
Man, this could be an innings! This could make life good.

       *   *   *

You see how he coming in, how he shoulder relax,
How he spin the bat, how he look up at the sun,
How he seem to breathe deep, how he swing the bat, swing,
How he look around like a lord, how he chest expan'.
You ever see the man wear helmet? Tell me.
They say he too proud an' foolish.
Nah! He know he worth, my boy,
The bowler should wear helmet, not he.
Remember long this day, holy to be here. See him
Stalk the high altar o' the mornin' air.

       *   *   *

You ever see such mastery in this world,
You ever see a man who dominate so?
This man don't know forebearance,
He don't know surrender or forgive,
He lash the ball like something anger him
Look how the man torment today!
He holding the bat, it could be an axe.
Look how he grinding he jaw again, my boy.
Look how he head hold cock an' high
And he smile, he gleam, like a jaguar.
Don't bring no flighty finery here, it gone!
Bring the mightiest man, he proud, Viv husk he.
He always so, he stay best fo' the best.

       *   *   *

I tell you, he smile like he hungry
You ever see this man caress?
He pound the ball, look at that, aha!
Like he vex, he slash, he pull, he hook,
He blast a way through the cover man,
He hoist the ball like a iron ball
Gone far and wild, damaging the enemy.
It be butchery today, bat spill blood,
He cut like he cutting hog on a block
Nobody could stop he in that mood.

*   *   *

That mood hold he, oh God, it feel good!
It bite he, the foe turn tremble,
Men step light, nervy, far, danger all about.
Almighty love be there! Almighty love, my boy.
We know he from the start, one o' we –
Something hurt he bad, you could see,
As if heself alone could stop we slavery!

Howard Fergus

The rain stood still above Antigua
To watch Brian Lara flail and cut them
Over and over with a blunt willow
He buried them under a ruin of ruins
In an Antiguan graveyard.
Inflating his countrymen, and absentee planter
Kissed Lara with 50 pieces sterling.

Playing with six stones
Like a broken rosary, two ombudsmen
Six feet deep in black and white
Performed last rites calling 'over and out'.

Digging their hell with a golden blade
Lara struck a jackpot among the shards
Where England sleeps, and raised both hands
In the shape of victory.
Mourners beat drums, drank deep
And a dirge of conch shells kept faith
For an uncertain resurrection
After 375 years of rain under Lara.

But the sun will not set
On the united state of the West Indies
And rain will come again.

Robin Lindsay

We salute the mighty Sachin,
Brightly shining Eastern star,
Lightening all both near and far;
His country's jewel, her Koh-i-noor –
India values Sachin more!
Modest in his life and manner,
Holding high his country's banner,
    God-like son of god-named father,
        Ramesh,
    Writer of such grace and beauty.

    Sachin,
    Player of such grace and beauty;
    His bat is like a magic wand,
    Or flashing sword of tempered steel,
    Or club of Shiva the Destroyer,
    Which sends the ball where'er he wills.
When he comes in to bat the stadium fills.

    Sir Donald Bradman,
Greatest batsman of all time,
From Australia's sunny clime,
Said that he had never known
Anyone whose style's more like his own
When he was in his younger prime.

    Fearsome bowler, Allan Donald,
When he's just been struck for four,
Stands with arms akimbo,
Wryly smiling, quietly saying,
'How I like it, give me more!'

Never since the game's beginning
In an earlier generation
On England's green and pleasant fields,
Has a player been more beloved
By so many in a nation;
    Thus it may be till time shall end.
For young and old, for rich and poor,
He's an imagined uncle, son, or brother,
    Or greatly valued life-long friend.

Greetings to his wife Anjali,
Skilful doctor, children's healer, caring mother,
And their lovely daughter, Sara.
May she show both grace and beauty
In whatever path she follows.
Welcome to their new-born son,
Their first-born son they've called Arjun.
May he be both brave and true
And his life an epic journey,
    A Mahabharata story.

We give whatever gods we worship
Grateful thanks that we have known him.

What will the future hold
When his time for playing ends?
We hope it will be good, for India,
For him, and for all his many friends.

VII

HOME AND AWAY

(National Boundaries)

~

This is a rhythmic tour of many of the cricketing parts of the globe – major and minor. The itinerary soon will be obvious.

Where better to start than with the cultured voice of John Groves as he explains the philosophy of the English game. Owen Seaman then gives an historical tour within a tour, as it were, at the same time displaying evangelical zeal and an enviable knowledge of ancient civilisations.

Richard Stilgoe looks back into the future at that hardy perennial between England and Australia with lines written for the 1977 Centenary Test. And having landed down under and experienced culture shock with the strident strine of O. C. Cabot's 'Bill', we are conveyed by an Oz verse quartet from Test cricket of some hundred or so years ago to more recent suburban and outback games.

The outback game in this case is at Wave Hill, which displayed the companionable features of so many cricketing venues in the wide open spaces. Wave Hill is a small settlement near the town of Halls Creek, on the border between Northern Territory and Western Australia. Sadly, at present, the club is in abeyance, for cricket matches were great social occasions and encouraged ringers, camp cooks, mechanics and others to travel many a mile to play in a game which could last for as long as a week. Adjoining the ground was Frank's Bar and Grill, with club captain Frank Dalton as resident licensee, and the number one ticket holder was none other than former Australian Test wicket-keeper Rodney Marsh. The verses on 'Wave Hill Cricket Club' were written by Peter Young, who became involved with the club when stationed nearby with the Northern Territory Police Force.

A journey now in distance and time back to 1871, where in South Africa, at Pretoria, the so-called 'Village of Roses', the cricket club accepted its first challenge from the old provincial capital of Potchefstroom and the excitement was such that it induced the poet laureate of the Transvaal, Allan Brodrick, to produce some lines on 'The Match'. This is complemented by an effusion in Xhosa (a Bantu language of tribes in the Transkei, where a system of clicks and tones distinguishes words that otherwise would sound the same). When the Champion Cricket Club from King Williamstown became the first inter-town winners in 1884, Xhosa literature was still in its infancy and making the transition from traditional oral praise poetry to formal written poetry. At the time, an excited supporter exclaimed in the manner of the *Mbongi* or praise singer, 'Ngxatshoke Qonce! Heke Champion?!'.

Another continental jump, and this time to join R. A. Fitzgerald's team touring Canada and the USA. At a banquet in Montreal shortly after their arrival, 'English Canadian educator', George Murray, was asked to propose a toast to the visitors. Accompanying the verses he composed was a rider: 'A song written on the occasion of a banquet given in 1872 to the twelve English cricketing "apostles" as they were called. The lines were written in a great hurry and the only reason they are worthy of being preserved is that they contain the names of all the Britishers, and were printed at their request.' Despite his doubts, the toast of the evening met with a hearty reception.

A year later down in Philadelphia the beautiful 'Cricket Field at Germantown' received deserved approbation from local magazine editor Arthur Petersen, who had Swedish ancestry. Around the same time the so-called 'Sweet Singer of Michigan', Julia A. Moore, was providing verses on the 'Grand Rapids Cricket Club'. Moore has been described as 'a gifted writer of bad verse with a national following'. Mark Twain was sufficiently impressed to base a character on her in *Huckleberry Finn*.

A clutch of Caribbean contributions follow, notably Poet in Residence at the BBC, John Agard's tribute to C. L. R. James, 'Prospero Caliban Cricket'. One is reminded that James himself wrote comic verse on the 1921 Intercolonial tournament in Trinidad and in particular the performance of Learie Constantine's uncle, Victor Pascall. 'Came Chabrol, Nurse and C. R. Browne, Men of wide fame and tried renown . . . and Pascall bowled!'

Anonymous verses announcing the appointment of Lord Harris as the Governor of Bombay preface a stay in the sub-continent. Among many a variety of poems that surround Indian, Sri Lankan and Pakistani cricket, inevitably our attention is taken by the character called Bob Shillington. 'He is imaginary', assures Dr. Srivastava, who wrote the poem, 'He is an amalgam of human behaviour observed over the years'.

The sequence of rhymes by A. P. Herbert written specially for the British Sportsman's Club luncheons at London's Savoy Hotel to welcome the tourists of the year bring this tour near to its close. A flavour of the game in Nigeria, a jaunt with the Lord's Taverners to Holland, some thoughts on how good the Chinese would be at cricket, and we finish where we nearly began: the old enemy at Lord's once more, an Anniversary Dinner and time for one of Roger Knight's original entertaining graces.

D. R. A.

John Groves

Cricket is an English game,
A game of quiet understatement,
Of gentle summer days,
Humming bees
And honey-teas
And gentle English ways:
Fever-abatement
Under another name.

It is not suited to hot-blooded races,
Although we export it to other places
In hope of therapeutic applications
In civilising more fomenting nations
And thus apply
A means to pacify.

But from this custom little has entailed.
In fact it must be said we've wholly failed,
For if indeed
It could be claimed we'd ever once succeed,
Not be a failure
(As in Australia),
It might have been our fates
To civilise the whole United States.

But, no.
True cricket is a game
Of gentle English scenes,
For poets dozing on quaint village greens
And not the same
As cricket where there's much more dash and din
And people play it so that they can *win!*

Owen Seaman

When wild in woods the savage ran,
Being a prehistoric man,
There is no record hinting at
His rude delight in ball and bat.
And, when, in times a shade more dressy,
People's amusements weren't so messy,
No trundler known to ancient lore
Got pagan Pharaoh leg-before.
Moses, who must have had a notion
Of heathen games as played in Goshen,
Has neither praise nor yet rebuke
Of Cricket in the Pentateuch.

No Old Phoenician "found a patch"
In any Tyre-and-Sidon match;
There is no story from Tibet
Of lamas slogging at the net;
No sporting annals tell us how,
During the dynasty of Chow,
The full-sized volley sped through space
And took Confucius in the face.

We hear not how Achilles spent
Whole weeks inside the scorer's tent;
Not read of Priam, stiff of joint,
Dropping a cert at silly-point;
Nor, on a nasty pitch that bumped,
Of Aristides being stumped;
Nor how, when Pheobus came out hot
At Salamis (a dampish spot),
The Attic skipper won the spin
And coolly put the Persians in.

No fable tells of Roman Cricket –
How well Horatius kept the wicket,
How brother Remus took first knock,
Or Fabius played against the clock;
Or Julius Caesar showed alarm
At Brutus "Coming with his arm";
Or Cicero in palmy days
Bowled with his head and broke both ways
Or Balbus – he that built the wall –
Played like it, blocking every ball.
Nor did our isles adopt the game
Till Christian missionaries came,
And even then the pagan sort
Failed to regard it as a sport.

No Viking, landing from his ships,
Was ever captured in the slips;
No Irish heathen learned the hat-trick,
Though freely coached by good St. Patrick;
No Pict, in legends known to me,
After the interval for "tea",
Lashing his sporran round his pad,
Appealed because the light was bad.

It was the same in our domains:
Not once on Bengal's tented plains
Did the great Nawab lift a googly
Halfway across the astonied Hooghly;
Nor yet was Cricket in his thought
When the high priest of Juggernaut,
Rain having fallen after drought,
Ordered the heavy roller out.

And, if at length the art of arts
Has wooed and won exotic hearts,
To Christian Cambridge it is due
Who of her Ranji made a Blue;
Taught him – what other creeds have missed –
His speed of eye, his sleight of wrist;
Taught him – who learned it like a lamb –
To cut and push and glance and slam
And live to be a perfect Jam.

Richard Stilgoe

Written for the Centenary Test in 1977.

In Melbourne on the Ides of March in 1877
The English team encountered an Australian eleven,
They couldn't see how possibly an English team could fail,
Although that chap behind the stumps could not get out on bail,
"We'll show the convicts how", they cried,
"We'll flay these chaps alive"
But as you know it wasn't so
They lost by forty-five.

In nineteen-seventy-seven to proclaim the century,
Another team of Englishmen went to the colony.
"Your Chappell's and your Lillees don't scare me," cried Tony Greig,
and Lillee chewed his gum and bowled, and hit him on the leg.
And Randall scored a century, but still t'was all in vain
T'was just the same, we lost the game by forty-five again.

In twenty-seventy-seven, when the bi-centenary's played
What bumpers will be bowled then, how many centuries made?
As in the Cornhill, Texaco, John Player, Dunhill Test,
The Aussies in their Brearley patent caps take on the rest.
As Arlott, Johnson, Frindall in the commentary box in heaven
Compare them to the English team of nineteen-seventy-seven
One things is sure, the final score, however hard they strive
Our national pride, the England side will lose by forty-five!

Attributed to Samuel J. Looker

Well done, Cornstalks! Whipt us
   Fair and square.
Was it luck that tript us?
   Was it scare?
Kangaroo Land's 'Demon,' or our own
Want of 'devil,' coolness, nerve, backbone?

O. C. Cabot

(Bill offers his opinion)

AUSTRALIA

First Innings 191

ENGLAND

First Innings – Hobbs, c Carter, b Hordern 178

(Fourth Test Match figures, Melbourne, 1912)

As a gen'ral rool me 'ealth's good, an me spirits is calm and 'igh;
I comes quite reg'lar for m food, an' never lets beer go by;
I runs me barrer, a 'uge success, as the picksher *spruikers* say,
An' wot wiv 'eadin' 'em, more or less I'm clearin' a quid a day!
But there's a fly in me meejam beer – the same as the papers put
W'enever they tries to make clear that sumfin's all my fut!
There's *sumfin'* up with our nashnal game – an' it's cost me a good few bobs;
Orstralian cricket is *not* the same – it suffers from too much 'Obbs!
I've played a bit in me time, see, although it's a long time past
I'm always there of a Saturdee – for I'm an enthoosiast.
I knows the players, an' all the scores they've 'it up for years an' years –
An w'en our fellers is sockin' fours it's me an' me mates as cheers!
But, strike me lucky! a sort o' blight 'as fell on our fellers now;
It may be, p'raps, that their *luck* ain't right – and Luck is a bloomin' cow!
Since 'Ordern googled the first Test game, an' outed them English nobs,
Orstralian cricket ain't been the same, because of a cove called 'Obbs!
Me cobber, Ginger – 'oo ain't no judge, compared to *me* and *you* –
'E says our fellows'd never budge, if 'twasn't for just them two.
Foster and Barnes, 'oo bowl like 'ell – 'an Foster's only a *toff!*
But I says: "*No!* It's the *runs* that tell, an' gettin' a good lead-off."
They've got this feller – I've watched 'im bat – 'e's good as any you've seen!
'E goes in first, an', strike me fat! 'e bats like a fair *machine!*
Our fellers give 'im the lightnin' ones, an' googlies an' swerves an' lobs,

But 'e makes 'is undred-an'-fifty runs w'ere *our* chaps is makin' *blobs!*
Them palmy days they torks about, w'en the Englishmen'd look
At Trumper knockin' 'em inside out, an' Darling like a book –
The days w'en 'arf our present team was in their pith an' prime -
'Ave vanished like a gorjus dream, before the 'and of Time!
It's *this* way! Our blokes ain't so young, an' one or two *ain't fit:*
If I may wag a troothful tongue, they're *quarrelin'* a bit!
An' some are polin' on their names, an' some are workin' jobs –
Orstralian cricket ain't the same; but 'taint *all* due to 'Obbs!

Simon Curtis

A fierce appeal. I heard the snick from here –
The scoreboard end on Dolphin – and he's out.
And Ryde has been reduced to two for ten,
With Randwick in the driving seat. Good shout.

The homely grandstand with its red tiled roof
And green well-watered grass just right for seam;
Close to my flat, the suburb's seafront ground,
And so, I guess, the Randwick team *my* team?

Beyond the pitch and Norfolk Island pines
And sandstone seawall and the Bay Hotel,
The heads of swimmers like so many dots
Bob in the surf and blue Pacific swell;

Whom I'm about to join, and thread my way
Past deli, RSL and Laundrette,
The haircut place with pennants on display
(*Juventus, Spurs, Toluca, River Plate);*

And thread by thread, I'm weaving what I feel
Aren't strands but ties – their team my team for real?

Peter Young

You may tread the hallowed precincts
Of the Oval or at Lord's,
You may see a Test in Sydney
Or join Melbourne's teeming hordes;

But you've never seen a cricket match,
I fear you never will,
'Til you've seen the boys in action
on a clay pan at Wave Hill.

Now Brisbane has the Gabba,
While Sydney has its Hill,
But the place that they all envy,
Is Frank's famous Bar and Grill.

You may speak about Don Bradman,
O'Reilly and Clem Hill,
But their exploits tend to pallor
With the mention of Wave Hill.

Our Number One is Rodney,
A keeper of great fame,
But we'd like to see him out here,
Just to polish up his game.

With their spirit never daunting,
Their fervour not denied,
I'm sure they'd play each other,
If it came to one a side.

You must take an extra cooler
If you've ne'er been there at all
'Cause you'll find that when you're leaving
One is hanging on the wall.

There's a reason for this practice,
As I'm sure you'll quickly learn,
See, you've always got a cooler,
Whenever you return.

They'll collect for causes worthy,
Or a mate who's down and 'flat',
And they'll gather up the proceeds
In Buck's old battered hat.

But when they've bowled the final over,
Or bad light has stopped play,
To Frank's Bar and Grill inviting,
They wend their weary way

Where the atmosphere is friendly,
Abounding with good cheer,
And we quaff the gallons lustily,
Of cold and welcome beer.

But the memories I will cherish,
I know I always will,
Are the hours playing cricket,
On a clay pan at Wave Hill.

Allan Brodrick

In 1874, the first challenge match between Pretoria and Potchefstroom induced the Poet Laureate of the Transvaal to produce the following lines:

In the midst of bills and worries, and all our countless cares
Of winding up of companies, in which we have taken shares,
A door is opened unto us, and pleasure lifts the latch;
Eleven bold Pretorians have gone to make a match.
No match that leads to Hymen; so ladies don't presume
To try a "catch," for CRICKET takes our "boys" to Potchefstroom
From school, from farm, and pulpit, and from the crowded store;
They're gone to add to salted "bays" one little "Laurel" more!

Oh! may the sun of victory shine on their bats and stumps,
Oh! may the team of Potchefstroom be left in doleful dumps,
They say that betting now is 10 to 8 against "our lot,"
It strikes me (being prejudiced) t'others will get it it hot!
Although we know that Ludorf bowls with fiery force and skill,
And Thomson is supposed to be a very bitter pill;
And Botha's (2), and many more, in fact a very host –
Yet listen half a minute and hear Pretoria boast.

There's Richard Coeur de Lion, indicative of scores,
And Noble, Rex, and Cartwright, whose every name ensures
A "battery" that almost makes their foemen "go to grass,"
Grace in their eye, their stroke a sort of *coup de grace,*
Marais, who studied "fielding," and then the jovial Hans,
And Rufus and brave Charlemagne, the rival Predikants!
With such a noble list I ask: How can Pretoria fail,
Unless fatigue upon the road their energies assail?
If they should win, of course they'll have the honours that they earn;
If they should lose, they'll have three cheers, and hopes for the "Return."

A. B. C.

The poet gives the teams surnames and these are Ndlambe and Ntlande. These are the names of well known men among the Xhosa and Sotho people who died a very long, long time ago. In praising the Crown Princes (Mighty Champions) the poet invokes the spirits of Ndlambe and Ntlande who are their dead ancestors. These ancestors who are peacefully sleeping are awakened by the poet's chanting. He acknowledges the presence of these ancestral spirits among the players for they can only play such an excellent game with the help of ancestral spirits. In addressing the dead, the poet acknowledges the excellent game and exalts the players. It is, therefore, fitting to give the teams the surnames of their ancestors well-known among the Xhosas and Sothoes. By doing this, the poet functions within a recognised and acknowledged tradition the Nguni people follow, when praising a person who has excelled in anything; for example the warriors were praised in this manner when they won a battle. Placing the players in a tradition known by all enables the poet to praise them fittingly. There is, therefore, no need to focus on the game as such, for the invocation of ancestral spirits sums it all up and then everyone knows that the players have done a splendid job.

Heke Champion?!

Champion'! Kumnkani abekiweyo yakulo
    Ndlambe nakulo Ntlade
Azu ube ucetywe nganina ube uzibutumele
    nje;
Bekungaziwana ukuba wena apa uwela ngo-
    mtantato.
Kuba lamanzi e-Qonce kuwe asuk'abe bu-
    buti.
Ucacante waya wafun' indlela kulo Gomp' e-
    Monti
Apo ibulalemfesi uye wayidla kona;
Gqwi, tendalela waya wel' ebalakisini e-Rini,
Apo ufike waqoshelisa amadinala
Aka rumanga kubuy' ubuyelela noko abusel'
    ukap' etafeni,
Kub' impondo ube ungekazisukuli zombini;

Bayaqala e-Bayi ukwanek' izitya kub' iyiso-
  polo,
Beva ngawe selu Handis' amawa ezants' ema
  Xambeni
Ude wenjenj' oku gxebe ubuz' uzonde ntoni-
  na,
Abakuzalelanga yinina oko ubuse Monti ezi-
  bukweni?
Ukuba lomhlab' uwumeleyo nakub' ungase-
  wako,
Usaziwa noko ukuba yayik' ingumhlaba ka
  Ntinde
Maud' onesikwa kwabaseza nts' ema Silamse-
  ni
Nowase balakisini ebongile nje akafumana-
  ng' enze,
Etelele ngokwese' emnqamlezweni wahleka
  nje naye,
Ibisey' ikufihla amehlo kuba naye enziwe isi-
  qwala.
Akuba ndandizalelw' e-Meliman Tawala,
Ndaba nami ndapefumlelwa ngomoya we-
  mbongi;
Kuba nami ngenamhla ngendigwentselela
  ndibonga,
Koko hay' lento ukuba mbi ukuvelel' emulu
  ngwini.

Glossary:

Qonce	King Williams Town
Ndlambe	Xhosa
Ntlade	Sotho
Monti	East London – Gompo is a location in East London
Rini	Grahamstown

SALUTE KING WILLIAMS TOWN!

Mighty Champions

Champion; Crown Princes
Crown Princes of Ndlambe and Ntlade
I wonder why they wake you from your peaceful sleep,
    for you are now dead. You died a long time ago;
I challenge you. If you can manage to cross this river
    walking on this chain bridge we would meet.
Because this water of King Williams Town River is like
    poison. If you fall into this river you will be dead.
You crossed the river walking cautiously on the tricky
    stones to find your way from Gompo in Monti
Where you had your breakfast;
Then you walked until you came to Rini,
Where you arrived and gathered up your tools.
You did not see it fitting to come and then go back for
    you had walked through the plain without a path,
For you had not yet sharpened both horns – all of your tools;
You started at Bayi to display your nets, and this was
    your strategy,
Then you provoked Handisi in the Southern cliffs at Xambeni,
Then when you came from there what were you angry for,
Did they not carry you at that time at Monti, at that place
    where you crossed the river?
In as much as you represent this land, it is no longer yours,
This land was known to be the land of Ntinde.
You are known among the people of the South, those at Silamseni
The poet is only an expert in his craft, he only praises and
    is not really supposed to play,
Visitors who had come to watch the game were also happy. They
    laughed as a sign of enjoyment,
They decided to shut their eyes wanting also to be crippled men.
If only I had been born at Meliman Tawala,
I could also have caught the Spirit of the poets;
So that even today I could be singing,
Showing my appreciation,
But the only thing that is not good is that this game originates
    from Europeans.

Translated by Thiyiwe Bafana Khumalo

George Murray

I've a toast to you – so, Gentlemen, hand on
The Mumm, and the Cliquot, the Moet and Chandon:
The toast that I offer with pleasure extreme
Is the health of "The Gentlemen Cricketers' Team."

And first, here's the health of their Captain, Fitzgerald,
Whose time-honoured name stands in need of no herald:
All know that he manages matches as well
As a match-making mother, with daughters to sell.

Next, here's to the Chief of the ball-driving race,
A Giant in cricket as well as a Grace:
Bat, bowler, or field, in himself he's a host,
All round, the best player that Britain can boast.

Here's to Hornby, who bears the *cognomen* of "Monkey",
All muscle and nerve – never feeeble or funky –
For pluck, skill and strength, he is hard to be beaten
By picked men from Winchester, Harrow or Eton!

Here's the left-handed bowler – that Lancashire swell,
Whom Ottawa batsmen remember so well –
He bowled a whole innings (and bowled like great guns)
In *Apple-Pie* order for – only three runs!

And here's to his *confrère*, spectacular Rose,
A rather quick bowler of dangerous "slows":
And now to the Lubbocks, a brave pair of brothers,
Who rank with the Graces, the Walkers and others.

Next, here's to four stars of the Oxford Eleven
(With all due respect for the home-keeping seven),
Here's to Harris and Ottoway, Francis and Hadow,
May Time ne'er decrease his Herculean shadow!

Here's to Pickering lastly – his name is enough
To prove that he's made of good cricketing stuff –
Warm welcome, I'm sure, he will even be shewn
For the sake of his Uncle, as well as his own!

So, here's to them singly, or taken together –
A finer set never yet hunted the leather –
Once more then, I pledge you, with pleasure extreme,
The health of "The Gentlemen Cricketers' Team."

Arthur Peterson

1

The field – the fair and level green
Which stretches off and all around;
The crowd, dark-circling round the ground;
The flags which overhead are seen!
High hauled into the noonday air
The red cloud of green England's love;
Beyond, with star-lit azure square,
And stripes of white and crimson wove,
Our standard, as a sunrise bright;
About the field, some near, some far,
White figures stand or run, and are
Now cheered, now watched with anxious sight.

2

I lie beneath the shade of trees,
An idler in this sportful fray;
Out in the sun the players play,
And lift their caps to feel the breeze.
My eyes go up to faces fair
Which look from under flags that flame
Afront the gay pavilion's stair,
Sweet queens who sit above the game.
A profile like a dream of Greece,
With hair in twinings statuesque;
A head like one which from the desk
Of Phidias might have gazed in peace,
Far up the rows soft colours warm
The air about a May-day face;
Gaily the half-uncovered arm
Waves the light fan which shares its grace.
And near, in white with northern hair,
Pale-yellow, parted low upon
A forehead exquisite, is one
For whom a man thinks he could bear

Death, torture: whose sweet girlhood seems
An Eden life, of some fair place
Far off, some garden of his dreams:
His blood, ere harm to her young face.

3

These ladies, lovelier than the morn
Of some rich hearted day in June,
Whose eyes are love, whose voices tune;
These banners, which the field adorn;
This music, sweetening all the air,
And making fairy-land below;
This luxury, this kingly show –
Is a dream of times that bear
The fame of Arthur on their front?
Is it the field of Camelot,
The glory of a joust, the hunt
For ladies' smiles through battle hot?

4

A shout from out the field – I lift
Myself from dreams of a far then
Into this waning day again.
Across the green begins to drift
The breaking crowd – the game is done.
I see bright ladies' colors flit;
I see the splendor of the sun
Of banners of gay buntings knit;
I hear a knightly march begun,
As when a victory is won!

Julia A. Moore

In Grand Rapids is a handsome club,
    Of men that cricket play,
As fine a set of skillful men
    That can their skill display.
They are the companions of the West,
    They think they are quite fine,
They've won a hundred honors well;
    It is their most cunning design.

Brave Kelso, he's considered great,
    Chief of the club he is found;
Great crowds he draws to see him bowl
    The ball upon the ground.
And Mr. Follet is very brave,
    A lighter player than the rest,
He got struck severe at the fair ground
    For which he took a rest.

When Mr. Dennis does well play,
    His courage is full great,
And accidents to him occur,
    But not much, though, of late.
This ball play is a dangerous game,
    Brave knights to play it though;
Those boys would be the nations pride,
    If they to war would go.

From Milwaukee their club did come,
    With thoughts of skill at play,
But beat they was, and then went home –
    Had nothing more to say.
Grand Rapids club that cricket play,
    Will soon be known afar,
Much prouder do the members stand,
    Like many a noble star.

Egbert Moore

*A Calypso by Egbert Moore (Lord Beginner), accompanied by Gerald Clark And
His Caribbean Serenaders: Recorded New York City, USA, 15 March 1935.*

The West Indians and the M.C.C. met once more.
I've never seen cricket so nice before.
The West Indians and the M.C.C. met once more.
I've never seen cricket so nice before.
For Mr Grant was really excellent,
Wyatt was magnificent,
Sealey and Headley was superfine,
And the heroes was Hylton and Constantine.

The first two matches at Barbados came to a draw,
And Hammond, England batsman, made a very great score,
Two hundred and eighty-one without a chance,
And the Barbadian bowlers had to sip and dance,
But when they came to Trinidad we got two hundred,
Not out from young Maynard,
Just fourteen runs again to complete,
So the time saved the M.C.C. from defeat.

I wouldn't say the first Test won by luck,
For Wyatt, England captain, really use his pluck,
The weather was bad, they had two days of rain,
So it was a match of only skill and brain,
I wouldn't say that our captain was a dunce,
For Wyatt have some experience,
And he showed his diplomacy,
With four wickets in hand, he won easily.

The second Test Match was the best to me,
It will always remain in my memory,
Nobody at all made a century,
Only ninety, ninety-two, and ninety-three,
The M.C.C. really did that fine,
By stopping them at the ninety line,
Ames played well, and Leyland blocked fine,
But was beaten with the fifth ball from Constantine.

It was the greatest excitement that we ever had,
In the history of cricket in Trinidad,
To see the last over, the second to last ball,
The last minute and the last man to fall,
Anxiety made ladies grind,
Shouting 'Give us it Constantine',
And the batsman put his foot in front of straight one,
Low and West Indians won.

Egbert Moore

Cricket, lovely cricket,
At Lord's where I saw it;
Cricket, lovely cricket,
At Lord's where I saw it;
Yardley tried his best
But Goddard won the test.
They gave the crowd plenty fun;
Second Test and West Indies won.

CHORUS:

With those two little pals of mine
Ramadhin and Valentine.

The King was there well attired,
So they started with Rae and Stollmeyer;
Stolly was hitting balls around the boundary,
But Wardle stopped him at twenty.
Rae had confidence,
So he put up a strong defence;
He saw the King was waiting to see,
So he gave him a century.

CHORUS:

With those two little pals of mine
Ramadhin and Valentine.

West Indies first innings total was three-twenty-six
Just as usual
When Bedser bowled Christiani
The whole thing collapsed quite easily,
England then went on,
And made one-hundred-fifty-one;
West Indies then had two-twenty lead,
And Goddard said, 'That's nice indeed.'

CHORUS:
    With those two little pals of mine
    Ramadhin and Valentine.

    Yardley wasn't broken hearted
    When the second innings started;
    Jenkins was like a target
    Getting the first five into his basket.
    But Gomez broke him down,
    While Walcott licked them around:
    He was not out for one-hundred and sixty-eight,
    Leaving Yardley to contemplate.

CHORUS:
    The bowling was super-fine
    Ramadhin and Valentine.

    West Indies was feeling homely,
    Their audience had them happy.
    When Washbrook's century had ended,
    West Indies' voices all blended.
    Hats went in the air.
    They jumped and shouted without fear;
    So at Lord's was the scenery
    Bound to go down in history.

CHORUS:
    After all was said and done,
    Second Test and West Indies won!

ON ANOTHER FIELD, AN ALLY:
A WEST INDIAN BATSMAN TALKS US
TOWARDS THE CENTURY

E. A. Markham

For Malcolm Marshall and Michael Holding, resting . . .

Into the nineties, into the nineties
Ten to go, don't panic . . .
Think Bradman . . . never got out when into the nineties

Nerves of steel, drive them through legs
Beginning to buckle *think* the three W's think Clive Lloyd
Think Richards and all those ruling heads

On the coin of cricket. And relax. Now, where am I?
Lost in the arms of voluptuous Anna. *Fin*
De siècle, recalling the days of immortal Kanhai

Hooking to the boundary from a prone position.
Cravats & decadence. Good ball. *Christ!*
Man in white coat weighing the decision

To point the finger, legalized gun
With power to run the 'Man of the Match'
Out of town. Not guilty. Not guilty, my old son.

If I say it myself. A lapse
In concentration quickly repaired by nailing
The Will against any further collapse

The side of the century. Here behind the barricades
Stretching from 'Clifton' and Gordon 'Le Corbusier' Greenidge
Through 'homelier' architects of our days

Of glory – the team's Frank Lloyd Wrights –
Up against pollution, thinning ozone, treeless forests
In the tropics, each run lifts you to the heights

Of vertigo. And for you down there. Miss X, Mrs Patel
At the corner-shop, this wicket guarantees
Orgasms, guarantees that this last exile suits you well.

And damn it, I'm out. *Out?* There's no morality to this game.
Protesting genocide and burying your head
In sweet Anna's thighs, it's all the same

The butcher of dreams, man in white coat
Offers no reprieve, his butchershop in Hounslow in need
Of more meat. Yet again I've missed the boat

Of the century. Breach in the wall.
Bowled through the gate. Marooned from the grand
Ocean liners: S S Sobers & Headley; not by formidable Wes Hall

Line of destroyers; no *chinaman* or finger lickin' spin
To obscurity – just a *gift* with your name on it
Lacking spite, Physics or Philosophy, innocuous as sin.

Like I say, there's no morality in this game.
Protesting genocide or burying your head
In sweet Anna's thighs, it's all the same.

John Agard

Prospero batting
Caliban bowling
and is cricket is cricket in yuh ricketics
but from far it look like politics

Caliban running up
from beyond de boundary
because he come
from beyond de boundary
if you know yuh history

Prospero standing
bat and pad
thinking Caliban is a mere lad
from a new-world archipelago
and new to the game

But not taking chances
Prospero invoking de name
of W. G. Grace
to preserve him
from a bouncer to the face

Caliban if he want
could invoke duppy jumbie
zemi baccoo douen all kinda ting,
but instead he relying
just pon pace and swing

Caliban arcing de ball
Like an unpredictable whip.

Prospero foot like it chain to de ground.
Before he could mek a move
De ball gone thru to de slip,
And de way de crowd rocking
You would think dey crossing de atlantic

Is cricket is cricket in yuh ricketics
But from far it look like politics.

Prospero remembering
How Caliban used to call him master.
Now Caliban agitating de ball faster
And de crowd shouting POWER

Caliban remembering
how Prospero used to call him knave and serf.
Now Caliban striding de cricket turf
like he breathing a nation,
and de ball swinging it own way
like it hear bout self-determination

is cricket is cricket in yuh ricketics
but from far it look like politics.

Prospero wishing
Shakespeare was the umpire,
Caliban see a red ball
and he see fire
rising with glorious uncertainty.
Prospero front pad forward with diplomacy.

Is cricket is cricket in yuh ricketics
But from far it look like politics.

Prospero invoking
de god of snow,
wishing a shower of flakes
would stop all play,
but de sky so bright with carib glow
you can't even appeal for light
much less ask for snow.

Is cricket is cricket in yuh ricketics
But from far it look like politics.

Krishna A. Samaroo

This is not cricket. A finger spun
a leather ball down a wicket
worn to the bone, cracked
like a skull unearthed by
a spade clearing space for
another soul in this cemetery
of dreams we call hope.
The umpire stood unmoved.
and the ball at the stroke
played, elbow squaring with shoulder,
bit into the flesh and flashed
to first slip; a quick grip
ended a career that spanned
passages beyond the boundaries
of this field; the slow gait,
the dropped head, the gritted teeth
tell the tale only too well;
the pattering palms in irony
flood with the horror of memory.

Morgan Dockrell

To commemorate Ireland's victory by nine wickets over the West Indies, 25 all out, at the Sion Mills ground, Londonderry, on 2 July 1969. What better verse mode than the heroic couplet to celebrate the Men of Ireland on this unique occasion! My outrageous play on players' names needs some explanation. For West Indies: J. Shepherd 0, B. Butcher 2, M. Foster 2. For Ireland: R. Waters 2, D. Goodwin (the Irish captain) 5 for 6.

M.D.

Some Contests acted out on humble swards
Are no less Epic-filled than those at Lord's.
Come Muse! Provide my pen with rhyming skills,
That I may sing the Field of Sion Mills,
(Whose fame may lie neglected and unsung
Unless some Aid Divine inspire some tongue)
Where Ireland's chosen, facing fearful odds,
Achieved a stature little short of Gods.

Oh to convey that Memorable Scene!
The pitch (see Wisden's note) was "em'rald green".
That claim for Girls and Diamonds I'll amend:
"An Em'rald Pitch is NOT a Carib's friend";
For Ireland's Heroes strove like men inspired,
While one by one the Visitors 'retired',
Their faces long, their crease-duration short,
Their Cause devoid of all Divine Support.
No Shepherd now appeared to lead the Flock;
No Butcher to attack, or slay, or block;
No louring cloud to foster hope's illusion,
Since nothing reigned but horror and confusion.

At 3 for 3, then 8 for 6 (no byes)
To Sion's hills in vain they raised their eyes.
At 12 for 9 the fact was plain to all
Their eyes had served them best by watching ball;
For such the ill success with which they played,
'Twas clear those hills withheld th'Expected Aid.

The tail wagged doggedly through snick and drive,
Progressing, (with one bye), to twenty five.
Those dark bare Mills and hills had caused such panic
The genius loci was believed Satanic.

The Irish now cut loose with pull and sweep,
Finding the troubled Waters far less deep.
Unrivalled Day! Good Win! Immortal Score!
Peace has its Victories more renowned than War.

Anon

The die is cast – my fate is sealed –
　　To India I'm away;
No more shall I the willow wield,
　　A nobler part I play.
No more, to make Australians yield,
　　Shall I prolong the fray,
I'm scoring in a wider field –
　　I'm going to Bombay!

In cricket I shall lose a 'pal'.
　　An' keen regret is mine;
But in a palankeen I shall
　　Find comfort most divine!
Or, seated in my bungalow,
　　I'll puff my nargileh,
(I hope I shall not bungle, oh!)
　　I'm going to Bombay!

Adieu, dear Kent and M.C.C.!
　　Bat, ball and stumps, adieu!
I go whence comes the proud Parsee –
　　Last bright recruit for you!
Yet I will banish all regret
　　At fate; – for – who can say?
I may become a Viceroy yet . . .
　　I'm going to Bombay!

Alan Vidern

On seeing three youngsters in a desolate back street in Mumbai in February 2001,
hypnotised by a television screen during a night game between India and Australia.

The sun has gone, 'tis time to dream
Their idols distant, out of beam,
The sprigs so earnest, quite entranced,
As mighty India's score advanced.
It matters not all can't be seen
Of those flickering figures on the screen;
For each among this group of three
Thinks as one, individually
His heroes are there throughout the day,
Part of him, when he's at play
And though he's sure they'll never meet,
He seeks to copy every feat.
The eventual roles, they will reverse,
The years flit by, indeed disperse,
The boy who watched them in their prime,
Will now, in turn, swift seize his time.
The screen has blurred, too soon grows dim,
He won't see them, but they'll see Him.

BOB SHILLINGTON PLAYS
CRICKET ALONE

Dr. Satyendra Srivastava

बॉब शिलिंगटन अकेले क्रिकेट खेल रहा है

बॉब शिलिंगटन अकेले क्रिकेट खेल रहा है
बॉब शिलिंगटन जिसके सफ़ेद/भूरे बाल बिखरे हुए हैं
बॉब शिलिंगटन जिसने गर्मी में भी तीन ऊनी कोट पहन रखे हैं ।
बॉब शिलिंगटन जो थोड़ी देर पहले ही सोकर उठा है.
            और उठते ही
        बगल में रखी लगभग खाली बोतल से
        रात की बची हुई दो घूंट शराब को अतड़ियों में डाल कर
        अपने दफ़्ती के बक्से को जो उसका बिस्तर और रजाई है
        तह कर, कोने में रखकर
        एक दो आने जाने वालों को भला बुरा कहकर.
        अब
            एक उठती अधूरी दीवार के
            सहारे तीन ईंटें खड़ी करके
            क्रिकेट खेल रहा है ।
बॉब शिलिंगटन अपने हाथों में
डेढ़ हाथ की एक पतली लकड़ी लेकर
उसे जमा कर, हटा हिलाकर
नीचे रखकर, आसमान को दिखा कर अब
बैटिंग कर रहा है ।

Bob Shillington plays cricket alone.
Bob Shillington, whose white and grey hair is blown all over
Who wears three woollen coats even in the heat
Who has just got up from sleep
And just as he gets up
Takes up the bottle beside him though almost finished
Empties the wine left last night into his intestines
Then the cardboard box which is his bed and bedding
Folds, keeps it in a corner
Abuses one or two passers by
Now, with the help of an unfinished wall,
Is playing cricket.
Bob Shillington in his hands
Takes a foot and a half long thin stick,
Holding it firmly, moving it up and down, lifting it sky high
Is now batting.
Bob Shillington
Lifting his bat a little higher

Is shouting
  Throw!
  Bastards! Throw all
  Throw one by one
  Throw fast
  Throw slow
  Throw a googly
  I will hit every ball
  Hit each and every one of them
  I will hit a four
  Hit a sixer
  Hit all
  Hit each and every one!

Bob Shillington is shouting
And playing cricket.
Bob Shillington is also feeling
That nobody is bowling
No-one is throwing the ball from any side.
After a while
Bob Shillington keeps his bat by the stumps of the bricks
And observing the people coming and going
Sometimes he laughs
And sometimes abuses.

Bob Shillington just saw an Asian.
Bob Shillington stopped him
Asked him for money for tea
And was turned down with cool Asian politeness
The Asian went and Bob Shillington kept looking at him
Then he shouted

  You son of a bitch!
  Come unwanted here
  Eat our bread
  And do not give us money!

Then Bob Shillington becomes quiet
And lifts his bat, offering it on all sides
Keeps batting
Keeps abusing
Bob Shillington abuses all
Except the children.
Boys sometimes throw stones, banana peel, or other things at him

Or go near him
Keep their hankerchiefs to their noses
And spit on his smelly coat
Even then
Bob Shillington utters not a word
Only laughs
And when they go away
The he shouts
    All will go! When the time comes they will all go
    And will pass unchanged
    Just as Peter went, open-mouthed, hands flung.
    Used to call himself a captain before me
    All will go! Yes, yes, all will leave
    As Hitler went, Stalin went
    As Major Livingston went
    Wanted to bowl me out, the rascal, betrayer
    Yes, yes, all will go, one by one they will all go
    As Maggie will go, Mother Theresa will go
    Came here calling London a Calcutta!

Like every day
Even today
Bob Shillington is playing cricket alone
Hitting hard and stong
Shouting loud and long, abusing
Throw!
Bastards throw!
Throw hard
Throw slow
Throw a googly
Throw
Throw with all your might!

K. V. V. Subrahmanyan

Despite all the multitudes that throng the cricket field
Some do run down the game with comments veiled,
Talking of ennui and waste of time the spectacle does yield
But on the might of the game their lips are sealed.

Who can deny the game inspires qualities of head and heart,
That call for discipline of mind and body of a high sort,
That spin bowling is a fine art,
That close in catches needs one to be agile and smart?

The sound and fury of pace and swing
Doth the death knell of many a batsman ring;
To face real pace one has to bring
Guts and gumption which is no mean thing.

The game reflects the philosophy of life
The ups and downs are mirrored in the strife
In the middle, where rivalry is rife
And everyone awaits a chance to snipe.

A renowned batter may make a duck
And throw all his ills on dame luck;
All because he didn't avoid the snick
And went for a venturesome flick.

History is made and records are broken
And all these denote a token
Of blood and sweat and limbs that are shaken
And dauntless deeds bespoke of efforts that didn't slacken.

Travails and trials are the tales of tastes,
Success or failure on a flimsy thread rests;
None dare hope to feather their nests
For all time to come and figure in the lists.

Exploits on the field have been sung by many a literary name
Battle of ball and bat has brought the wielders fame;
Cardus and Gardiner have penned the glory of the game;
For the true connoisseur success or failure is all the same.

For witnessing the Test in cricket
There will be many a pest for ticket;
For the thrill of the fall of a wicket
The addict would fain empty his pocket.

Whatever the critics may ascribe
And deride the game in terms to describe
The true devotee would continue to subscribe
To the game, with worthy mementoes to inscribe.

Dom Moraes

Green is the grass, the first young shoots
Are bursting in fulfilment on the ling.
And lo! the sap in tree-trunk and the fruit
Cry out in harmony: ''Tis Spring: 'tis spring.'
And what a spring; in perspect I recall
The melting music of tall Worrell's batsmanship . . .
So green a spring – oh, when shall it befall
That one may take spring's cup, and gently sip
Of its amazing freshness, and on lip
Savour the first fine thrill of cut or drive
And welcome Kenny's hit that goes for five?
Never again so green, so green a spring –
And for my spring, may I not shed a tear?
In not-so-distant time: well, I may sit
In grey pavilion, with no lustre on the grass
So even now I think it passing fit
That I have made mine own work on the stars.
The stars that do in High Olympus sit
They gild our cricket with a grace divine
This, with my admiration; it is writ
For them; but still, the thrill . . . the thrill is mine.

Jay Quill

Who said the Sinhalese couldn't play cricket?
Did they ever see Douglas at the wicket?
Do "Babsy" and "Bonny" mean nothing at all?
Why, then, no bat ever hit a ball!
Gunasekeras and other giants of the game
Have won for their Club enduring fame.
Of E. Weerasooriya we've heard men tell,
Of C. E. Perera and S. B. L.,
R. E. S. Mendis and Albert (M. K.)
And the great "Sargo", much nearer our day . . .

S. S. C. men to none would yield
When leading teams in a wider field.
Through all its fifty years and more
This Club could well be proud of its score,
And embodying the spirit of the glorious game
Is its Premier-President's peerless name.

Paul Weston

In heat to make a camel swoon,
Opposed by those who scorn restraint,
Can England brave their own 'high noon'
Where none can hide whose hearts are faint?

When Jayasuriya the Oval trod
He split the field asunder:
His bat remains a lightening rod
But can we steal his thunder?

Can Murali still make leather warp;
Shall Athers play the victim?
Or will he just be food for Thorpe
And Duncan purr: "We've licked 'im!"

Sri Lanka face the wrath of Gough,
The wiles of Giles and Caddick's feet;
At least we've spared them Tufnell's cough,
If not Trescothick's ample seat!

Our doughty tourists 'know the ropes'
But who can forecast how they'll fare:
Will they succeed, or will their hopes
Recede as fast as Nasser's hair?

John Snow

Behind the limpid dust-clothed trees
the pointed tower,
Moulvi waiting,
stands faded red against the blue.
Above a Cheel, eying wheeling,
also views the sunbaked ground,
sees standing people kameez clad
and women burqa'd seated,
ochre-blue-red canopied,
shaded from sun's prying too.
Charred afternoon.

Stewart Brown

Cerulean and jet, the Tuareg
from the Sahel with his bow and arrow
stalks the dusty outfield
which is his heritage, his history,
like a wraith in some Gothic drama,

squats at deep mid-wicket
to watch the strange *baturé* ritual,
the inexplicable dances
of the white men in their bleached
ceremonial robes.

Soon play continues,
the intruding spectator ignored,
merely a local hazard
like the gully-oak at Broadhurst
or the boundary stream at Brook,

and with eyes closed, behind
mosquito screens, the pavilion's
ceiling fans rustling an artificial breeze,
the sounds of leather on willow,
of 'come one', 'no, wait',

and 'How-was-that-umpire!?'
appeal to racial memories,
recall the ancestors and holy places
of the tribe's formation . . .
Canterbury, Lords, the County Ground at York.

Such meditation would explain
our dancing to the nomad from Niger,
but neither he nor we will probe
beneath the fictions that our eyes create,
our shared humanity obscured

by vocabularies of such conflict
that their lexicon is silence.
So, at stumps, nomad and exile
pursue their disparate paths,
amicably separate, rooted in certainties

centuries old, our rootlessness
a fragile bond that will not bear embrace.

Peter Swan

The sons of the prophet are brave men and bold
and quite unaccustomed to fear
but the bravest by far, in the ranks of Allah,
is Abdul, the spinner, Qadir.

When England invaded, in confident mood,
each looking the part in his gear
with a flick of the wrist we soon were dismissed
by Abdul, the spinner, Qadir.

Umpires with a twitch, a terrible pitch,
no wonder our batsmen felt queer;
which way it would turn they never did learn
From Abdul, the spinner, Qadir.

'Our chap Gatting should stick to his batting' –
the authorities made it quite clear –
'give the umpires a rest, and get after that pest
called Abdul, the spinner, Qadir.

Lahore to Karachi – in search of a win
our cricketers reached their nadir.
For wherever they went on the sub-continent
was Abdul, the spinner, Qadir.

LUNCHEON TO THE PAKISTAN
CRICKET TEAM, 1954

A. P. Herbert

Warm welcome, Pakistan,
Captain Kardar in the van!
    (The rhyme, I fear,
    May hurt your ear –
Do better if you can).
Warm welcome, Pakistan!
You are tigers, every man,
    And we always sing a song
    When our visitors belong
To the one great cricket clan.
Warm welcome, Pakistan!
All runs that Ranji ran!
    All the bowling we can mix
    You may put away for six –
We shall still be Paki's fan.
Warm welcome, Pakistan!
Since this little isle began
    We have suffered with a smile
    Every wickedness and wile
That the weather men could plan.
But we have it from the Queen –
There's to be a change of scene:
    Until you go
    On rain and snow
There is a ban.

151 LUNCHEON TO THE SOUTH AFRICAN CRICKET TEAM, 1960

A. P. Herbert

Here comes a friendly cricketer,
   And we are glad to see you, Sir.
   Brave Captain, Dangerous D. McGlew,
   You have some mighty men with you –
GODDARD and ADCOCK, DUCKWORTH and McLEAN,
We've met before – and hope to meet again –
   TAYFIELD – and WAITE, of course, who loves
   His bat as fondly as his gloves.
Then to the new boys, welcome, though you win –
GRIFFIN, McKINNON, FELLOWS-SMITH, O'LINN.
CARLSTEIN and WESLEY – do they bat or bowl?
Well, one, at least, should shake us to the soul.
And last, throughout their long itinerary
May PITHEY do as well as POTHECARY!
   To all we wish especial suns –
   A happy time – and reasonable runs!

LUNCHEON TO THE
NEW ZEALAND CRICKETERS, 1958

A. P. Herbert

I have the most insanitary cold:
It snows. I feel exceptionally old
(I notice also, through the snowy blast,
The Cambridge crew is rowing slowly past).
But I must write some happy verse for you
About the cricketers of Zealand (New).
(This is to please my printer friends. But blow it!
Nobody seems to think about the poet).
  Cricket! New Zealand! Well, with rapture true
(Though sneezing sadly) I salute the two.
Welcome, dear Britons from the Beauteous Isles
(Distant, I think, about 12,000 miles)!
How wonderful that you should come so far,
But be at home (at least, we hope you are)!
The Finns, the Swedes, may dump their butter down,
But they have no eleven in this town.
Quick runs, quick wickets, REID! Be bright and bold –
And God preserve you from the British cold!

Paul Weston

The use of saliva,
That great ball reviver
So relished by Roger G. Twose,
Can hardly be placed
At the forefront of taste,
But, damn it, what else could he use?

Yet drily reviewing
The act of bedewing,
A practice one shrinks from condemning,
How strange that the function
Of smarming the unction
Was never entrusted to Fleming.

But none who can whittle
The truth from the spittle
Will ponder its influence lightly:
The ball told a story of gloom and of glory,
One side shining much the more brightly.

Richard Stilgoe

Written for the Lord's Taverners' visit to the Hague in 1985.

We all went off to Holland upon a Saturday –
Hoping to play cricket before acid rain stopped play.
For the great Liefdadigangshow – we'd a team so big and strong
We could reach the number one spot (like the Popy Jopy song!)
Like a happy crowd of rabbits being let out of the hutch –
We went to 's-Gravenhage to play against the Dutch.

The eleven from the Hague, had a very sporting air –
They'd an athlete and a skater, an Olympic hockey player –
The Minister of Farming – called Ad Ploeg for his crimes –
And Eef Kamerbeek – decathlon – allowed to bat ten times –
But Snow and Rumsey bowled – and they never got a touch
When we went to 's-Gravenhage to play against the Dutch.

Now cricket in the Netherlands is full of fol-de-rols.
Because after every over they give you a new Bols –
The umpires give you Warninks – avoid them like the plague –
They often give you herrings – but they never give you Haig –
They gave us lots of herring – but we didn't manage much
When we went to 's-Gravenhage to play against the Dutch.

Two-oh-one the score was when we broke the final dyke
Then we stopped to meet the Princess (alas, not on her bike).
We stood in the marquee – and it was lucky we were there
Because outside the Belgians parachuted from the air.
So we chatted to the Dutch – to what's his name and such and such
When we went to 's-Gravenhage to play against the Dutch.

Oh what a fuss to get on pads, what hustle and what bustle –
The runs came thick, the runs came fast from Frost and Osman (Russell)
Cowper got his thirty-odd, Rushton's stay was brief –
Then taking time from paying bridge – out came Omar Sharif
(Omar Sharif – is feeling so down in the dumps
He looked around – and then he found that he had three no-stumps).
The strokes played by the Taverners were quite beyond description
The day we went to 's-Gravenhage, to play with an Egyptian.

The final ball came round – One run was needed, that was it –
I shan't say, out of modesty, who made the winning hit –
And everyone from both sides – all the Dutch and English Chaps,
For playing so extremely well, were given their Dutch caps.
The Day we went to Holland to play against the Dutch –
We had a really smashing time – so thank you very much.

David Phillips

The *chinaman* and *chinese cut*, so coined
when 'trick' was deemed analogous to 'chink'
for any gambit that seemed odd
by cricketers not paid to think
and half the world was British Empire pink.

And Peking might have been a Martian moon
for all your English county player knew,
both Eaton toff and yeoman batter
connived in ignorance that grew
into a game appealing to so few.

The Chinese would I think be good at cricket,
stamp the sport with their own playing style,
find some aspect they'd excel at,
grace the game with speed and guile,
compete and no doubt stuff us by a mile.

Roger Knight

We give thanks for our guests from Australia
And the pleasure their visit affords.
As there's no Ashes Tour that's a failure
We look forward to matches at Lord's.
As we all look ahead to the cricket
And we pray for a summer of sun,
Though we know that it's tough at the wicket,
May we hope that the players have fun.
Bless us all at this MCC dinner
Every cricketer present or past.
Bless each batsmen, each keeper, each spinner
And those fortunate men who bowl fast.
Make this evening one more for our treasures
Bless the food that we eat and the wine
Make us grateful for all cricket's pleasures
As we sit down together to dine.

VIII

THE HUMOUR OF CRICKET

(Short-legs and Long-stops)

~

Everything is funny as long as it has happened to somebody else – so we are told.

Whether or not that is true, one suspects many of the following pieces are based on personal experience; which is not to deny the possibility of a spot of *schadenfreude*. The mood of the earlier poems is wide-ranging: gleeful verse from Norman Gale; mock-snobbery (at least, one hopes it is that) from G. F. Bradby surrounding strict protocol in the upper echelons of cricket; and quaint confusion from a gallant unnamed Anglo-Indian versifyer whose ponderings were originally published in a Calcutta newspaper during the 1890s. Transferred *to The Lady Cricketers' Gazette*, these verses were encapsulated in an article drawing the attention of readers to schoolgirl cricket at the Peacock Fields, Bedford Park, 'becomingly dressed in reseda, with bright yellow sashes and white caps', and contests between 'actresses . . . actors and journalists' at the Paddington Recreation Grounds; the latter, no doubt, an excuse for a touch of bonding . . .

The mixture of type with the poetry is equally eclectic. In general terms there are a number of poems that fall into the category of having period gentility with a discreet chuckle behind the hand in vicarage tea-party mode. These contrast sharply with an individual and accurately aimed poke at blokish behaviour from John Whitworth in 'Coarse Cricket'; and a fetching few lines 'on cricket, sex and housework' from the popular Jamaican 'dub' poet Jean 'Binta' Breeze which are, well . . . different.

Throw in some amusing doggerel; cognizance of the sale of Lord's old lawn; Richard Stilgoe's witty tribute to that irrepressible funster Brian

Johnston; and we have just enough time to carry out Morgan Dockrell's
'Last Instructions of a Cricketer':

Smile, please!

D. R. A.

Norman Gale

I bowled three sanctified souls
   With three consecutive balls!
What do I care if Blondin trod
   Over Niagara Falls?
What do I care for the loon in the Pit
   Or the gilded Earl in the Stalls?
I bowled three curates once
   With three consecutive balls!

I caused three Protestant 'ducks'
   With three consecutive balls!
Poets may rave of lily girls
   Dancing in marble halls!
What do I care for a bevy of yachts
   Or a dozen or so of yawls?
I bowled three curates once
   With three consecutive balls!

I bowled three cricketing priests
   With three consecutive balls!
What if a critic pounds a book
   What if an author squalls?

What do I care if sciatica comes,
   Elephantiasis calls?
I bowled three curates once
   With three consecutive balls!

Coulson Kernahan

I.

I ran for a catch,
    With the sun in my eyes, Sir;
Being sure at a 'snatch',
I ran for a catch; . . .
Now I wear a black patch.
    And a nose *such* a size, Sir!
I ran for a catch,
    With the sun in my eyes, Sir.

II.

I stepped in to drive
    And the umpire said, 'Out, Sir!'
Being last to arrive,
I stepped in to drive,
For we wanted but five,
    And had made them, no doubt, Sir;
But I stepped in to drive,
    And the umpire said, 'Out, Sir!'

159   A VILLAGE CRICKET MATCH
(A TRUE STORY)

W. N. Cobbold

One day a friend of mine was playing cricket,
   And came in last with 'one' required to tie;
A single; he was 'home' beyond the wicket,
   As anyone could see with half an eye.

That he was 'in' the batsman never doubted,
   Delighted he'd escaped the dreaded 'blob' –
When suddenly 'How's that?' was loudly shouted;
   The umpire answered 'Out! *I wins five bob!*'

J. S. Fletcher

The Aldermere cricket-players came one day
Unto the Village of Hogley, a match for to play
At cricket, which is a very noble game,
Unless you should happen to be blind or lame.
The match was played upon the village green,
Which is a most beautiful and charming scene,
And everybody was there of high degree,
Including the Parson and the Noble Quality.
The Aldermere cricketers went in first,
And Squire Chuffleigh laughed until he was nearly burst,
When Billy Wheezer bowled a man out first ball,
After which the wickets did very suddenly fall,
And Parson Jones, of Aldermere, near had a fit
Because the Hogley bowling couldn't be hit.
So the innings ended, and all they'd got
Was four-and-twenty, which is not a great lot.
After that there was ale, in cans and jugs,
And also porter, in barrels and mugs,
And when everybody had drunk in moderation
Squire Chuffleigh proposed "The Glorious British Nation!
God bless the Queen and every pretty wench;
Health to our noble selves, and damn the French!"
And that being over, Hogley fell to bat,
And every player wore a new top-hat,
But whether it was the ale or else the porter
Every Hogley man did what he didn't oughter,
And in the end, which produced a deal of fun,
The Aldermere players beat them by a run.
So that's the story of this famous game,
Now told to you by one of mighty fame,
Who now will say farewell, but ere he goes,
Will once more lift his glass toward his nose
Pledging the bat, the ball, and eke the wicket,
With three times three – for England and for cricket!

MONOTONOUS BALLADE
OF ILL-SUCCESS

Alfred Cochrane

Behold me batting as I fail
Once more to stop the crafty slow;
I hear the click of smitten bail,
The wicket-keeper's tactless crow;
I have been in and out, and lo!
My aggregate remains the same;
Another naught! – six in a row;
And yet it's an uncertain game.

Behold me bowling tired and pale
I see the striker's visage glow;
He hits them to the boundary rail,
He hits them high, he hits them low,
For he is playing like a pro,
While I have lost my length and aim;
Another four! I told you so;
And yet it's an uncertain game.

Behold me fielding – thick as hail
Come balls to stop where'er I go,
And still betwixt my shins they sail,
Snick, drive, or cut, or overthrow;
The while I gallop to and fro,
Bombarded with loud shouts of blame;
Another miss! The word was 'blow';
And yet it's an uncertain game.

Envoi

Friend, cricket is a fraud, I know,
Trading on legendary fame;
I find it very certain woe;
And yet it's an uncertain game.

F. A. J. Godfrey

You may have paid your Income Tax
   And bought the wife a hat;
Adjusted each domestic bill;
   Reduced anxiety to nil.
Quite likely, too, you've made your will;
   But – *have you oiled your bat?*

Perchance on questions ponderous
   In conference you've sat;
Mayhap you've met a potentate
   And settled grave affairs of State
That call for tact and cannot wait;
   But – *have you oiled your bat?*

Your conscience may be crystal-clear
   On togs and things like that;
You may be waiting – unafraid –
   To turn out, spotlessly arrayed,
Complete with blazer (newly made);
   But – HAVE YOU
        OILED YOUR BAT?

P. G. Wodehouse

The sun in the heavens was beaming;
The breeze bore an odour of hay,
My flannels were spotless and gleaming,
My heart was unclouded and gay;
The ladies, all gaily apparelled,
Sat round looking on at the match,
In the tree-tops the dicky-birds carolled,
All was peace till I bungled that catch.

My attention the magic of summer
Had lured from the game – which was wrong;
The bee (that inveterate hummer)
Was droning its favourite song.
I was tenderly dreaming of Clara
(On her not a girl is a patch);
When, ah horror! there soared through the air a
Decidedly possible catch.

I heard in a stupor the bowler
Emit a self-satisfied "Ah!"
The small boys who sat on the roller
Set up an expectant "Hurrah!"
The batsman with grief from the wicket
Himself had begun to detach –
And I uttered a groan and turned sick – It
Was over. I'd buttered the catch.

Oh ne'er, if I live to a million,
Shall I feel such a terrible pang.
From the seats in the far-off pavilion
A loud yell of ecstasy rang.
By the handful my hair (which is auburn)
I tore with a wrench from my thatch,
And my heart was seared deep with a raw burn
At the thought that I'd foozled that catch.

Ah, the bowler's low querulous mutter,
Point's loud, unforgettable scoff!
Oh, give me my driver and putter!
Henceforward my game shall be golf.
If I'm asked to play cricket hereafter,
I am wholly determined to scratch.
Life's void of all pleasure and laughter;
I bungled the easiest catch.

G. F. Bradby

You saw that man. You wonder why
I passed him with averted eye,
Although he nodded affably?

It was a Test Match – anxious days.
Somehow he had secured a place
With us, with the habitués.

We were all there. I mean by "we"
The Old Guard of the M.C.C.,
And, with us, but not of us, *he*.

He talked and laughed, as if unused
To serious cricket. He confused
Fosters with Fords, and seemed amused.

You know the story of the match;
The brilliant start, the rotten patch,
And, last, the unaccepted catch:

Mid-off; a gift; no spin at all;
Pure nerves. He fumbled with the ball,
Retrieved it – and then let it fall.

Lord Nestor gave a groan, the rest
Sat silent, overwhelmed, oppress'd
And he, that fellow, made a jest!

That man, who muddled up the Fords,
At such a moment played with words!
In the pavilion!! and at Lord's!!!

Dorothy Spring

A cricketer Lord's-bound from Yeovil
Turned up by mistake at the Eovil;
    So he said 'Never worry,'
    And batted for Surrey,
Though this met with some disappreovil.

R. Whieldon Baddeley

Not of that sort is he
    Which lounges by the tents to kill
The time with levity;
    Nor loudly boastful of his skill
Telling how (in a match you didn't see)
    He drove a slow for six, or smote to leg
A four, or cut a three,

    Or over, a tent peg
Tumbled, but made his catch – not boastful thus
Is the STOUT CRICKETER, nor frivolous.
Yet you may see him smile
    At his own joke, may hear him air his wits
Most pointlessly and slowly, while
    Heavily on a bench he sits
Smoking a pipe, and with a critic's gaze
    Upon the younger batsmen of his side,
Recalls the old cricket memories from the haze
    Of time, not loudly to deride
But calmly to disparage the wild play –
'Which, sir, the youngsters of the present day –'
'Smith!' 'Where's old Smith?' 'Now Smith!'
    For innings Smith doth boune;
In waistcoat black and beltless trousers, with
    His braces not let down,
He, walking stumpwards, doth the lean earth lard;
    His gloves, or as he funnily calls them, 'mits',
Are buttoned by the umpire, he takes guard,
    Most likely on the bat then gravely spits,
Plays the first balls with not untroubled mien,
    But somehow scrapes a score up, say fifteen.

He bowls – swift under-hand,
    And has been seen to previously apply –
As though he had some mysterious magic planned –
    The ball unto his eye.
A smile, yea e'en a chuckle from him breaks,
    When with a lucky length he floors the stumps;
Off then his hat, his head to rub, he takes,
    Shows how he pitched the ball where the ground bumps;
But piteous looks, and stolidly perplexed,
    If his 'best pitch' 'just suits' the man who comes in next.
At dinner he is great,
    Drinks beer and sherry, pays for a friend's wine;
Grows genial and proceeds to state
    'He never yet saw a ball so fine
As that which bowl'd him'; liberal then
He 'stands' the umpire's dinner, nor yet stays
    His generous hand, but for four seedy men,
Who somehow claim a dinner, next he pays
    Those losels help him, struggling, to get peel'd,
When he, alack! must after dinner field.
    Sometimes on tented plain,
The only veteran there,
    I have seen him, running, mirthful plaudits gain
From athlete youth, or girl-spectators fair;
    And I have pitied him as seeming strange,
Misplaced among the rest, to him mere boys,
    And fear'd his memories might sadly range
Back to fled youth and unreturning joys;
    But these fine fancies don't, I think, occur
    To my respectable STOUT CRICKETER.

A gallant Anglo-Indian poet

Ladies' cricket, as you know,
   Now-a-days is all the go,
Whence a question comes, tho' answer it I can't,
   And it possibly might hurt you
If you're jealous of your virtue,
   Yet desirous to be courteous and gallant.
If I heard a little lady
   Using language rather shady
At a batting glove or bow she couldn't tie,
   I'd not hesitate a second,
But before "one two" you reckon'd
   I would help her, or at any rate I'd try.
Her sash I'd knot with taste
   Round her dainty little waist;
I would even tie her shoe,
   But this question drives me mad:
"When she's putting on her pad
What's a modest, yet polite, young man to do?"

168 SIX AND OUT (A STREET IMPRESSION)

G. D. Martineau

The pitch was only smooth in parts;
It sank at either crease,
And motor vans and baker's carts
At times disturbed the peace.

The bowlers found it hard to hit
The lamp-post's slender stem.
The broader wicket, opposite,
Was cleared at 6 p.m.

It was a keen determined school,
Unorthodox and free;
Harsh circumstance oft made the rule,
And not the M.C.C.

The scorer, seated by the wall,
Kept up a fire of talk;
He was both umpires, crowd, and all,
And plied a busy chalk.

So, standing, musing on the scene,
I let the moments pass:
How well he drove it to the screen . . .
And then – the crash of glass!

I watched the players as they ran,
And heard, while yet they fled,
The loud voice of an angry man,
The Law's majestic tread.

Unknown

Supposing Durston went in first
    And carried out his bat;

Supposing Sutcliffe's hair rose up
    And Waddington's lay flat.

Suppose a Surrey partisan
    Imagined Hobbs was Peach:

Supposing Parkin lost his voice,
    And Woolley made a speech.

Supposing Fender took the field
    Without his old silk scarf;

Supposing Tate looked solemn,
    And Hearne was heard to laugh.

Supposing Carr was cautious,
    And Mann renowned for blocks;

S'pose Lee and Dales got reckless
    And broke the Pavilion clocks.

Supposing Strudwick stood quite still
    That agile wicket-keep;

Supposing Hendren slept at slip
    And slumbered in the deep.

S'pose Louglas gave up gardening
    And became a rapid hitter;

Suppose our skipper won the toss,
    And Hammond dropped a sitter.

Suppose the Oval shilling seats
    Were filled with sleek top hats;

And oh! suppose that Warner came
    To Lords without his spats.

Ralph Wotherspoon

In Festivals or Cricket Weeks
Muffled or intermittent squeaks
Denote the presence of a band,
But what I fail to understand
Is why half-hearted use is made
Of local instrumental aid.
If you have music, I submit
That you should make the most of it.
The band might play the batsman in,
That stirling march from 'Lohengrin'
Would fill the bill; now how about
A tune to play the batsman out?
No difficulty here at all,
Handel's C major 'March in Saul'.
'The Rosary' 'Lest we forget'
'Funeral march of Marionette',
'Goodbye for Ever' (this to be
A second innings threnody) . . .
Such melodies as these I think,
(Culled and arranged by Herman Finck),
As incidental to the action
Should merit general satisfaction.

Paul Weston

After the theft of Ranji's turban from Ilkley.

A spectral song affrights the owls
And stills the whirring gnat;
Whence come those undulating vowels;
What oriental banshee howls
On Ilkley Moor bah t'at?

Consenting zephyrs waft the strain
From rural parts to urban.
It rises, falls, then soars again,
Foreshadowing the bleak refrain
'Some Tyke has nabbed my turban!'

R. J. O. Meyer

The great Maurice Tate
Used to swing very late
Not just now and then but
Again and again

For Larwood and Voce
Silly points stood in close
For me they would beat
A hasty treat

They say Brian Close
Could be somewhat verbose
Not so with Bob Wyatt
Who kept pretty quiet

Said the 'Skip' to Alf Gover
Who had begged one more over
'You heard what I said Sir!
Hand over to Bedser'

'Quod erat demonstrandum'
Declared coach Andy Sandham
'Just do as I say
And you will stay in all day.'

John Whitworth

Chancers all at the back of the bus! I
Drop a half-dollar – this game's a racket.
Christopher grins, he's winning a packet,
    Bastard, far too fly.
These stumpers, all need thumped occasionally.

Posh pavilions, but where's the beer-tent?
Someone gets 40. I get duck – it
Comes off the toecap, clangs like a bucket.
    Umpire's blind, or bent.
I bum a 'bine and soak up sympathy.

90 for 9 – Jeeze! Murder their tea though,
Egg and lettuce and cucumber sandwiches.
    Skittle the sods for 33, go
    Horsing with Chris in the shower.
    Bloody sex-maniacs, and which is
    Better, the kings of an hour.

Jean 'Binta' Breeze

I have never liked ironing

but there's something steamy here
that softens the crease
and although I played it straight
I fell
to your googly

I came out slightly crinkly

perhaps it's the strange things
your fingers do
around my seams

CRICKET WIDOW

Kit Wright

Out of the love you bear me,
By all its sweet beginnings,
Darling heart, please spare me
The details of your innings.

David Phillips

When batting you must concentrate the mind,
shoo every pure and impure thought away;
a catchy tune looped in the head I find
allows the brain to focus on each ball
                              and helps me play.

Don't need at all to be a highbrow cheese
for any nagging phrase will serve to milk
the bowling, and patently this useful wheeze
makes no distinction between Beethoven
                              and Acker Bilk.

Neville Denson

He runs the village pub, at drink
And food works long and hard
Yet every Wednesday in the nets
He comes and takes his guard;
He turns his arm a time or two
He'll chase balls wide and far,
Then back he'll go at nine o'clock
To 'keep' behind the bar.

He's way down in the averages
He's slower in the field,
He would have been out-leg before
If someone had appealed
But everyone took pity on
This ageing number seven
Though on his form he wouldn't make
An under-nines' eleven

His bowling was atrocious
He couldn't hit the sticks
He'd sixteen no-balls, fourteen wides
And none for ninety-six.
But everyone took pity on
This ageing man of spin,
And said that dropping him would be
A shame, a crime, a sin.

Such is the heart of cricketers,
Compassion won the day;
We'll nurse him till his form returns –
Oh yes, and by the way,
Our feelings are not influenced
By the fact – let's make it clear –
That after games he treats both teams
To dinner and free beer.

Morgan Dockrell

As a fielder batsmen love me
For I'm such an idle stroller.
I'm each bowler's favourite batsman,
And each batsman's favourite bowler.
Only honesty compels me
To make public this admission: –
My popularity extends
Just to the OPPOSITION.

Geoffrey Johnson

This is a grim to-do:
To be grabbed for the village side,
Which has met its Waterloo
And to suffer on holiday too
This blot on my blazer's pride.

Out total is now eleven
And extras in it are nine;
Big hitters of ours were seven
But for all their swipes to heaven
Their ducks have an ominous sign.

What a hangman's leer I call
That bowler's at this end;
So gaily he flips the ball
He would not scruple at all
To bump off his best friend.

Will no one send me a wire,
No last-minute next of kin,
No splendidly merciful liar
Send news my house is on fire?
For I am the last man in.

Anon

Written on the shell of a duck's egg and found on the cricket field of
Amersham Hall, 17 July 1886, after a match

Two balls I survived,
　　But the third one came straight,
For the bowler contrived
(Seeing what I survived)
To bowl at a rate
　　I did not contemplate.
Two balls I survived,
　　But the third one came straight.

Norman Gale

When the doctor pulls up as you pass in the street,
        You know he will say: –
'Well Rodgers, I hear that you suffered defeat –
        How many today?
Not a hundred, I fear; but you always do well,
        And doubtless you struck?
It is hard to admit that you could not excel
        A 'duck.'

For the bowling was easy, the wicket was true,
        And had it not been
That you thought the slow trundler was guilty of *screw*
        You had driven it clean!
How galling to read in the *Sportsman* next day –
        What horrible luck! –
'H. Rogers (the Captain) caught Grinstead, bowled May,
        A 'duck."

But 'tis worse when your Uncle and sweet Cousin Bell
        Come over to watch
All your wonderful deeds as a very great Swell –
        The hope of the match!
And Bell asks your score with a traitorous smile,
        More knowing than Puck;
And you say (looking straight in her eyes all the while)
        A 'duck.'

But when Fogson, your rival, makes Four after Four,
        And Three after Three,
And next a grand drive, that adds six to his score,
        Right over the tree,
Bell's eyes with excitement delightedly flash –
        She praises his pluck!
So you think that the worst of emphatical trash
        Is 'duck.'

Anon

He played cricket on the heath,
The pitch was full of bumps:
A fast ball hit him in the teeth,
The dentist drew the stumps.

J. S. Fletcher

A fig for your doctors, their pills and their plaisters;
There's nothing like cricket for liver or brain!
A trot o'er the turf, 'twixt the wickets, my masters,
Will soon make a sick man a sound man again!

Barclay Hankin

If lawn is now so badly worn,
At Lord's some hallowed turf,
A twelve inch square will cost ten pounds,
A chance, for what it's worth!

You'll think of all those famous knights,
That may have trodden there,
Sir Gubby Allen, Sir Jack Hobbs,
Make haste, the offer's rare!

For twenty pounds for nine square feet,
Yes, a cheaper rate,
A thrill for you of Larwood's skill,
Or six from Maurice Tate!

You may remember Leslie Ames,
A keeper of renown,
A batsman too, so chosen well,
To score, and keep runs down!

Do you remember Botham now,
Who bowled and scored so fast,
And many more who trod the turf,
Which can be yours at last!

If you're retired and left to watch,
Your cricket on T.V.,
You could enjoy your special link,
And dream of M.C.C.!

Richard Stilgoe

Written for Brian Johnston's Memorial Service at Westminster Abbey, 16 May 1994.

Eternal paradise at first glance, looks very nice –
This is heaven. Every moment is sublime.
For the first few weeks it's great, then it starts to irritate –
Eternity's a hell of a long time.

But heaven's dull perfection's had a recent shock injection –
A muffled titter's running through the pews.
The cause of all this change'll be the maverick new angel
With ears like wings and co-respondent shoes.

The cherubin and seraphin are starting to despair of him
They've never known a shade so entertaining.
He chats to total strangers, calls the angel Gabriel "Ainjers"
And talks for even longer of it's raining.

He had told them all his stories – the countless broadcast glories –
They listen as the narrative's unfolding.
Motorcycling through a wall, the crazy gang, but best of all
They like the line that starts "The bowler's holding . . ."

He'd have liked to play the halls, or be Ralph Lynn or Tom Walls,
But actors almost always end in hell.
So he wrote himself a role, and with all his heart and soul,
Cast himself as him, and played him awfully well.

He made twenty million friends, for the broadcast voice extends
Far beyond those you encounter face to face
And those he never met have a chance to meet him yet
For all of us end up in the same place.

And when St. Peter's done the honours he will pass you on to Jonners,
Who will cry "Good morning – welcome to the wake.
You're batting number seven for the Heaven fourth eleven.
While you're waiting have some Angel cake!"

So if you think that Heaven's like a wet weekend in Devon
When you get there he'll be sure to change your views
Up there the big-nosed cherub'll be telling really terrible
Old jokes while wearing co-respondent shoes.

186 LAST INSTRUCTIONS OF A CRICKETER

Morgan Dockrell

When Umpire Time sees fit to raise his Finger,
Cremate me with my cricket gear, don't linger.
And further, please don't question, but obey:
Dispose of my urned ashes in this way:-

Scatter some ash upon that earthy bed
Whose inmates rarely heard my living tread,
That dust of mine perpetually dozes
In, symbol of my life, a bed of roses.

The rest, reminders of my wit's bright flashes,
Should stand by WISDEN, apt abode for Ashes,
Placed on a little clock: be this my fate,
That I should be on time while being late.

IX

CRICKET PARODIES

(On-and-Off-Beat)

~

Parody usually starts with admiration of the subject, even if the object of the exercise is ridicule. In the examples that follow the inherent element of exaggeration necessary for parody is kept on a tight leash – underplay is nearly always more effective – either because the material has been used with serio/ironical intent or because the composition is sufficient unto itself as an impression of the *genre.*

We start with 'the first finder of our language', Geoffrey Chaucer, and Simon Barnes's inventive re-interpretation of the 'Prologue to Canterbury Tales'. The aesthetic Francis Thompson is then seen adopting a ribald role for his double take on 'The Rubaiyat of Omar Khayyam': a double take in the sense that the source material had already been adapted so freely by Edward Fitzgerald that it could almost be considered his own work regardless of doubts about the original being attributed solely to the eleventh/twelfth-century Persian poet.

After the homophonous 'Rime O' Bat Of O My Sky – Em', A. M. Robertson finds the punning and black comedy of Thomas Hood to his liking in 'The Cricket Match'. Hood once wrote, 'Of all games and sports cricket appears to be the most trying to the temper, for a player cannot lose his wicket without being put out.' 'The starry soul that shines when all is dark', so described by an admirer, was much influenced by Keats who wrote of cricket several times in his letters. And it is to Keats that we turn next with his poem 'The Mermaid Tavern', the source for an adaptation by John Pugh which was read at an equally famous Tavern, the one at Lord's, a number of years ago. The occasion was the Annual Dinner of the Buccaneers Cricket Club. Keats was also the backdrop for sometime Sri Lankan Ambassador to Belgium and the Netherlands, D. A. de Silva, who tendered his apologies to the poet for borrowing the framework of 'On first looking into Chapman's Homer' to express his joy 'On hearing of Sri Lanka's first Test victory', against India in 1985.

Again de Silva, using his middle name Alan, makes token apology, only in this case to Wordsworth for the parody of 'On Milton' which appeared in 'Poet's Corner' in *The Cricketer* in the spring of 1988, entitled 'Cardus'. De Silva's diatribe against the state of the game is in stark contrast to G. H. Vallins's use of the same poem in the mid-1950s. Vallins extols the prowess and literary bent of Frank Tyson.

Vallins spread his labours liberally in *Punch*, where his method was described by R. G. G. Price as 'usually, but not always, an imitation of older writers. It was pastiche rather than strict parody, and really derived from an earlier tradition. For example, he applied Chaucerian verse to contemporary types like the Air Raid Warden. The anachronism was perhaps too slight a peg for humour, and the reader's pleasure came from the skill with which Vallins wrote in the styles of different men rather than from amusement.' Here, the two Alfreds, Tennyson and Housman, were among those captured by his pen. The former, with a rather ruminative feel of his fabric, and the latter, with a skit at his 'Shropshire Lad', who in this verse has migrated to Marylebone.

Walt Whitman's 'Leaves of Grass' was once considered so radical in content that its author was thought to be a revolutionary, which would not have mattered a jot to R. W. Raper, who dedicated 'The Innings' to the nineteenth-century American poet and essayist. One of Whitman's most enthusiastic supporters was his countryman and fellow writer, Ralph Waldo Emerson, and it is Emerson and the Scot, Andrew Lang, who are acknowledged by Herbert E. Clarke as he endows 'Cricket' with a *persona* to remind that the game can make fools of us all.

Before that, A. M. Robertson makes play with the Lord Chancellor's Song from 'Iolanthe' in 'A Nightmare Innings'. Despite W. S. Gilbert's disparaging assessment of himself as 'a doggerel bard' the parodist has the advantage of desuming the mind of arguably the wittiest librettist of any age.

P. G. 'Plum' Wodehouse was very much of Gilbert's ilk, in that he collaborated on more than thirty plays and musical comedies. Before

World War One, Wodehouse wrote a number of poems under the name of 'Mr Parrot' which appeared in the *Daily Express*. In 'The Outcast' he turns his attention to ladies' cricket, which, at the time and in the wake of the White Heather Club, had gained ground in Australia, New Zealand and even Kenya. The poem is a satirical swipe at the last-ditch saloon style of 'The Shooting of Dan McGrew' by 'the old sourdough' Robert W. Service. Waal, whadya know!

On Christmas Eve 1982, on the second day of the third Test Match between India and England at New Delhi, Geoffrey Boycott broke the then Test aggregate record of 8,032 runs held by Garfield Sobers. Boycott's typically patient innings of 105 had taken 440 minutes. In lieu of a match report the *Guardian* correspondent Frank Keating sent back parodies of a handful of well-known carols. 'Hark does *Hindu Herald* sing' and 'We Three Tweaks' were two of them.

'The Tragedy of Prince Botham – Part Two' is, once again, the work of Simon Barnes, ably assisted by William Shakespeare. The short extract focuses on Hamlet's eternal soliloquy, 'To play or not to play . . .'.

'The Cricketing Versions' by one of the leading poets of today, Wendy Cope, is not so much a parody as a literary joke. Attending a dinner-party she overheard a snippet of conversation from the far end of the room: 'There isn't much cricket in the Cromwell play', to which she came out with the riposte, 'There isn't much cricket in *Hamlet* either'. The theme was developed and dedicated to a friend and fellow guest, Simon Rae.

Rae himself pokes gentle fun at the spirit of cricket in company with Dylan Thomas's signature ode to bring the sequence to a close.

D. R. A.

PROLOGUE TO THE
TESTE MATCHE TALES

Simon Barnes

(Geoffrey Chaucer)

Whan that Aprille with his sonne bright
The chille of March hath halfway put to flighte,
And folken in their gardens start to swinke
And poshen folken Pimmies start to drink,
The dayseyes in the outfield gan to flowre
And groundsmen lepe astride the rattlinge mowre,
So grass is short and daies growe evre longe
And tea-ladyes all bursten into songe,
Thanne longen folke to go and watch crickette
And see the batter cope with greene wickette.

Bifel thatte in this season on a day
In London at the Tavern as I lay
Redy to wenden to a cricket match
The second Teste I was all set to watch.
But natheless whil I have time and space
Er firther in my match report I pace
And er I tell yow of the three one-dayeres
I first shal something tell of all our playeres.

The captaine first, and he a worthye man,
That from the time that he first bigan
To play the game, he lovede tactics,
Leadership, psychologie, and tricks.
A doctore of philosophie, this fellowe,
And when at batte he hummede of the cello.
His haire beneathe his helmette al was greye
But he could lede the yonge folke al day.
He had taken many a soverein pris
An thoghe thatte he was worthy, he was wis.
He was not talle, like a church's steeple,
But this man had a degree in peple.

A battere ther was, a wontoun and a jollye,
But sometimes given o'er to fits of follye.
He mighte scor an hundred runnes full quicke
Or get out flashing by the offe-sticke.
To play defensively he had no luste,
Alway with him twas shitte or buste.
He had a hede right full of golden curles
And knewe the way to talke to pretty girles.
Scoring runs he found a thing quite fine
Yet seemede to preferre drinkinge win.
Of gritte and effort he did seem to lacke
And of his nature he was ful laid-backe.

We had with us was an al-roundere,
A mightye manne, a bit of a boundere,
He scorerde much wherever cricket playede,
Not only ronnes, or so the paperes sayde
He coulde muchel of wanderinge by the weye
Long-haired he was and playede at cardes al day.

Long yeres ago, the mighty deeds wer done,
And always playede the game as if for fun.
His crickette left he pretty much to chaunce,
He could of love the old daunce.

We had with us a fast bowllere,
Whose port was alway ful of sad doloure,
His deeds had made the crickette world amazede
With whirling arms and with his eyes all glazede,
His run-up was a windmil prance
He semeth like a man caughte in a trance.

A spinnere too we had, a sorry knave
Who knew not how our cricketteres behave,
A left-handere few batsmen knew to matche
And for a sponsor he could wear a Swatche.
He loved rancour, enmity and feud
And alwaye to his captaine he was rude.
He had a tricky bitche for a wife *
And chose a mightye man to write his life.

And thus we gan to riden on our weye
To see the cricket for the next five day.

* *This line contributed by my old friend Frances Edmonds. S. B.*

Francis Thompson

(After Omar Khayyam)

Wake! for the Ruddy Ball has taken flight
That scatters the slow Wicket of the Night;
    And the swift Batsman of the Dawn has driven
Against the Star-spiked Rails a fiery Smite.

Wake, my Beloved! take the Bat that clears
The sluggish Liver, and Dyspeptics cheers:
    Tomorrow? Why, tomorrow I may be
Myself with Hambledon and all its Peers.

Today a score of Batsmen brings, you say?
Yes, but where leaves the Bats of yesterday?
    And this same summer day that brings a Knight
May take the Grace and Ranjitsinhji away.

Willsher the famed is gone with all his 'throws'.
And Alfred's Six-foot Reach where no man knows;
    And Hornby – the great hitter – his own Son
Plays in his place, yet recks not the Red Nose.

And Silver Billy, Fuller Pilch and Small,
Alike the pigmy Briggs and Ulyett tall,
    Have swung their Bats an hour or two before,
But none played out the last and silent Ball.

Well, let them Perish! What have we to do
With Gilbert Grace the Great, or that Hindu?
    Let Hirst and Spooner slog them as they list,
Or Warren bowl his 'snorter'; care not you!

With me along the Strip of Herbage strown,
That is not laid or watered, rolled or sown,
    Where name of Lord's and Oval is forgot,
And peace to Nicholas on his bomb-girt Throne.

A level Wicket,as the Ground allow,
A driving Bat, a lively Ball, and thou
    Before me bowling on the Cricket-pitch –
O Cricket-pitch were Paradise enow!

2

I listened where the Grass was shaven small,
And heard the Bat that groaned against the Ball:
    Thou pitchest Here and There, and Left and Right,
Nor deem I where the Spot thou next may'st Fall.

Forward I play, and Back and Left and Right,
And overthrown at once, or stay till Night:
    But this I know, where nothing else I know,
The last is Thine, how so the Bat shall smite.

This thing is sure, where nothing else is sure,
The boldest Bat may but a Space endure;
    And he who One or who a Hundred hits
Falleth at ending to thy Force or Lure.

Wherefore am I allotted but a Day
To taste Delight, and make so brief a stay;
    For meed of all my labour laid aside,
Endeth alike the Player and the Play.

Behold, there is an Arm behind the Ball,
Nor the Bat's Stroke of its own Striking all;
    And who the Gamesters, to what end the Game?
I think thereof our writing is but small.

Against the Attack and Twist of Circumstance
Though I oppose Defence and Shifty Glance,
    What power gives Nerve to me, and what Assaults, –
This is the Riddle. Let dull bats cry 'Chance'.

Is there a Foe that domineers the Ball?
And one that Shapes and wields us Willows all?
    Be patient if Thy Creature in Thy Hand
Break, and the so-long guarded Wicket fall!

Thus spoke the Bat. Perchance a foolish Speech
And wooden, for a Bat has straitened Reach:
    Yet thought I, I had heard Philosophers
Prate much on this wise, and aspire to Teach.

Ah, let us take our Stand, and play the Game,
But rather for the cause than for the Fame;
    Albeit right evil is the Ground and we
Know our Defence will be but lame.

O Love, if thou and I could but Conspire
Against this Pitch of Life, so false with Mire,
    Would we not Doctor it afresh, and then
Roll it out smoother to the Bat's Desire?

A. M. Robertson

(After Thomas Hood)

Now list, and I will tell you
    How a scratch eleven came
To play Durham County miners
    In a Minor Counties game.

It rained all through the morning,
    Which meant an hour's loss;
It was agreed to toss at one
    And Durham won the toss.

The miners' skipper cried 'Aha!
    Your fate is surely sealed'.
So Durham took first innings
    And the others took the field.

To start with, they could muster eight
    (This happens in all sport);
They'd left behind their three short men
    Which left them three men short.

But their captain had three sisters
    And framed a cunning plan;
He sent the second shortest girl
    To field at deep third man.

She said: I can propel a ball
    200 yards you know,
So please don't throw me over
    If I make an overthrow!'

The shortest girl was active
    Although not very strong.
He fielded her at long-stop
    But she didn't stop there long.

She frisked about the outfield
 Like a young and lively pup;
She wasn't really backing down,
 But only backing up.

The tallest one there was all at sea
 To stand she knew not where.
Her father had to move her round
 Until she was quite square.

The umpires, as to stature
 Did very ill assort.
The short man stood at deep long-leg
 When the other cried: 'One short!'

Bill Butty played for Durham
 (He didn't play for fun)
And, if he liked one number.
It sure was number one.

So when he saw the order
 It made him fiercely frown,
For there were six wickets up
 He was sixth wicket down.

The skipper saw him scowling
 And said 'Is this agreed –
I'll let you lead the innings
 If we get first innings lead?'

Bill's turn soon came for batting
 For the innings was a rout.
The early bats were given in
 And so were given out.

One man had done the damage
 (A Wily bird was he);
He'd taken 3 for 25
 By 25 to 3.

What happened to his first ball
 Bill never could have told,
But though he felt quite confident
 He found he wasn't bold.

He said: 'I had it covered –
  It neither sot nor bumped;
But if you ask me how I missed
  I must confess, I'm stumped!'

The next one was a yorker
  Straight on his middle peg.
Bill's leg began to tickle
  So he tickled it to leg.

They took a risky single.
  Thought Bill: Beyond a doubt,
If my zeal outruns my caution
  I soon shall be run out!

I must play very steady
  And mustn't have a dip;
If my patience slips a second
I'll be caught at second slip.

I must avoid that umpire, too.
  One ball, I'm pretty sure,
That hits my bat before my leg
  And he'll give me leg-before.

(That other time, when rain began,
  He put me out of joint:
I pointed to the covers
  And was caught at cover point.)

Ah now here comes a bumper
  To fill my sorrow's cup,
But I needn't take it lying down:
  The 'keeper's' standing up.

But still, it wasn't pleasant
  (I hate this kind of play).
I fear my nerve may peter out:
  I am not Peter May!'

But somehow Bill got settled
  Once he had cracked his egg.
And bowled a maiden over
  With a lively glance to leg.

He'd been there forty minutes;
    Then, just as he'd supposed,
Though the match was still quite open
    They declared the innings closed.

Said Bill: 'This is a pity –
    I felt like runs galore.
My score is on the board, I see,
    And borders on a score.

But I'll take it like a sportsman –
    I mustn't moan or shout.
I really don't mind going in
    As long as I'm not out.

If the bowler takes his sweater
    And the fieldsman takes his hat
And the stumper *will* keep wicket,
    Why, I'll carry out my bat!'

He got no second innings
    (That hope was quickly gone)
For when the miners took the lead
    The others followed on.

But he had some consolation:
    He helped to win the match,
And the skipper caught him by one hand
    For his neat one handed catch.

190 LINES BASED UPON JOHN KEATS' POEM, 'THE MERMAID TAVERN'

John Pugh

Read at the Annual Dinner of the Buccanneers Cricket club at the Tavern, Lord's Cricket Ground, 8 January 1947.

Souls of Cricketers dead and gone
What Elysium have ye known
Happy field or mossy cavern
Choicer than this classic Tavern.

Have ye tasted drink more fine
Than this evening's Bowlers' Wine
Or is food of Paradise
Choicer than our sugared spice

And meat without right generously
Served as though great W. G.
With Alfred Mynn and good Lumpy
Would sup and browse form horn and can?

If as must come on a day
Mine host's signboard flies away
No one will know whither till
An astrologer's old quill

To a sheeps-skin gives the story
Says, he has seen you in your Glory
Beneath a Heavenly Tavern sign
Sipping beverage Divine

And pledging with contented look
Divine late-cut
Elysian hook.

Souls of Cricketers dead and gone
What Elysium have ye known
Happy field or mossy cavern
Choicer than this classic Tavern

Has your company more good cheer
Than feasting with a Buccanneer
Or do you envy me and my
Fellow guests their company?

Just a little I'll be bound
As you glance this room around
And spy the talent that these gay
Bold bad Buccanneers betray.

Well through the sky chinks you may peep
And praise the company I keep.

Souls of Cricketers dead and gone
Join with us at feasting time
To thank the President, the Proposer and the *club*
And the landlord of this – Tavern.

191 ON FIRST HEARING OF SRI LANKA'S
1ST TEST VICTORY

D. A. de Silva

(With apologies to Keats)

Long have I dwelt in cricket's noble realm
And many goodly games and players seen.
Round many a wayward wireless have I been
To catch a broadcast of some distant game.

And always, hope did not stay long suppressed
That cricketers from one resplendent isle
Would bring resolve to bear on skill and style
And breach, in time, the barrier of a Test.

Once, on that green and hallowed field at Lord's,
Sri Lanka's light shone brightly through the game;
Yet later burned with only fitful flame
And triumphs were denied us by the Gods.

And so it seemed, when there began, anon,
Another quest for that elusive grail.
As sadly, nature's elements prevailed
To rob us of a victory all but won.

Then fortune smiled – and Justice long delayed
Moved to redress the balance of her scale.
Great India bowed; Sri Lanka did not fail.
The Test was won and history was made.

When memory recalls, in future years,
The moment when our cricket reached its prime,
We will remember, too, a troubled time
When we could smile – if briefly – through our tears.

Alan de Silva

(With apologies to Wordsworth)

Cardus! thou shouldest be living at this hour
The game hath need of thee; it is a fen
Of squalid waters; petty, peevish men
Grown arrogant with money, fame or power,

Have squandered cricket's ancient, precious
    dower
Of inward happiness. Obscenity abounds
Where once were heard the glorious sounds
Of knightly combat – hour by blessed hour.

Your soul was like a Star, and dwelt apart;
It shed brilliant light upon a game
Which honest men did nothing to defame.

Your heroes heeded Honour's courtly code:
Grace under pressure, steadfastness of heart.
Now, pygmies pirouette where giants strode.

G. H. Vallins

It is reported that Tyson, the England fast bowler, is in the habit of quoting Wordsworth to himself as he runs up to the wicket.

Tyson! 'tis well thou livest at this hour;
Hutton hath need of thee: thy pounding run
Tireless beneath the blazing summer sun
Or where the gathering clouds in thunder lour,
Hath made a friendly foes discreetly cower
With inward fearfulness, as one by one
They come and go, by swinging bolts undone
Hurl'd by thy cunning arm's relentless power

Yet thou, an England star, dost dwell apart
From those triumphant fields; by Peter Bell
Thy wandering thought is stirred, or Heartleap Well,
Or Michael, lifting ne'er a single stone;
Simon and Ruth and Lucy fill thy heart,
And Newton, on his seas of thought, alone.

ALFRED, LORD TENNYSON UMPIRES
A VILLAGE CRICKET MATCH

G. H. Vallins

So in the leafy heart of June
   I donned, to judge the mimic strife,
   The white coat of a blameless life,
And stood, the sunlit afternoon,

Counting the pebbles, fixt in thought,
   And watch'd the battle ebb and flow,
   Where one would come, and lightly go,
Too soon returning, bowl'd or caught;

And one keener eye would wield
   The unrelenting blade, and smite
   The flying ball to left or right
In splendid arcs about the field.

With anxious but unerring eye
   I judg'd the careless wide, and spread
   The outstretch'd arms, and o'er the head
Uprais'd the hand to mark a bye.

But on a sudden, lo! a shout
   About mine ears; and high upflung
   The eager arms with silent tongue
Made question whether in or out.

I stood; I paused a moment's space,
   And in the sudden hush I heard
   A counsellor that in me stirr'd
And said "'Twere better far to face

The lifted brow and faint surprise
  Of him who waits thy stern decree
  Than watch the incredulity
Mirror'd in two-and-twenty eyes."

I rais'd the finger; as he went,
  The eager crowd, according well,
  Relax'd, and on their faces fell
The silence of a deep content.

G. H. Vallins

(Alfred Edward Housman: from A Marylebone Lad)

Out? so quick, so clean an ending?
  Oh that was right, lad, that was brave;
'Twas best not waste the time defending
  The side you could not hope to save.

Fear no longer slip or cover,
  Or the ball that moves away;
Get you gone: your reign is over
  No forgiving, no delay.

Now your debt to brighter cricket
  Lies discharges, past fear and doubt;
Fading light and fiery wicket
  Will not harm a man that's out.

Safe from silence, moil, and pother,
  Watch the swerve and sudden break,
Where through tedious hours another
  Makes the runs you scorned to make.

R. W. Raper

(Dedicated to Walt Whitman)

1.

To take your stand at the wicket is a posture of haughty defiance:
To confront a superior bowler as he confronts you:
To feel the glow of ambition, your own and that of your side:
To be aware of shapes hovering, bending, watching around – white
    Flannelled shapes – all eager, unable to catch you.

2.

The usually fine weather,
The splendid silent sun flooding all, bathing all in joyous evaporation.
Far off a grey-brown thrush warbling in hedge or marsh;
Down there in the blossoming brushes, my brother, what is it that you are
    Saying?

3.

To play more steadily than a pendulum; neither hurrying nor delaying,
    But marking the right to strike.

4.

To slog:

5.

The utter oblivion of all but the individual energy;
The rapid co-operation of hand and eye projected into the ball,
The ball triumphantly flying through the air, you too flying.
The perfect feel of a fourer!
The hurrying to and fro between the wickets: the marvellous quickness
    Of all the fields:
The cut, leg hit, forward drive, all admirable in their way;
The pull transcending all pulls, over the boundary ropes, sweeping
    Orotund, astral:
The superciliousness of standing still in your ground, content, and
    Masterful, conscious of an unquestioned six;

The continuous pavilion-thunder bellowing after each true lightening
    Stroke
(And yet a mournful note, the low dental murmur of one who blesses not,
    I fancied I heard through the roar
In a lull of the deafening plaudits;
Could it have been the bowler? or one of the fields?)

6.

Sing on, grey-brown bird, sing on! Now I understand you!
Pour forth your rapturous chants from flowering hedge in the marsh,
I follow, I keep time, though rather out of breath.

7.

The high perpendicular puzzling hit: the consequent collision and miss:
    The faint praise of 'well tried.'
The hidden delight of some and the loud disappointment of others.

8.

But, O bird of the bursting throat, my dusky demon and brother,
Why have you paused in your carol so fierce from the flowering throng?
Has your music fulfilled the she-bird? (It cannot have lulled her to sleep);
Or see you a cloud on the face of the day unusually fine?

9.

to have a secret misgiving:
to feel the sharp, sudden rattle of the stumps from behind, electric,
    incredible:
to hear the short convulsive cap, announcing all is over.

A. M. Robertson

(With acknowledgements to W. S. Gilbert)

When you're right out of touch, and your record is such
    that you're bound for the Second Eleven,
You can bet your best hat you'll be sent in to bat at precisely
    five minutes to seven.
It's a horrible light, and you're shaking with fright, and your
    arms and your legs are all shivery;
The bowler looks grim and your vision goes dim as you wait
    for the fatal delivery.
Then forward you grope in a desperate hope (you're thankful
    it isn't a bumper!),
But you took the wrong guard, so you miss by a yard, and
    the ball has gone through to the stumper.
You face up again, but by now it is plain that your status is
    that of a rabbit,
And the fieldsmen close in with a sinister grin, as if saying:
    'One touch and we'll grab it!'
So you lash the next ball, give your partner a call (if he's
    backing up well it's a gamble),
And you sprint up the track, but the fool sends you back,
    and you get to your crease with a scramble.
You recover your bat, give the wicket a pat, and pretend to
    be weeding out clover
(This elaborate mime helps to spin out the time) – then
    thank goodness, the Umpire calls 'Over!'

Herbert E. Clarke

(With apologies to the shade of Emerson and Mr. Andrew Lang)

If every player thinks he plays
　　Better than most men you can name,
I prompt him to these little ways;
　　I am the glory and the game.

I am both centuries and ducks,
　　Defence, leg-break, lob, bailer, bail;
I am the coin and the captain chucks,
　　And one to me are head and tail.

He reckons ill who gets me out;
　　I am the ball he upward flings;
I am the crowd who groan and shout,
　　And call the umpire many things.

I am the snick, the drive for four,
　　The overthrow that makes it seven;
And I am he who saith, Give o'er,
Or lose your place in heaven in the eleven.

THE OUTCAST: A TALE OF A LADIES' CRICKET MATCH

P. G. Wodehouse

(Robert W. Service)

Out in the silent Rockies,
  Tracking the Teddy-bears,
There's a man whose brow is furrowed,
  Whose hairs are silvered hairs.
Folks in that far-off region
  Know him as 'Jaundiced Jim';
And now I'll tell you his story,
  How well do I know him? I'm him!

Once I was gay and mirthful,
  Ready with quip and jest,
Strongmen shook at the stories
  That I would get off my chest.
I knew no doubts nor sorrows;
  I was filled with the joy of youth.
But I dished my life in one second
  Through a morbid passion for truth.

Angela Grace Maguffin
  Was the belle of the county then.
Suitors? Including me – well,
  There must have been nine or ten.
But I put in some tricky work, and
  Cut out the entire batch
Till the fatal day that undid me –
  The day of the Ladies' Match.

Cricket was not my forte.
  I never won a match
With a fifty made against time, or
  A wonderful one-hand catch.
Rude men called me a rabbit;
So I thought it were best that day,
Lest Grace should have cause to despise me,
  To umpire and not to play.

(Why did not guardian angel
   Down to my rescue swoop,
And hiss in my ear: 'You juggins!
   Desist or you're in the soup!'
Why did the Fates permit me
   To tackle that evil job?
Why did I offer to umpire?
   Why did – excuse this sob.)

Everything went like clockwork;
   The sky went a gentle blue;
The sun was shining above us,
   As the sun is apt to do.
Everything went as stated,
   Like wheels of some well-made clock:
There wasn't a sign of disaster
   Till Grace came in for her knock.

Nature seemed tense, expectant,
   All round was a solemn hush,
She murmured: 'What's this, please, umpire?'
   I said two leg,' with a blush.
Down to the crease moved the bowler . . .
   Ah! Fate 'twas a scurvy trick.
My Grace swiped out – and I heard it . . .
   Yes, an unmistakable click.

' 'S that?' cried the cad of a bowler.
   'How *was* it? Yelled slip, the brute.
For a moment I stood there breathless –
   Breathless, and dazed, and mute.
'*How* was it?' All creation
   Seemed filled with a hideous shout,
I wavered an instant, gulping . . .
   Then hoarsely I muttered: 'Out!'

Down where the grizzly grizzles;
   Out where the possums poss;
Where the boulders fall from the hill-side,
   And, rolling, gather no moss;
Where the wild cat sits in the sunshine,
   Chewing a human limb,
There's a thin, sad, pale, grey hermit:
   Folks know him as 'Jaundiced Jim'.

Frank Keating

Hark! Does *Hindu Herald* sing
Glory to our Yorkie King,
Peace on earth, 'cept Kapil's wild,
Geoff and history's reconciled.

Joyful all ye nations rise
(E'en the Doctor in the skies);
With your morning toast proclaim,
'Boycs the best in all the game.'

[Repeat opening two-line chorus]

Frank Keating

We three tweaks of Orient are
Bedi, Venkat, Chandrasekhar.
We rejoice in, can we join in
Applause for y'Ayatollah?

Oh, Star of Wonder in bad light
Star who wears White Rose so bright,
Hairpiece preening, sweatbands gleaming
Surely He will soon be Knight?

from PART TWO OF THE
             TRAGEDY OF PRINCE BOTHAM

                    Simon Barnes

PRINCE BOTH: To play or not to play: that is the question.
Whether 'tis nobler in the mind to suffer
The blows and bouncers of outrageous fortune
Or to take up arms against an over of troubles
And by hooking, end them. Duncan, prince?
Fearnley, king? My lord of Worcester soon to
    be
The King of England and I to aid him?
I that on the field of Heading Lee
And thrice again, and thrice times thrice once
    more
Did earn the right, if any man e'er did
To wear such garlands as a victor should!
Dare I then to wear that gilded garland
Which the noble brow of England doth adorn?
Or shall I settle for a pauper's prize:
The thanks, the smile, and the forgetting
Of a treacherous king? Of vengeance!
As rebel I do stand before the world;
A greater rebel am I in my heart!
I shall cheat on cheating. I shall treachery
    betray,
Murder murderers and I shall rebel
Against rebellion. So shall I advance
In holy blasphemy and in villainy
Most noble.
Soon the watching world will have it's king!
Ian Hotspur, mighty Botham, shall be king!

Wendy Cope

(for Simon Rae)

'There isn't much cricket in the Cromwell play.'
      (overheard at a dinner-party)

There isn't much cricket in *Hamlet* either,
There isn't much cricket in *Lear*.
I don't think there's any in *Paradise Lost** –
I haven't a copy right here.

But I like to imagine the cricketing versions –
Laertes goes out to bat
And instead of claiming a palpable hit,
The prince gives a cry of 'Howzat!'

While elsewhere the nastier daughters of Lear
(Both women cricketers) scheme
To keep their talented younger sister
Out of the England team,

And up in the happy realms of light
When Satan is out (great catch)
His team and the winners sit down together
For sandwiches after the match.

Although there are some English writers
Who feature the red leather ball,
You could make a long list of the plays and the books
In which there's no cricket at all.

To be perfectly honest, I like them that way –
The absence of cricket is fine.
But if you prefer work that includes it, please note
That now there's some cricket in mine.

* Apparently there is. 'Chaos umpire sits,/ And by decision
more embroils the fray.' *Paradise Lost*, Book II, lines 907–8.

DO NOT GO GENTLE INTO THAT PAVILION

Simon Rae

(i.m. the spirit of Cricket, with apologies to Dylan Thomas)

Do not go gentle when you're given out.
The batsmen burn and rave at close of play:
The umpires are both bent without a doubt,

The fielders cheats who raised that awful shout.
Fall to your knees as though about to pray.
Do not go gentle when you're given out.

Though wise men at their end have all the clout,
We'll challenge them whatever they may say.
The umpires are both bent without a doubt.

Good bats, the last stroke played, will often pout:
"I'd score a century if I could stay."
Do not go gentle when you're given out.

Wild men who spin and flight the ball can rout
An English batting order any day.
The umpires are both bent without a doubt

's a kind of consolation to the stout
And googly-blinded batsmen on their way.
Do not go gentle when you're given out.
The umpires are both bent without a doubt.

X

CRICKET IN NARRATIVE

(Timeless Tests)

~

There is nothing like a good story and one of the joys of these narrative poems is that in each of the nine tales there is a beginning, a middle and an end, which together with plot and characters, is the essence of any good story.

To define 'Cricket (Hearts and Wickets)' purely as narrative would be a misnomer. It is, in fact, the complete libretto (together with all the stage directions) of a charming thirty-minute musical written by Tim Rice, with music by Andrew Lloyd Webber, which is published here for the first time. The work was commissioned by HRH Prince Edward for Her Majesty, the Queen's sixtieth birthday party.

The traditional story concerns love and romance behind the sightscreens at the beautiful cricket ground within the borders of the Earl of Headingley's country seat. (Cue music) . . . and really there is no need to say much more before you take your seats, except that cricketers would appear to be no match for racing men in the corruption stakes and for further related moral preachment please pay attention . . .

The next four offerings emphasise the importance of beer and belly timber when it comes to cricket.

After an encounter between Sunbury and Hampton in 1830, dedicated 'with the deepest respect to the worthier sex' by an anonymous Sunburian (grovelling, no doubt, after a night on the tiles) the jarveys with their coaches and fours collected his team to take them back to College. We are told that: 'For our horrid din we showed no remorse, For on the roof and in the shafts was a "hoarse", And every man, his bed and slumber storming, Shouted with all his lungs "We won't go home till morning".' A lone policeman in the vicinity wisely makes himself scarce.

'The Kentish Cricketer' was written about fifteen years earlier and is in the dialect of the hop county, one of many regional varieties of speech that were later largely eradicated with the spread of both the railways and educational opportunity. The great cricketer William Beldham once remarked to historian James Pycroft: 'There was no mistaking the Kent boys when they came staring into the "Green Man"' (the cricketers' house of call in Oxford Street). 'A few of us had grown used to London, but Kent and Hampshire men had but to speak or even show themselves, and you need not ask which side they were on.'

Another cricket historian, Charles Box, would appear to have had some clue as to the identity of the author of this 'very curious song', but was unwilling to speculate in print in his weighty tome 'The English Game of Cricket'. According to Box, the story of this 'lay', as it was also called, was based on fact. 'As a literary production, it possesses no merit whatever,' he wrote, dismissive in the extreme, 'tending in some quarters to elucidate the manners and actions of the uneducated classes, from which rough and ready cricketers are upon a pinch drafted.' Oh dear! As the Kentish yokels' 'My Lard' might have said, 'Pass the port'.

Another anonymous narrative in verse appeared in 'Ironbark's Southerly Busters', Sydney, in 1878. 'The Great Cricket Match' between the Brewers and the Publicans was another drunken outing with the result never in doubt. After much elbow raising, a mass hangover was won by the Licensed Victuallers' Association.

The theatrical script-writer Jay Hickory Wood, whose working life bridged the Victorian and Edwardian eras, was renowned for his burlesques and recitations. 'The Cricket Club of Red Nose Flat' he describes as 'a yarn of "Ole' Frisco"'. We are introduced to a figure few can fail to recognise, the spectator in the next seat who can cap any anecdote with a superior one with which he was involved. In return for fodder, 'baccy and liquor, this character from the New World relates a tall tale of intimidation in a match between some British expats and a side from Philadelphia down 'Frisco way. An umpire who made an unpopular decision got the bullet.

Charles Clive-Ponsonby-Fane's bucolic of the devious village landlord has a ring of authenticity which is not only the sound of the cash register behind the bar. There are hidden shafts towards territorial rights, local development and class privilege – important issues to some in a small community.

Away from the clink of glasses, schoolmaster Gerard Martineau has a dig at progressive education in his previously unpublished 'Ballad of the Incorrigible Cricketers' where pupils Tom Willow and Pamela Duke are seduced by the lure of 'ORGANIZED CRICKET, A DISCIPLINED GAME' and so are faced with expulsion from their modern 'Co-Ed', Laxaby Hall.

The chapter concludes with two powerful socio-cultural commentaries from the Caribbean and it is worth enlarging a little of the background in order to place them in context.

'Rites' by Kamau Brathwaite is set on Brown's Beach and at Kensington Oval during the first Test Match of the 1947/48 MCC tour to the West Indies. (There is also an insertion of incident with a fowl hawk, which is based on an occurrence on the same ground in a match between Barbados and Trinidad in 1944.) The setting though, is relatively unimportant in what is an allegory about the exchange of political power during an uncertain period of West Indian history. We are treated to a brief reunion with those legendary figures Worrell, Weekes, and more lengthily with Walcott, who is seen combating the wiles of the England spinners, Wardle and Laker. The game represents the battle for self-government against Imperialism although the narrative cleverly communicates on other more local levels as well. While the plot reflects the social situation in the Caribbean at the time, the story as a whole makes judgements on national character, citizenship, and the qualities necessary for leadership. This density of allusion and an underlying darkness beneath the satire, present no obstacle to an all-pervading humour. Brathwaite's use of the Caribbean vernacular and what is currently called 'Nation Language' with its strong drum-based rhythms, makes an intense impression. 'Rites' is a remarkable achievement.

Whereas in 'Rites' Brathwaite captures the eye in his page-presentation of words, in 'Tanti at de Oval' Paul Keens-Douglas takes a prisoner of the ear. That is not to say that P. K.-D. does not enjoy engaging our attention with computer word-processing techniques, deliberate mispellings, onomatopoeia and graphic renditions of the rhythm and syntax of agitated everyday speech. But essentially he is a proponent of the African oral tradition and therefore his work is for aural consumption. Performance is the key to Keens-Douglas's delivery. His dialect is generically West Indian with Trinidadian overtones, and that only serves to enhance the story's universal appeal as an embodiment of Caribbean culture.

The actual match described in 'Tanti at de Oval' is that between Trinidad and Tobago and the Combined Islands in the Shell Shield at Queen's Park Oval, Port of Spain, in April, 1975. The game finished as a draw with the scores equal and the Islands' last pair at the wicket, though in the poem, differing opinions about the result of the match are all part of the fun of the piece.

Keens-Douglas's own special blanket of humanity and heart is wrapped warmly around 'Tanti' and nobody can fail to empathise with the narrator's mock indignation and suffering as he relates his vain efforts to cope with his rambunctious relative in a series of hilarious incidents. The characters are wonderfully alive in what is surely a classic of its kind.

D. R. A.

Tim Rice

The world premiere of 'Cricket (Hearts and Wickets)' (music: Andrew Lloyd Webber, lyrics: Tim Rice) took place on 18 June 1986 at Windsor Castle in a private performance for HM the Queen and the Royal Family. The cast included Ian Charleson (Donald), Sarah Payne (Emma), Alvin Stardust (Vincent), Ian Savident (The Earl), George Harris (Winston B. Packer), Cantabile (Chorus) and HRH Prince Edward as Wittering.

1. The Summer Game

The beautiful cricket ground within the borders of the EARL OF HEADINGLEY***'s country seat. A hot bright afternoon in June. A match is in progress and the*** EARL***'s team have just started their innings, the visitors having made 89. Our hero,*** DONALD HOBBS, **the home side's number 4, is next man in. The score is 23 for 1.**

EARL & CRICKETERS (*watching the game*)
    Another golden afternoon
    An idyllic sporting scene
    A tapestry in green
    Willow heroes
    And in pavilioned splendour nationwide
    The game and its laws bestride
    The best of England

    Bat on ball
    The manly thwack of blade on leather
    Players all
    So worthy of the crowd's acclaim
    And although
    Protected in their regions nether
    Batsmen know
    The dangers of the summer game

(**A wicket falls.** DONALD **leaves the pavilion.**)

And walking bravely to the crease
A man with much to do

EARL (*solo*)
We're 23 for 2, needing 90

EARL & CRICKETERS
And watching bravely from the boundary ropes
A sweet English rose whose hopes
Stride out there with him

(*They mean* EMMA KIRKSTALL-LANE, *the* EARL's *daughter.*)

Now the test
Of character and application
At his best
He's man enough for any cause
Round the ground
In civilised appreciation
Comes the sound
Of dignified informed applause

Bat on ball
The noblest of all competition
Players all
In attitude and drive the same
Steeped in grace
And mindful of the game's tradition
They embrace
The glory of the summer game

EARL
I'm very worried about my daughter. She's not giving Donald the
support he needs. No ball! This is a vital match for Headingley C.C. we
need all the runs we can get from my future son-in-law.

2. As The Seasons Slip Fruitlessly By / 3. The Sport Of Kings

Further along the boundary, EMMA *watches her man walk out to play his
crucial innings. Her fair countenance is however clouded.*

EMMA
My Donald's at the wicket thinking only of his side
And though my gentle bosom fills with longing and with pride

And I applaud his strokeplay and commend his cover drive
I wonder between overs if our passion can survive
For love seems less important to my lover than his scores
From April to September and for longer if he tours

But nonetheless he's all that I want
Every match my love grows deeper
I love him so, he's all that I want
As my captain and my keeper

But I see other couples sharing everything they do
And never spending weekends in a gang of twenty-two
I wonder am I doomed to live my life at deep fine leg?
Should I dissolve our partnership since I'm too proud to beg?
I do not feel it's sharing when I'm marking out the pitch
I ask myself which way to turn and echo answers which

As the seasons slip fruitlessly by
He ignores my true requirement
Is it my fate to sit hopelessly by
In the shade 'til his retirement?

(EMMA *has been unaware of the nearby presence of a racing man,* VINCENT
ST. LEGER.)

VINCENT
My dear I could not help but overhear your heartfelt beef
To solve your grim dilemma take the bit between your teeth
If cricket cannot satisfy you turn to higher things
May I suggest you switch allegiance to the Sport of Kings?
My glamour world of racing offers all you've missed to date
Sophistication, pounding hooves, and girls participate!

From Epsom to Uttoxeter, from Cheltenham to Ayr
The thrills and spills are legion in a stable atmosphere
This rather dreary setting won't improve when you're a wife
Come throw away your Wisdens, open up The Sporting Life!

The Sport of Kings!

EMMA
As the seasons slip fruitlessly by
He ignores my true requirement
Is it my fate to sit hopelessly by
In the shade 'til his retirement?

VINCENT

You can't compare a cricketer for breeding with a horse
Shake off your inhibitions and come with me to the course
My box awaits, champagne's on ice, the limousine is booked
I'll give you 6 to 4 that you'll be well and truly hooked

The Sport of Kings!

EMMA

Perhaps you're right, I need to break free
I've always felt that those who could, should
Perhaps my heart should fly and take me
To Market Rasen or to Goodwood

(EMMA *is weakening.*)

VINCENT

This rather dreary setting won't improve when you're a wife
Come throw away your Wisdens, open up The Sporting Life!

The Sport of Kings!

(EMMA *tears up her scorecard and takes* VINCENT*'s hand. They run off.*)

4. The Art Of Bowling

WINSTON B. PACKER, *the visitors' lethally fast West Indian bowler, prepares to bowl.*

WINSTON

The art of bowling
Is very subtle
For those who doubt it
Here's a rebuttal
You can't just chuck them
You have to aim them
You need a brain if
You want to maim them.

There is nothing within the laws
That prevents an approach like this
Still they claim it's unfair because
They get hit every time they miss

(*He bowls. A batsman's howl of pain is heard off stage.*)

Back in the old days
We hit the wicket
We shattered stumps, man
Such boring cricket
We had to change, man
The crowds were waning
We now hit batsmen
More entertaining

(*An injured batsman hobbles past* WINSTON *on his way back to the pavilion. 23 for 3.*)

All I have is a tiny sphere
To establish my point of view
They are armed with the latest gear
It's so hard to get my message through

(*He bowls again – another cry of anguish is heard off stage.*)

WINSTON
The art of bowling
Is now a science
We don't take prisoners
Brook no defiance
From Lord's to Sydney
Or in Barbados
Batsmen remember
When they have played us

(*A batsman is carried past* WINSTON *on a stretcher to the pavilion. 23 for 4.* WINSTON *repeats the last verse with added gusto.*)

5. All I Ask Of Life

DONALD *is now batting. He suddenly notices* EMMA *leaving with* VINCENT. *The score is now 56 for 4.*

DONALD
Emma! With that racing person!

Since flannels first were worn
Has any batsman borne
The strain of losing his intended
While facing vicious pace?

Would Bradman, Hobbs or Grace
Have left the matter unattended?
I must get out . . .
I must stay in!

(*As* DONALD *sings his aria, he is bombarded with fast deliveries that do him considerable damage.*)

All I ask of life
Is the chance to show
I can face vicissitudes
Standing tall against the cruellest blow
But the keenest knife in its velvet glove
If I may mix metaphors
Is the one plunged in and turned by love

My choice is Hobson's now
Do I bat on, allow
The one I love to desert me?
But when I see the score
We still need 34
I can't let selfishness divert me
I must play on
I have a dream
I have a team
All life asks of me
Is to play my part
Let them hurl their worst my way
None can break my wicket or my heart

(*A particularly vicious ball fells him. As he lies in agony on the ground, figures from his past gather round him in a ghastly dream. He hears:*)

WINSTON:
The art of bowling is now a science . . .

EMMA:
As the seasons slip fruitlessly by he ignores my true requirement

VINCENT:
If cricket doesn't satisfy you turn to higher things . . .

EMMA:
Perhaps he's right, I need to break free . . .

ALL:
The Sport of Kings!

(DONALD *staggers to his feet. As he prepares to face yet more fast bowling, he proudly sings, supported by his team-mates.*)

DONALD & CRICKETERS
Let them hurl their worst my/his way
None can break my/his wicket or my/his heart!

(*He strikes a ball perfectly via an immaculate cover drive.*)

6. Fools Like Me

The tea interval. EMMA *has returned, full of remorse. The score is now 80 for 9. The* CRICKETERS *are preparing for the game's final phase.*

CRICKETERS
Bat on ball
The manly thwack of blade on leather
Players all
So worthy of the crowd's acclaim

EMMA
Vincent deceived me! Racing has been my ruin.
How could anyone possibly enjoy it?
I've won nothing and lost everything

Who could take pity on fools like me?
Only another fool and I know
There's none who'd admit to mistakes like mine
Careless and selfish all down the line
No-one to blame but me

Who'd show compassion to fools like me?
Who'd give the time of day to someone
Who threw herself into a mad affair
She rushed right in, she just didn't care
Neither, alas, did he

How come I don't hate him
I don't want to implicate him
In my sadness? It's quite simple
It's me – blame me

Who will be tender with fools like me?
Who'll tell me all this could have happened
To anyone, anywhere, anytime
Being so stupid is not a crime
Who will be tender with me?
A poor little fool like me

7. A Ban For Life / 8. Wittering's Final Innings

The CRICKETERS *walk back along the pitch.* DONALD *catches* EMMA*'s forlorn eye, but coldly ignores her. The* EARL *storms up to his daughter.* VINCENT *is loitering sheepishly nearby.*

EARL

Not only is the family name now tarnished in this shire
My daughter's reckless gambling debts have dropped me in the mire
Which means that on Bank Holidays and every fourth weekend
I'll have to let the public in – how low can we descend?

VINCENT

May I point out –

EARL

And as for you, you reprobate, you've had your wicked way
I trust that you enjoyed it, sir, for now you have to pay
As Steward of the Jockey Club I hereby warn you off
All courses, flat or steeplechase, you'll have to take up golf!

A ban for life!

(*The irate* EARL *departs.*)

VINCENT

You never said your father was such
An important force in racing
Without the turf my life isn't much
Can you conceive the angst I'm facing?

EMMA

You never said my horse wouldn't win
I put my faith in your selection
It came in tenth – how can I begin
To win back papa's affection?

(*A howl of pain from the wicket interrupts the conversation. A* CRICKETER *rushes back to the pavilion.*)

CRICKETER
Wittering has been struck!

OTHER CRICKETERS (*hurrying to grab a stretcher*)
Wittering struck? Wittering struck?

EARL (*rushing back to the scene*)
You mean Wittering, our gallant last man, cannot continue?

(WITTERING *enters, horizontally on a stretcher, carried by two team-mates. All gather round him anxiously.*)

WITTERING
I'm sorry I let you down – think only this of me –

EARL
Think what Wittering?

(*But* WITTERING *is still. His arms are folded for him, his cap placed over his face and his bat rested on his chest.*)

EARL (*continued*)
Good man, Wittering.
But we still need 10 to win –
And now there is no man remaining who can take
Wittering's place alongside Donald
This is a black day for the Headingley family and for Headingley C.C.

(*As "The Summer Game" music strikes up "Bat on ball . . ." who should step forward but* VINCENT.)

9. The Making of St. Leger

VINCENT *begins to strap on a pad. The others watch in amazement.*

VINCENT
Don't despair!
The game ain't lost until it's won
Let me share
The fury of the opposition
I can't fare
Much worse that poor old Witt'ring's done

ALL

    Bat on ball
    The noblest of all competition
    Players all
    In attitude and drive the same
    Steeped in grace
    And mindful of the game's tradition
    They embrace
    The glory of the summer game

(VINCENT *walks out to join* DONALD.)

10. The Final Stand

VINCENT *and* DONALD *attempt to score the final 10 runs, watched anxiously by the* EARL, EMMA *and* CRICKETERS.

CRICKETERS

    To think that we dismissed him as a parasite and cad
    When now it's plain for all to see St Leger's not all bad
    But all the same he faces an unenviable task
    To stay out there with Donald is an awful lot to ask

EARL

    My goodness Donald's played a rather reckless shot to leg –

CRICKETERS

    The ball is in the air – he must be caught mid-wicket

    He's dropped it! Only 8 to win, we'll make it after all
    But then again St. Leger has to face another ball
    He's soaking up the punishment, there goes another tooth
    He seems to thrive on pain, a great example to our youth

EARL

    But now he's calling for a run that surely isn't there

CRICKETERS

    He's doomed – the match is good as lost, so near and yet so –

    He's made it, we can breathe again, there's only 6 to get
    This partnership of brain and brawn is not dismantled yet

EARL

    Reminds me of the final Test of 1935
    When whatsiname and someone else did wonders to survive

CRICKETERS

    Look, Donald's rushing down the pitch –

EARL

    That's right, come on my son!

CRICKETERS

    A perfect stroke, a massive blow

ALL

    It's six at least, we've won!

(*Wild excitement and cheers as* DONALD *and* VINCENT *return to a heroes' welcome.*)

    None can break his wicket or his heart!

EARL

    St. Leger, you may race again
    You've gained your peer's respect
    I cannot recollect
    A braver gesture

DONALD

    He's not the only one to see the light
    I think from now on I might
    Play less on Sundays

EMMA

    We could go racing

VINCENT

    While I play cricket

WINSTON (*coming off the pitch*)
    I'll try slow bowling

WITTERING (*emerging from the pavilion*)
    I'm feeling better

11. One Hot Afternoon

DONALD

The only thing I'm sure of
Is nothing's ever certain
You think you know
The score, but no,
You're learning
And the moment life seems easy
Then some no-good moves the sightscreen
The very ground starts turning

DONALD & EMMA

If lazy games of summer
Were all that really mattered
I'd chase that ball
Until they all
Stopped cheering
But as I've just discovered
The running gets you nowhere
A lot can change in one hot afternoon
How can you be so good to me
When I tried so hard to let you down?
When you knew I was playing games
And was getting nowhere

EMMA

The world beyond the boundary
Is only for the daring
Until today
I wouldn't say
That meant me
But you have played superbly
You've shown me I can go there
And nothing will prevent me

BOTH

I'll never make another
Confident prediction
Except for one
All said and done
Worth hearing
That the narrow minds of morning

Will be breaking out this evening
A life can change in one hot afternoon

EMMA

But you have played superbly
You've shown me I can go there
And nothing will prevent me

BOTH

I'll never make another
Confident prediction
Except for one
All said and done
Worth hearing
That the narrow minds of morning
Will be breaking out this evening
A life can change in one hot afternoon

(***All return and gather around the happy pair.***)

ALL

All I ask of life
Is to play my part
Let them hurl their worst my way
None can break my wicket or my heart

THE END

SOMETHING ABOUT
A CRICKET MATCH

Anon

(Sunbury v Hampton, 1830)

It was a beautiful morning
And the sun was just adorning
When we went to Hampton by the ¼-to-10 buss,
Umpires and scorers, and all of us;
For in truth it was a glorious day,
And we went to a CRICKET MATCH to play –
Eleven heroes filled with horrid zeal
Each paid their sixpence to Sir Robert Peel.
When the jovial crew arrived at the inn
They began the ball to spin.
The wickets were pitched about eleven –
The sun was shining in the Heaven.
We sent to the wickets the great Mr. Taylor,
Where he stood till he got a ball called a nailer;
Then in the proffered jug of bitter beer
The mighty flyman dropped a monstrous tear.
Many went in with eager bats,
And came out looking no end of flats;
But "Gore" by making a stunning score,
Proved himself to Hampton a terrible bore.
Next Isherwood came, who would have won the match,
Only unfortunately he was out by a catch;
And yells of triumph made the long reeds quiver,
And Cygnets shudder by the distant river;
When Mr. A. B. went in with a clay,
He had an idea of stopping all day – . . .

. . . And when the Sunbury their innings had done,
The Telegraph told of sixty-one.
And the Sunburian forces swore
That the proud men of Hampton should hold the palm no more.
Each to the other ones confusion wished,
Scowled on the foe, and shook the manly fist,
Then to the booth the cricketers did run,
Each man feasting beef a ton –
Every thing they did devour
In the short space of half an hour.
Mr. Lawrence he said, with a horrible leer
That he never sold in his life such a lot of draught beer.
Peace to the tenants of the silent tomb,
Six waiters perished in their early bloom –
Then the second innings they began to play,
Thinking the College would win the day.
It is needless to say how both sides did their duty,
As the ground was graced both by rank and by beauty,
And lovely woman caused a sudden joy
To thrill the bosom of the smallest boy.

The Hamptonians made a very long score,
So of our defeat wc will say no more,
But rather draw a gentlemanly veil
Over the sequel of the tragic tale,
And of the Lion collect the forces,
To talk of victory and losses.

Now gracious Muse, assist poetic sinners
To sing in verse the jollities of dinners,
How chickens vanish'd as a pleasant dream,
Before the onslaught of the hungry team;
How fled the beef with melancholy cries,
And "spare us!" faltered persecuted pies,

Ye Gods! It was a memorable sight!
Gore at the top – "the Moffat" on his right, –
The moments flew by with uproarious fun,
And many a song was very well sung;

All the persons who were present did say
That they had had a capital day;
Toasts were drunk of men not a few,
Honour was paid to whom honour was due,
And moisture dimm'd the College eyes,
When Bob the boy announced the flys.
Two splendid steeds, with coats of glossy brown,
Conveyed the heroes thro' the sleeping town,
The bright moon shone upon the parish pales,
And tinged with silver their erratic tails,
Crack went the whip, stirrup cups did flow,
Loud swore the jarveys, and away we go,
For our horrid din we showed no remorse
For on the roof and in the shafts was "*hoarse*",
And every man, his bed and slumber scorning,
Shouted with all his lungs "We won't go home 'till morning."
A lost Policeman, on his lonely round,
Heard in the distance a peculiar sound,
Sound, as of demons bent upon a lark,
Saw the cigar lights flashing thro' the dark,
And, seized with horror and tremendous dread,
Pull'd off his boots, and fell upon his head.
At last were seen by our benighted pates
The well-known features of the College gates,
And soon to rest our wearied heads
We each were couched in our neglected beds,
And there was only heard from sleeping muff,
"No more sherry, thank you, I've had enough."
Fare well, dear reader, if our lowly lay
Shall serve to chase an idle hour away,
Not the great praise that to our perfect song
So worthily, so justly, doth belong,
Will half the pleasure verily impart,
As your approval, to the Poet's heart.

Anon

My feyther and mother be boath dead and gone,
　　And ha' left only me and our Mary,
So I goes up to Lunnon, leaves sister at hwoam,
　　To look a'ter de dogs and de dairy:
For Lunnon I heerd was a wunnerful place;
　　So ses I tu myself, I'll run up for a race,
And how I got onner'd I'll tell ye de case.
　　Tol de rol lol de rol li do.

Now de first thing I heerd, and that made my 'art glad,
　　Was a wunnerful gurt match o' cricket;
Fur in Kent you all know dere is hardly a lad
　　But is famous at bat, ball, an' wicket.
An' den as I heerd an arterwards found,
It was tu be played on my Lard's cricket ground:
Deng it, I foun' em out, and de stumps dey cum down.
　　Tol de rol de rol lol de rol li do

Dey stood hankerin'about, for wot I cudden't tell
　　Till my Lard he said to de bye standers,
Be dere any a lad as can play pretty well?
Because I am shart of a hand, Sirs.
So den I stept in; dear heart, how dey did grin;
　　Says I tu myself, to be grinned at's no sin.
(*Loquitur*) Well, Sir, my Lard he cum up to me and asked me if I cud
play or nay. 'I doan't know, my Lard' I ses, ses I, 'I bean't no gurt spaiks
of a player; mine's an aukerdish kind of a knock, a sort of lapper right
round de field.' 'Well, my man,' ses he, 'can ye boal?' 'Aha, my Lard, Sir,'
I ses, 'I jest can; I always het de man or de wicket to a dead sartinty.'
Well, my Lard then ses he, 'Yu're de man jest for me.'
　　Tol de rol de rol lol de rol li do

We shartly strip'd in, and de geam did begin,
  An' at fust it went on pretty rightish;
Till we'd been in twice, an' it looked rather queer,
  For they knock'd her about pretty tightish,
'Bout losing de geam, we thought one an' all;
  when my Lard ses to me, 'Cannot you take the ball?'
(*Loquitur*). And be darned if I didn't too, and a teejeous good boul I
made on it, for I broke so many heads, arms, legs, bats, wickets, de
geam was nation soon ourn.
An' t'other chaps then were all hospital men,
  Tol de rol de rol lol de rol li do.

The folks that stoody by, dey were pretty much 'mazed,
  An' struck by a nashional wonder;
To think, as dey said, sech a bumpkin as I
  Shud come up dere, and make 'em knock under,
An' de winners dey laaft, an' de losers dey swoor,
And both on 'em called I a gurt Kentish boor . . .
(*Loquitur*). Well, my Lard, he laaft tu, an' axed me wot my neam was.
'Well Sir,' ses I, 'my neam's Giles' 'Well, Giles,' ses he, 'for what you've
done for us, here's a five pun note for you.' 'Na, na, my Lard, Sir,' ses I,
'you will defend me, ef ye du. I han'nt come up here to yarn money;
have trubble enuf in doin' that at home. I've come up to see sites an'
curiosities, Newgate, an' Cripplegate, an' Billingsgate, an' all de gates
fur wot I know; but ef ye like to ask me whoam to dinner wid ye, all's
well an' good.'
So we went, one and t'other, like brother an' brother,
  Tol de rol de rol lol de rol li do.

Now when we got there, the table was spread,
  With everything heart an' mouth wishes;
I was teejously vex'd tu know what tu have first,
  Sich a huge nation site of Frinch dishes.
An' dey aked me sich questions, such plaguery hard words.
  (*Loquitur*) 'Deng it all, my Lard,' ses I, 'your talk bean't nothing like
wot ourn is, down in de country' ; an' I felt nationly 'bashe'd too, till I had
drinkt two of three glasses o' dat sham sham sham cider stuff, what de
gentry drink at dinner-time, and I den began to titter at de ladies; An' de
ladies, d'ye see, dey all tittered at me,
  Tol de rol de rol lol de rol li do

After dinner, my Lard, in a wunnerful speech,
    Gets up an' thanks me for my trouble.
But I bows to de Pason instead of my Lard;
    For my eyes, dey began to see double.
De ladies all nodd'd an' winked at each other,
    And into de drawing-room went, one arter t'other.
(*Loquitur*). And I gets up, an' ses I, 'Here's arter ye; I beant a gwene tu
lose my sweetheart reckly minit arter dinner.' An' den one o' dem dandy
butterfly chaps stopt me, and asked me how long I had been out o' de
company o' de wild beastes. 'Dang ye' ses I, 'I beant bed a wild beast nor
yet a monkey, and I'll take good care not to stop long enuf among ye to
be made one neither; if this be your fashion tu turn de ladies out of de
room directly after they've had their dinners, I'll be off to de country agen,
where I can have a ceek by jowl for my life.'
So wid ne'er a good-bye, tu de country cum I,
    Singing *tol de rol de rol lol de rol li do.*

208

THE GREAT CRICKET MATCH,
BREWERS V PUBLICANS

Anon

From Ironbark's Southerly Busters, Sydney, 1878.

The day was wet, down poured the rain
   In torrents from the sky;
Great coats, umbrellas, were in vain.
   But every lip was dry.

The clouds seemed disinclined to part,
   The wind was from the *West*,
Yet worked each brewer's manly heart
   Like (y)*east* within his breast.

Along the road each brewer spent
   His coin in frequent drains,
For mere external moisture went
   Against those brewers' *grains.*

And with a bright triumphant flush,
   Their Captain, Mr Staves,
Swore they should crush those suns of lush
   Who dealt in 'tidal-waves' *

For, speaking of the L. V. A., *
   The brewers said, and laughed,
'A most efficient team were they
   For purposes of *draught.*'

'Twas thus they talked upon the way
   Until they reached the ground;
But in their friends the L. V. A.,
   Rum customers they found.

I havn't space to speak of all
   The glories of the match –
Of every well-delivered ball
   And every well-caught catch.

I fain would tell of Mr Keggs
   (they *spiled* and *bunged* his eye)
of *Barley*-corn, and how his legs
    got twisted in a *rye*;

How Stoups, the umpire, stood too near,
    And came to grief and harm;
How, when he fell they gave him beer,
    Which acted as a *barm*;

Of Hope, who keeps the Anchor bar
    And vendeth flowing bowls
(My feet have often been that far
    And anchored fast their *soles*)

Mark how he bustles, snorts and spits –
    His brow he mops and wipes,
And though I couldn't praise his hits,
    I'll gladly praise his '*swipes*';

Of Corks, who funked the second ball,
    And by a sudden turn
Received the straightest one of all
    Upon his ample stern.

He raise a loud and fearful roar –
    With fury he was blind,
And, though they called it '*leg-before*',
    He felt it most *behind!*

Of Marks, the scorer – best of men!
    Sure everybody talks;
He chalked the runs correctly when
    He couldn't *walk* his *chalks*.

Despite the flasks of monstrous size
    He'd emptied to the dregs,
He scored 'wides', 'overthrows', 'leg-byes',
    And runs attained *by legs*.

For all the ceaseless rain which flows,
    The rival teams care naught;
Though *runs* were made by many a nose,
    And many a cold was *caught*.

Inside and out they all got wet –
   Each drank what they could hold;
I'm sure a bowl was overset
   For every *over bowled*.

The daylight fails; at length 'tis gone:
   There's little left to tell;
For as the shades of eve drew on
   The stumps were drawn as well.

Then to the tent each man resorts;
   On food intent were they.
Who won the sport? the pints and quarts –
   The gallant L. V. A.

Beneath the canvas let us pass –
   Old Bottle-brush was there,
And well he filled his empty glass,
   And well he filled the 'chair'.

(* Tidal Wave – a large glass of colonial beer.)
(* Licensed Victuallers' Association.)

209

THE CRICKET CLUB OF
RED NOSE FLAT

J. Hickory Wood

(A Yarn of Ole 'Frisco)

I met him at a cricket match – he came
    and sat by me
And he chatted in a manner most agree–
    able and free.
He borrowed my tobacco, and he wasn't
    slow to ask
If I'd let him share my sandwiches, my
    matches, and my flask;
And, in return, he told me some most
    interesting tales
About lassoing wild horses and harpooning
    monstrous whales.

He narrated fearful combats in the
    "Rockies" with a bear,
And blood-curdling scalping histories that
    nearly raised my hair;
And though, to all appearances he hadn't
    lost a limb,
Yet all these fearful incidents had hap–
    pened unto him.

Now when a man identifies himself with
    certain acts,
It's very rude for any one to doubt that
    they are facts.
There are only two ways for it – you
    believe him, if you're wise;
If you're not, and he is little, then you tell
    him that "he lies."

So, as my friend was taller than myself by
        quite a head,
And a toughish-looking customer, I swal-
        lowed all he said.
But when at last he paused for breath,
        and also for a drink,
I thought I'd change the subject, so I said,
        "No doubt you think
That cricket is a sport very womanish
        and tame
Compared with scalping Indians. Do you
        understand the game?"

"Do I understand the game?" he said.
        "Wall, stranger, you may bet
What I don't know 'bout cricket – wall, it
        ain't invented yet.
Perhaps you ain't aware, my friend, that
        'way down Ole 'Frisco
We had a slap-up cricket club?" I said
        I didn't know.

"Wall, now you know," he answered,
        "and I'll tell you 'bout a game
We played there just a year ago as warn't
        so plaguy tame."
And this is what he told me – of course it
        mayn't be true –
But as he told the tale to me I tell the
        tale to you: –

      .   .   .   .   .

"The boys 'way down in 'Frisco, though
        all a reckless lot, –
They'd most come out from England, –
        and had a tender spot.
That spot it were the village green, where
        as boys they'd bowl and bat,
So we all made up our minds we'd have
        a club at Red Nose Flat.

We didn't have no captain – leastways we
    elected four,
But some one allus pistolled them, so we
    didn't vote no more.
You see, them captains allus tries to boss
    the blessed show,
Which ain't a healthy thing to do, 'way
    down in Ole 'Frisco

Wall, we went ahead a-practising, as
    happy as could be,
Till Thunder Jack shot Blood Red Bill for
    hitting him for three.
And we held a general meeting, and we
    Passed the following rule:–
'A member pistolled on the field by
    members in the cool,
Providing he is up to date in payment of
    his "sub.",
Is planted at the sole expense of this 'ere
    cricket club.'

We heard as how a lot of chaps from
    Philadelphia
Was out on tour, so we challenged 'em to
    Come along and play.
Our challenge was accepted, and one day
    they came around,
All ready for to play us, so we took 'em to
    the ground.

Joe Blazes says to me, says he, 'Ole pard,
    I'll tell you what,
There ain't a single shooting iron in all
    the blessed lot.
What do you mean a-coming here, ex-
    pecting for to win?
It ain't half good enough, ole pard, a jolly
    sight too thin.'

They tossed for choice of innings, and you
      bet we won at that;
We all was whales on tossing, and we
      started for to bat.
'Twas just as well we won the toss,
      because I'm bound to say,
That even if we'd lost it, we'd have
      batted any way.

Wall, first of all I starts to bat, along o'
      Thunder Jack,
The bowler sends his ball along, I makes
      a mighty smack,
But, somehow, 'stead of hitting that there
      ball with that there bat,
I hits it with my leg. The bowler shouted
      'How is that?'

And that there blessed umpire started for
      to answer 'Out,'
When he saw my shooting iron – so he
      guessed there was a doubt;
And he'd heard as how the batsman
      always got the benefit,
Which plainly showed as how that
      blessed umpire knew a bit.

You'd have thought as t'other umpire
      would have had some common
      sense,
But he went and said as Jack were out,
      On the following pretence:–
Old Jack had made a mighty swipe, and
      if he'd hit the ball,
I guess we hadn't never seen that ball no
      more at all.

But, then, you see, he missed it, and his
      wickets they was downed
By the wicket-keeping chap, who said as
      Jack was off the ground,
And 'stead of speaking up and saying as
      there was a doubt,
The umpire said as Thunder Jack was
      very plainly out.

Then Jack he pulled his shooter out, and
      drew on him a bead,
And there the blessed umpire he went
      very dead indeed.
We shouted out 'Fresh Umpire,' but,
      somehow, no one came,
So we guessed we'd do without one, and
      we then resumed the game.

Wall! After that they took to bowling very
      nice and slow,
And, if a fielder caught a ball, he allus let
      it go;
So Jack and I, we slogged away as lively
      as could be,
Until my score was ninety-seven and Jack's
      was ninety-three.

Wall, we had to close our innings, so's to
      give us time to win,
And, as they couldn't get us out, we said
      they might go in;
They didn't seem so anxious for to bat as
      you'd have thought,
But we talked to them persuasive, and
      convinced 'em as they ought.

We told 'em as good cricketers should
      sooner die than yield,
And we loaded our revolvers, and we
      started out to field.
We'd Rifle Bill, a deadly shot, a-fielding
      near the rails,
And when Bill means to shoot a chap he
      very rarely fails;

We'd Blazing Bob at cover point, and
      Mike was near the stand,
And Thunder Jack kept wicket, with his
      shooter in his hand,
And Lord! Them Philadelphy chaps, they
      couldn't bat a bit;
I bowls 'em nice and easy just to tempt
      'em for to hit,

But 'stead of smacking at the ball, they
    kept on looking back,
And seemed most interested in the ways
    of Thunder Jack.
One chap did hit a ball to leg, and started
    on a spurt,
But Rifle Bill just fetched him down, and
    he retired hurt.

Of course we beat 'em hollow; why, they
    never scored a run,
But they admitted freely as it had been
    splendid fun;
So we challenged 'em to come again,
    and play us a return,
And, p'r'aps it may be fancy, but they
    didn't seem to yearn.

However, we persuaded 'em to play it out
    next day,
But, when the morning came, we found
    as they had gone away.
We've challenged other clubs since then,
    but one and all they states,
As, they're very, very sorry, but they have
    no vacant dates.

So we swept the decks completely, and we
    calculated that
The boss of all the cricket clubs was ours
    at Red Nose Flat."

      .   .   .   .   .

And this is what he told me – of course
    it mayn't be true –
But as he told the tale to me I've told the
    tale to you.

Charles Clive-Ponsonby-Fane

The Major bought an old Farm House.
    And in the field near-by,
He thought he'd make a cricket ground.
    (At least he'd have a try!)
And all the village wondered when;
    They also wondered why?

But first he had to buy the land
    To start his Cricket Club.
He found the devious owner was
    The Landlord of the Pub.
A wizened, shrivelled, mean old man,
    A real Beelzebub!

The Landlord waited for the day
    When calling, cap in hand,
The Major told him all about
    The Cricket Ground he planned.
And how the opening match would be
    En fête and **very** grand.

The Landlord ruminated long,
    As though he'd been struck dumb.
And furiously he tried to think
    Of what colossal sum
He might extract for his old field.
    The Major just said, "done".

The Landlord then, with wicked grin,
    A proposition found.
He'd field a team of lads to mark
    The opening of the Ground.
The loser then would have to buy
    The pints of beer, all round!

And just to see fair play was done
    He made a gesture bold.
"I used to do some umpiring;

I know I'm not too old."
(The Major had a sneaking thought
　　He might have been steam-rolled.)

At last the task was safely done.
　　The pitch was passed as fit.
The Major placed an easy bench,
　　Where pensioners might sit.
The Landlord said it wouldn't do.
　　Then felt he'd done his bit!

The opening game. A gala match.
　　The Cricket Ground decked out.
A BP garage loaned some flags,
　　And scattered them about.
The Landlord said, "It's bound to rain!"
　　And others said, "No doubt."

"Look sharp you chaps, all gather round!
　　Now listen well to me!
I've done the lunch – please help yourselves.
　　The Pub will do the tea.
And when I say we start at two.
　　I do not mean **at three!**

"I've organised the cricket stumps,
　　The bails, the pads, and ball.
I've carried all the folding chairs
　　Up from the Village Hall.
I've even found an umpire's coat.
　　You'll find it's **rather** small.

"I've rolled the pitch. I've mown the square.
　　The crease has been marked out.
I've fixed the tallywag to be
　　Done by a small Boy Scout
Good manners please, to one and all,
　　And courtesy throughout!"

The Major gave his little speech
　　With flourish and panache.
By now his face was mottled red
　　Beneath his trim moustache.
The village Landlord turned and said
　　"What utter balderdash!"

The Major let the others bat,
 With modesty galore.
He came in last, all padded up,
 His pride he nobly bore.
He sallied forth to win the match
 With just a simple four.

He squeezed into his IZ cap.
 He pulled his gloves on hard.
He moved the sight-screen to the right,
 No more than just a yard.
And with a glance around the ground,
 He nervously took guard.

He stood and waited for the ball,
 As thoughts poured through his mind.
At last his dreams were coming true,
 From years and years of grind.
A simple four to win the match
 And glory unconfined!

A callow village youth ran up,
 With cricket skills quite raw,
And bowled a ball with all his force.
 (It made his right arm sore.)
He hit the Major's IZ cap!
 Then yelled out, "**leg before** . . .?"

The village Landlord scratched his nose
 And tickled his right ear,
With utter innocence he asked,
 "Did you appeal, my dear?
'Cos if you did, I says it's out!
 'Tis opening time, I fear!"

"Hey, you! I say! That isn't fair!
 You're venal, through and through!
You've made me lose my Cricket Match.
 Please say it isn't true?"
The grinning Landlord winked – and said,
 "The drinks are **all** on **YOU!**"

G. D. Martineau

Phil Willow, the sculptor, whose fearless designs
Expressed the new vision in bulldozer lines,
When seeking a soul-mate, departed from these,
And married Belinda, a star of strip-tease.

By nature compliant, round-featured and fair,
Her mind and her body were equally bare.
She bore a fine body, waxed maternally proud,
But also conceded that one was a crowd.

Hence, little Tom Willow – sole shaft in the quiver –
Grew up among shapes that made thoughtful folk shiver.
Unthwarted, unfriended, he wandered at will.
His training and guidance a problem for Phil –

Whose notion for schooling was "freedom for all",
The principle honoured by Laxaby Hall,
A modern "Co-Ed", where the pupils were taught
To exercise freedom in word, deed and thought.

Thus Tom learnt new terms, which he carelessly used,
And came to his senses both scratched and contused;
For boy-and-girl freedom, too freely applied,
Is apt to reveal its less genial side,
Releasing reactions corrosive as crude
When youth can swop swear-words or dance in the nude.

Now Laxaby Hall would not own a "headmaster"
Denoting Control – for Control spelt Disaster.
The "Leader" was Julian, bearded and shorted;
The "Partner" with whom he (quite freely) consorted,
Was Lillian – blonde and brunette in rotation –
Whose shorts had him beaten for sheer elevation.
All formal politeness was wholly rejected,
And "Julie" and "Lil" were the styles they affected.

Both Julie and Lil held routine in disdain:
You went into class if you felt in the vein,
And *organized games* were so scorned at the Hall
That nobody *mentioned* a bat or a ball.

Thus, little Tom Willow sat watching T.V.,
Or plunged through the woods, climbing tree after tree,
Or bathed in the lake – when the girls were elsewhere,
For some of them seemed so *aggressively* bare.

"A Full Self-Expression" preached Julie and Lil,
was "only attained by a Life of Free Will".
Yet full self-expression may turn the wrong way:
Tom Willow – alas! – grew more bored every day,
Until by God's favour (which some call a fluke)
He met a rare spirit in Pamela Duke.

Rear-Admiral Duke, not so many months dead,
Had left a young widow, who went off with her head,
And, in this condition, quite failed to recall
Where Pam had been entered . . . thus, Laxaby Hall
Received a dark maiden, who, left to fare free,
Expressed herself roundly in terms of the sea.

Now, Pam hoarded treasures, and, deep in the wood,
She built a headquarters like some Robin Hood,
Though no bows and arrows met Tom's puzzled gaze,
But simply some gear from her father's young days:
A bat and some stumps and an old leather ball –
The trappings of cricket – at Laxaby Hall!

With Pamela coaching, Tom Willow first played
The National Game, in a still forest glade . . .

But cricket, though quiet when crowds are not near,
Conveys a sweet echo to any quick ear –
A song of the summer, enchanting in tone,
A quickening note, with a spell of its own;

And, drawn by enchantment, those neophytes came
Who, having espied, begged to join in the game,
Till Pamela, finding the secret revealed,
Took charge, like a captain, and set them to field;

But secrets so shared become secrets no more,
And Julie and Lil waxed offended and sore.
Such Sin in their Garden they hardly believed:
Tom Willow – an Adam! Pam Duke – his dark Eve!
Their apple, a ball – one of palpable weight –
The tree of their knowledge – a Willow – 'twas fate!

Where now was Free Will? Tom and Pam, to their shame,
Had ORGANIZED CRICKET, A DISCIPLINED GAME.
Old Laxatives heard the grave tale of disgrace,
And urged that the pair be expelled from the place.

Phil Willow, reacting, called Julie a fool,
And somehow got Tom into Manborough School,
Where all self-expression was under control,
And hundreds of boys learnt to field, bat and bowl,
While poor Mrs Duke, conscience-stricken indeed,
Remembered that Pam should have gone to Roemead.

The change in their lives which thus tore them apart
Woke passions that moved from the crease to the heart:
Exams and degrees being past, they were plighted,
And duly and truly in marriage united,
A Duke and a Willow! Symbolic – sublime –
Though sophists averred they'd been "bats" all the time . . .

And when they had twins, it transpired, as their due
That both boy and girl proved keen cricketers too:
Young Peter at Lord's gave all bowlers a skinning,
While Mollie at Colwall sent ball and bail spinning,

Till Grandfather Willow, a figure of fame,
Dragged Grannie Belinda to study the game,
And thus was inspired to those sculptural gems
Which only the rigid precision condemns:

"The Wicket", a masterpiece shaped like a pylon;
"The Ball", an ellipsoid for spinners to smile on;
"The Bat" – a creation whose mood was in keeping,
Since no one could doubt that this willow was weeping.

                    *   *   *   *

Thus, out of the errors to which man is prone,
Youth, Learning, and Art entered into their own;
And may we be spared freedom's false affectations,
And Cricket bring joy to untold generations.

Kamau Brathwaite

Many a time have I seen him savin'
the side (the tailor was saying
as he sat and sewed in his shop).
You remember that tourney wid Brandon?
What-he-name-now
the big-bale-water-policeman –

de one in charge o'de Harbour Patrol . . .
You mean Hop–
a-long Cass! Is because a cow

give he mother a kick before he did born
that he came foot out so.
Yes, I know

but it is not what I was talkin' about. Ol'
Hoppy was bowlin' that day
as if he was hurricane father.

Lambert went in, play –
in'he know all about it as us'al
an' *swoosh!* there he go fan –

nin' outside the stump-off an'
is *click!*
he snick

de ball straight into de slips.
'Well boys it look like we lossin'
this match', says the skipper,

writin' nought in the exercise book
he was keepin' the score in; 'you think
we could chance it an' sen' Gullstone in

before Charlie or Spooks?'
So Gullstone went in.
You could see he face whitenin'

under he tan an you know
that that saga-boy frighten: bat
tappin', feet walkin' 'bout like they talkin'

wid ants; had was to stop meself axin'
meself if he ever play cricket on Brown's beach before.
An' I tole him,

I tole him over an' over
agen: *watch de ball, man,* watch
de ball like it hook to you eye

when you first goes in an' you doan know de pitch
Uh doan mean to *poke*
but you jes got to *watch what you doin'*;

this isn't no time for playin'
the fool nor makin' no sport; this is cricket!
But Gullstone too deaf:

mudder doan clean out de wax in he ear?
Firs' ball from Cass an' he fishin';
secon' ball an' he missin', swishin'

he bat like he wishin'
to catch butterfly; though the all Gullstone ever could catch
pun dis beach was a cole!

But is always the trouble wid we:
too fraid an' too frighten.
Is all very well when it rosy an' sweet,

but leh murder start an' *bruggalungdung!*
you cahn fine a man to hole up de side.

Look wha' happen las' week at de O–
val!

At de Oval?
Wha' happen las' week at de Oval?

You mean to say that you come
in here wit dat lime-skin cone

that you callin' a hat
pun you head, an' them slip slop shoe strap

on to you foot like a touris';
you sprawl you ass

all over my chair without ask–
in' me please leave nor licence,

wastin' muh time when you know very well that uh cahn fine
enough to finish these zoot suits

'fore Christmas' an' on top
o'all this, you could wine up de nerve to stop

me cool cool cool in de middle
o'all me needle

an't'read; make me prick me hand in me haste;

an' tell me broad an'bole to me face

THAT YOU DOAN REALLY KNOW WHA' HAPPEN
AT KENSINGTON OVAL?

We was only *playin*' de MCC, man;
M-C-C
who come all de way out from Inglan.

We was battin', you see;
score wasn't too bad; one
hurren an' ninety–

seven fuh three.
The openers out, Tae Worrell out,
Everton Weekes jus' glide two fuh fifty

an' jack is de GIANT to come!
Feller name Wardle
was bowlin'; tossin' it up

sweet sweet slow-medium syrup.
Firs' ball . . .
'No . . .o . . .o . . .'

back down de wicket to Wardle.
Secon' ball
'N . . .o . . .o . . .'

back down de wicket to Wardle.
Third ball comin' up
an' we know wha' goin' happen to syrup:

Clyde back pun he back
foot an' *prax!*
is through extra cover an' four red runs all de way.

'You see dat shot?' the people was ahoutin';
'Jesus Chrise, man, wunna see dat shot?'
All over de groun' fellers shakin' hands wid each other

as if was *they* wheelin' de willow
as if was *them* had the power;
one man run out pun de field wid a red fowl cock

goin' quawk quawk quawk in 'e han';
would'a give it to Clyde right then an' right there
if a police hadn't stop 'e!

An' in front o' where I was sittin',
one ball-headed sceptic snatch hat off he head
as if he did crazy

an' pointin' he finger at Wardle,
he jump up an' down
like a sun-shatter daisy an bawl

out: 'B . . . L . . . O . . . O . . . D, B . . . I . . . G B . . .
O . . . Y
BRING ME HE B . . . L . . . O . . . O . . . D'
Who would'a think that for twenty–

five years he was standin' up there
in them Post Office cages, lickin' gloy
pun de Gover'ment stamps.

If uh wasn't there to see fuh meself,
I would'a never believe it,
I would'a never believe it.

But I say it once an' I say it agen:
when things goin' good, you cahn touch
we; but leh murder start an' you cahn fine a man to hole up de side.

Like when Laker came on.
Goin' remember what happenin' then
for the rest o'me life.

This Laker a quiet tall heavy-face fellow
who before he start to do anything ser'ous
is hitch up he pants round he belly.

He bowlin' off-breaks.
Int makin' no fuss
jus' toss up de firs'

one an' *bap!*
Clyde play forward firm
an de ball hit he pad

an' fly up over de wicket.
Boy, *dis* is cricket!
Laker shift weight

an' toss up de secon',
it pitchin' off-stump an' comin' back sharp
wid de men in de leg trap shinin' like shark.

Clyde stretchin' right out like a man in de dark
an' he kill it.
'N . . . O . . . O . . . O', from de schoolboys, 'hit it, hit it'.

Boy, dis is *cricket.*
Then Laker come down wid he third
one. He wrap up de ball in de palm

o' he han' like a package
AN' MAKE CLYDE WALCOTT LOOK FOOLISH.
Mister man, could'a hear

all de flies that wa buzzin' out there
round de bread carts; could'a hear
if de empire fart.

An' then blue murder start:
'Kill one o'dem, Clyde', some wise–
wun was shoutin', 'knock he skull off;

doan let them tangle you up in no leg trap;
use de feet dat God give you!'
Ev'ry blabber mout' talkin',

ev'ry man jack givin' advice'
but we so frighten now at what happenin' there
we could piss we pants if we doan have a care.

'*Swing de bat, man*', one feller was shoutin',
an' Clyde swing de bat but de bat miss
de ball an' de ball hit he pad

an' he pad went *biff*
like you beatin' bed
an' de empire han' stick

in de air
like Francis who dead
an' de bess o' we batsmen out.

The crowd so surprise you int hearin' a shout.
Ev'ry mout' loss.
But I say once an' I say it agen:

when things goan' good, you cahn touch
we; but leh murder start
an' ol man, you cahn fine a man to hole up de side . . .

Paul Keens-Douglas

Yes, ah come back.
Ah bring back Tanti Merle too.
Look, woman, don't ask me no foolish question – yu hear?
Where yu see ah sit down here, is trouble yu lookin' for.
Yes, ah know Trinidad lose.
Yes, ah know Combined Islands beat we,
Yu should ask Tanti Merle 'bout dat, she should know.
Why I vex? Who tell yu ah vex? Yu find ah look vex?
Yu didn't study dat
When yu make me take Tanti Merle to de Oval?
Ah know we been through all dis already,
But never me again, never, never, never
Ah not takin' no relative with me to de Oval, not me,
Next time is me one alone an God goin' in de Oval.
Ah mean to say, yu had de whole year
To send Tanti Merle to de Oval,
But why today, eh? Today of all days,
Trinidad versus de Islands, ah big match like dat,
An' you want me to take Tanti Merle to see cricket match.
Ah know is she birthday,
Ah know she from St. Vincent,
Ah know she always talking 'bout de Islands,
But Tanti Merle livin' in Curepe fifteen years
An' she never put foot in de Oval,
So why today, eh? why today? tell me dat.
Yu have Transistor,
Yu have Radio,
Yu have Television,
Right here in dis God-bless house,
Tanti Merle could ah well come an' enjoy de match,
Instead of dat, yu take de woman an' sen' she
Quite in Port of Spain to see cricket
An' nearly kill me dead, dead, dead
Dis April month of de Lord, 1975
An' Tanti Merle is sixty five years old.
Woman, yu don't know what confusion yu put me in, eh?
Woman, yu don't know how yu nearly lose a husband , eh?
Yu see dat woman yu callin' Tanti Merle?

Well, let me tell yu 'bout she . . .
First of all, we leave late.
Ah tell Tanti Merle to get ready for ten o'clock,
Match startin' eleven,
We had ah good hour to reach de Oval,
But Tanti Merle wouldn't leave de house,
She only tittivaying, packin' basket with ah set ah food,
Sayin' how nobody eh go' starve she in Port of Spain.
An' yu know who end up carryin' de basket . . . me!
Ah man like me who does go in de Oval
With me money in me side pocket,
Ah petit-quart in me back pocket,
An' me two hand swingin' free.
But see me now, looking like some kind ah market vendor,
People only askin' me' what yu sellin'?
An' of course Tanti Merle had to take she parasol too.
Ah tell she de stands have roof, but not she,
She eh takin' me on at all,
Talkin' ah whole lot ah stupidness 'bout sun-stroke,
An' on top of dat is ah pink parasol she bring.
Imagine me in de Oval with ah pink parasol.
People must ah tought it was Carnival.
Any way, ah take de basket.
De nex' set ah horrors was de taxi.
You self know how taxi hard to get in Curepe,
Every time I stop one, Tanti say she not goin' in,
Either de driver look too funny,
Or de passengers look too low-class,
Or de car look like it go fall down.
So ah tell she "choose yu own taxi".
She say she want ah red taxi.
Now tell me why your Tanti Merle must drive
In ah red taxi
Yu see dat woman is like she wukkin' Obeah yu know
Is like yu tanti is ah real bad Obeah woman.
Tank God ah taxi come dat lookin' kind ah red,
Because she decide to take it.
An' yu know how she do dat?
De woman just step off de pavement
Right in front de taxi, an' say 'hold dat!'
Well yu could imagine brakes,
Ah never hear ah taxi-man cuss so yet.

But Tanti Merle eh take he on,
She just freeze him with one "bad eye"
Haul open de back door,
An' take over de whole backseat
As if she is de Queen of Sheba.
An' me self with dis big basket, smellin' like ah snackette.
Nex' ting de taxi-man switch on music, reggae.
Tanti Merle tell him take it off,
She say she want to hear cricket.
Well, dat was de only good ting she say,
From de time we leave Curepe
To de time we reach in de Oval.
De taxi-man put on de cricket,
An' from dere on Tanti Merle take-over.
Nobody mus' talk, Islands batting,
Tings in de Oval goin' good an Tanti Merle grinnin',
Hear she, "dats me boys an' dem, dey go bus' allyu tail".
De taxi-man made de mistake an' ask she
Where she come from.
Well is who tell he say dat,
We get de whole history of St. Vincent,
How it came Hiroona an' one set ah ting.
All dis time I vex, match start an' ah missin' play,
An' on top of dat Tanti Merle carryin' on 'bout St. Vincent.
Ah eh know how de taxi-man eh turn over de taxi
De way he begin to drive fast,
Ah never seen ah man drive so fast yet,
Fus he want to get Tanti Merle out de taxi hurry.
He take we straight to de Oval, non-stop.
Den Tanti Merle start to talk 'bout fifteen cents.
Well ah sure dat taxi-man must be tink she mad,
Is me wha' had to put peace again,
Ah just hand he five dollars
An' tell him tank you.
Yu tink wha' ah just tell yu bad?
Wait till yu hear wha' happen in de Oval.
Dat Oval was something else, is den story start.
Tanti Merle try to go through de people gate
With she parasol open,
Because she say she 'fraid she catch 'sun stroke'.
Well you self know how de gateman an'dem in de Oval stop,
Some ah dem does jus' watch yu hand with de money,

Dey doesn't even watch yu face
Fus dey couldn't care less, 'bout yu,
Is just de hand de money an' de ticket,
De hand de money an' de ticket,
Well dey had to watch Tanti Merle,
She nearly jook out dey eye with she parasol.
All dis time I apologisin',
An' yu know what one ah dem turn 'round an' tell me?
Why ah eh leave me wife home if she 'fraid sun.
He eh say aunt, he eh say granny, he eh say cousin,
He say wife. Yu know how ah feel? Yu laughin'!
Is because ah make de sign of de cross
When we reach inside de stand an' get we seat.
An' guess who is de first man ah see?
Boysie an ah whole side feteing up with one set ah rum,
An' me with Tanti Merle.
An' when dey see me, yu could imagine de scene.
"How de madam?"
"Ae, ae boy, where yu get dat one"
"Make sure she have ah will."
"How yu selfish so, yu can't introduce de boys?"
"Where yu get dat nice woman, boy?"
"Dat is de one yu always tellin' us 'bout?"
An' dey start to carry on.
Is tank God de cricket so hot
Dey eh have time to take me on for long.
Islands battin' an' Trinidad bowlin',
Islands have runs to make,
Trinidad have wickets to take,
Time runnin' out an' is excitement in de Oval,
If Islands win dey get de shield
Tension in de place like steel.
I settle down to watch de game,
An' is den Tanti Merle start up.
She tell ah fella in front she to take off he hat,
She say it barrin' she.
Well he start to cuss she, an she start to cuss he
An' I trying to put peace but ah frighten,
Because is ah real 'Bad-John' Tanti interfere with.
Tank God jus' den Richards get out stupid,
Cause dey say he not in he crease
An' de ball fall out de bowler hand an' hit de wicket

An' so he stump out stupid, stupid so.
Well Tanti Merle forget de 'Bad-John an' start with de umpire,
She say how he blind like ah bat,
She say is how he have lumbago,
She say is how is teaf he teafin' for Trinidad,
She say how he lucky she eh out dey
Because is wha' she would do an' wha' she wouldn't do to he,
An' she start to carry on.
But she quiet down when Allen start to blade ball
An' de score start to move
An' every run dat make de crowd makin' noise,
Tanti like dat.
Next ting braps!! Shillingford gone,
Braps!! Eddy gone, braps!! Coriette gone,
Imtiaz an 'Jumadeen spinnin' ball like joke,
An' wicket fallin' like smoke.
An' every wicket dat fall de crowd makin' noise,
Tanti eh like dat, she get vex,
She say how de crowd too hypocrite,
One minute dey cheerin' de Islands,
De next minute dey cheerin' Trinidad,
Den she turn round an say how Imtiaz stonin'.
Well ah fella tell she how spinner can't stone
An' ask she where she come out.
Well who tell he say dat.
We get de whole history of St. Vincent again,
Only dis time she stan' up on de people seat to explaciate.
Ah had to beg she quick, quick, come down Tanti
Open de basket, let we eat.
Dat was de fus time ah glad we bring dat basket.
She open up de ting, an' was like Christmus, if yu see food.
Den Tanti start to share out, was like ah picnic, everybody get,
She even give de 'Bad-John' piece.
Nex' ting ah know Allen out at ninety-six tryin' to vup
An' everybody forget food, tension high in de Oval.
Finlay an' Roberts battin', thirteen runs needed.
Den Tanti decide she want to change she seat,
She say de pole barrin' she.
So I behind, Tanti down front.
Roberts attempt ah six an' he out, the crowd roar,
Den Tanti start to shake she fist at Gomes for takin' de catch.
She say de way Gomes jump is like he eat Dominica Mountain chicken.

Ah man tell she move, an' was go' drop ah lash on she,
But jus den Willet out an' town in ah mess.
Islands need seven runs, with nine balls to bowl
An' one wicket to fall.
Dis time I forget 'bout Tanti Merle
Excitement in de Oval like yu never see in yu life,
Gore come in to bat an' is den de action start.
Nine balls seven runs to go . . . noise in de place.
Eight balls six runs to go . . . Tanti start wavin' de basket.
Seven balls six runs to go . . . Tanti on top de seat.
Six balls five runs to go . . . Tanti fall off de seat.
Five balls five runs to go . . . Tanti wavin' de parasol.
Four balls four runs to go . . . police cautionin' Tanti.
Three balls three runs to go . . . Tanti climbin' over de fence.
One ball three runs to go . . . Tanti on de people field.
Gore hit de ball, an' he an' Finlay pelt down de wicket for two run,
An' is den de bacchanal start, score tie at 283
An' everybody say Islands win.
Nex' ting ah see
Is Tanti parasol high up in de air,
An' she in de middle of one set ah people,
An' dey on de people pitch singin', an' dancin', an' carryin' on,
Ah whole heap of small-island people, and Tanti in de middle,
An' Tanti parasol only goin' up an' down, up an' down, up an' down.
Nex' ting loudspeaker say match eh tie, it draw
So Islands eh win de shield is Guyana.
Well who tell dem say dat, Tanti nearly cause ah riot.
She start to carry on.
She say dey teaf,
She say dey eh like de Islands,
She say change de rules,
She say tie and draw, same ting,
She say she forming delegation to see de Doctor,
She say she declare war,
An' she have one big, big crowd round she,
An' she on top one ah dem ting dey does roll de pitch with.
Dat same Tanti Merle dat look as if butter can't melt in she mout.
It take me 'bout two hours to get she out de Oval,
She lose de basket an' de parasol mash up,
But she eh study dat, is noise de whole way home.
An' yu know what dat woman have de heart to ask me when we reach de gap?
When nex' we goin' back in de Oval?

XI

PRACTICALLY SPEAKING

(Ins and Outs of the Game)

~

Here are presented cricket's component parts. There is a sense of inspecting the engine-room of the game with glances at the individual bits and pieces. Each is a portion of the whole. Both on and off the field a picture emerges of how the cricketing world functions at large. There are reminders of the preparatory slopes during schooldays. There is the reluctant volunteer called to make up a team. There are the crafts of the players and their different positions. There is a look behind the doors of the committee-room. And reflection of the remote control of ancient wireless and modern TV. Even the bookish charms of those who write about the game. And right up to date, a lip is curled at the corporate suits in the hospitality boxes with their backs to the play rather like the King in *Hamlet*.

This is a deeply personal chapter. In a way it uses the cricketer's lot as a mirror of the human condition and as such it is social commentary. The common thread is humour and much magical imagery.

Who would have thought there was so much to say about, what is, after all, (as Daniel Healey points out at the beginning) only 'six bits of stick, a bat and ball, and two and twenty asses . . .'

D. R. A.

Daniel Healey

Well, what is cricket after all,
　　That so delights the masses?
Six bits of stick, a bat and ball,
　　And two and twenty asses.

Yes, two and twenty donkey-men –
　　I wish I could impound them;
Yes, asses, I repeat again,
　　With thousands more around them.

And then the asses howl and bat,
　　Knock down, or keep a wicket;
And run, and cheer, and shout, and that –
　　Why, that's the game of cricket.

Philip Hodgins

The way a dream of sporting glory dissolves
when early morning light seeps grimly back
into the room, so too this half-constructed aviary
with its slabs of wire mesh and concrete floor.
Instead of dirty Tipp-Ex worms the droppings
are red raw skid marks mostly in the middle
where some of the unhelmeted batsmen lost sight
of just the ball they needed to keep an eye on.
Their bats are like the pitch in miniature.
Each one is badly scarred with the hot spots
and rashes of that disease which spreads beyond
the playing victims to their wives and kids –
the sempiternal pain of a middle-order collapse.
But perhaps worse are those more personal wounds:
the split webbing after a dropped slips catch,
two broken toes from practising in sandshoes,
and everyman's nightmare of turning full-on
to an awkward ball without the vital box.
When banishment from next week's team is likely
the anatiferous number three will come back
to this uncovered nave and go through strokes
with all the devotion of a former sinner.
Watching the one who used to be their idol
groups of school children will hang along the aisles,
their fingers poking dangerously through the wire.
An act of public penitence is always fraught.
The padded man who finds himself exposed
to such a swaying congregation is never sure
which ball is going to cut sharply off the seam.
The only choice is to practice a straight bat
as if the life of chance could be theorised.
Not that these children pushing against wire
would ever be impressed with a return to form
which only happened before the five real days.
They know that that's the attraction of the nets.
It doesn't matter how many times you're out.
You'll always carry your bat. It's like a dream.

Thomas Hutchinson

If you would be a cricketer,
    You must have lots of pluck,
And though you wield the willow well,
    A tiny bit of luck.
Don't be afraid to cut or drive –
    Stone-walling soon grows flat;
But if you mean to make a score,
    Play – a – straight – bat.

A duck's all right at dinner-time,
    But not when playing cricket,
Hit out-like thunder, if you like,
    But don't – don't hit your wicket.
And when a ball comes down to leg,
    Give it a mighty pat;
But if you mean to make a score,
    Play – a – straight – bat.

Take heed of slip and second slip,
    Of point and cover-point,
But don't lose heart if caught, and say
    The times are out of joint:
Be wary, and next time you're in,
    Watch, as its prey a cat,
And if you mean to make a score,
    Play – a – straight – bat.

And should a lightening ball, alas!
    Send flying all your stumps,
Don't ape the melancholy Jacques,
    And mope in doleful dumps:
Defy misfortune with a smile –
    Don't dance upon your hat,
Then if you mean to make a score,
    Play – a – straight – bat.

L'Envoi.

The war was won, so we were told,
  Upon the playing field,
Where men and officers alike
  Were trained how not to yield:
And although treachery might succeed,
They never thought of that –
Winning or losing, they did aye
  Play – a – straight – bat.

Then let us prove our kith to them
  Who for their country bled;
And if we have to fight, fight fair,
  As did the glorious dead.
Come victory or defeat, with scorn
  We'll ne'er be pointed at,
If all through life our motto is –
  Play – a – straight – bat.

Fred Ponsonby

Bowlers, when they first begin,
Should study straightness, pitch, and spin.
Without attention to these three
First-class in bowling none can be:
With measured step but springy tread
With steady eye and upright head
Advance, when back-foot's near the crease,
Deliver boldly but with ease,
Use well your legs, arms, wrists and all
And throw your body with the ball,
Exert your brains more than your strength
To vary slightly pace and length,
Sometimes higher, sometimes lower,
Sometimes faster, sometimes slower,
When the ball drops exactly right
The batsman will be puzzled quite,
Caught in two minds an accident
Will be a probable event.
But if by chance or skill he stay,
Closely observe his style of play,
Remember that you've got a field
Work his weak points and he must yield,
If not, though, bowling well enough
Don't grumble if you're taken off,
For rested soon in arm and brain,
You're ready to set to again:
So let us end as we begin
Attend to straightness, pitch and spin.

Siegfried Sassoon

O Batsman, rise and go and stop the rot,
And go and stop the rot.
(It was indeed a rot,
Six down for twenty-three.)
The batsman thought how wretched was his lot,
And all alone went he.

The bowler bared his mighty, cunning arm,
His vengeance-wreaking arm,
His large yet wily arm,
With fearful powers endowed.
The batsman took his guard. (A deadly calm
Had fallen on the crowd.)

O is it a half-volley or long-hop,
A seventh-bounce long-hop,
A fast and fierce long-hop,
That the bowler letteth fly?
The ball was straight and bowled him neck and crop.
He knew not how nor why.

Full sad and slow pavilionwards he walked.
The careless critics talked;
Some said that he was yorked;
A half-volley at a pinch.
The batsman murmured as he inward stalked,
'It was the extra inch.'

Danny Gardner

From an early age
The echoes beckon,
In the spring-fired gathering
Of upright, flannelled forms,
Their shrill reports,
The crisp 'chock' of willow smiting leather,
Arrowing the summer torpor.

Nothing moves the heart
Like quickening pulse, of taking block,
When heated brow and clammy hands
Are witness to ambition
And its dark shadow, fear.

Electric then, the sweet shock of contact,
And the red missile whistling
Between diving, white guardsmen,
Is a cherished wish
Spreading its wings.

So begins the long pilgrimage
Across uncertain terrain,
Though youthful hope is flirtatious,
Wanting thousands to acknowledge
What a mere twelve others will commit to memory.
Though their yarns become
Those echoes that beckon
That lesson not
With their repetition.

'Til achievement embraces admiration,
Or folly falls midst cruel deception,
A spread-eagling of stumps
Terminates those called early.

And when that first walk out
Mists into the last,
An old master meets,
One more cherished time,
The boy he once was.

Basil MacDonald Hastings

Hurtling them down in a dancing light – skip and a dancing run –
Seeing the batsmen come and go – bowled out one by one –
Driving the leg-stump out of the ground – knocking the middle flat –
Catching the sound of a click in the wind – yelling a frenzied 'S that?'
    'How's that?'
Watching the rise from an awkward tuft – turn and break and spin –
Leg and keep and cover and slip
Keen as a staghound under the whip –
O the delight of a morning bright – slinging 'em in!
First and second and third and fourth length balls on the stumps –
Fifth a yorker – dead on the leg – bagged the ace of trumps!
Next man stoops for an easy glide – missed it – leg before!
Six for ten – a dropping slow bags one victim more –
    'One More!'
Knocking the dust-clouds off the pitch; fighting hard to win;
Leg and keeper and cover and slip
Itching to pounce on an uppish tip
Spherical lightning shivering sticks – slinging 'em in!

John Groves

Slope?   *Slope?*   *What* slope?
We speak of a slight eccentric inclination,
An impetus to skill – an inspiration
To those who come with more than craven hope,
Being not content to yield
To such as want a level playing field,
Or yearn for comfort of a sterile dome.
Good Lord, man, this is England, this is *home!*

Try thinking of it as *a sweet undress,*
As Nature's bold, freehand configuration.
No self-respecting ball would dream of rolling
Down it, save in maladroit distress
Of bowling,
Or unless,
Behind it, a sudden force of bat.
Well then, I ask you – where's the harm in that?

John Groves

No ticket for the Test?
Can't get to Lord's,
The Oval or Trent Bridge?
Reduced to drinking beer from your own fridge,
Starved of what Headingley affords?

Of course it's best
To share the drama of the game
With the like-minded chap who thrills the same
In all those places Englishmen forgather
And share their passion for it with each other.

Perhaps you don't hanker for where people bellow?
Want to be nice and quiet, like Richie Benaud,
Recalling, in the interval for Tea,
An age-old triumph, "how it used to be"?

Then commandeer the best seat in the house,
Switch off all other flannel,
Switch on (despite a loud-protesting spouse)
To God's Own Channel
And watch a big-sky epic, wrought by Kings,
The camera's eye beholds, then spreads before . . .
And so say thank-you, thank-you all the more
For wizardry and artistry that brings
The game for free
                              – with love from Channel Four.

C. J. Dennis

I reckon (said Dad) that the country's pests
Is this here wireless an' these here Tests.
Up to the house and around the door,
Stretchin' their ears for to catch the score,
Leavin' the horses down in the crop,
Can you wonder a farmer goes off pop?

I'm yellin' at Jim or I'm cursin' at Joe
All hours of the day, but it ain't no go –
Leavin' their work and hangin' around
When they think I'm down by the fallow ground;
Sneaking away when I start to rouse,
An' as soon as me back's turned, back at the house.

'Who got Wyatt? Is Sutcliffe out?'
Wot do they care if I rave an' shout?
Bribin' young Bill for to leave his job
To twiddle the switches an' twist the knob.
'Has he made his century? Who's in now?'
And I bought that machine for the price of a cow!

There's a standin' crop, an' the rain's not far,
An' the price is rotten, but there you are:
As soon as these cricketin' games begin
The farm goes dilly on listenin' in;

Not only the boys an' the harvester crew,
But Mum an' the girls gits dotty too.
An' I reckon (said Dad) that a man's worst pets,
Is this here wireless an' these here Tests.

Gerald Brodribb

All smooth and elegant
The stylish strokes flow from the blade,
And even the defensive pokes come
Sweet upon the air
In soothing serenade.

And you will say (as you stand behind the net):
Here is a child whose fifteen years
Defy the span of time, recall a touch of Palairet,
And prophesy a glorious prime.

You will be wrong.
For all this talent, flaming at the nets,
Fritters to nothingness . . .
Out in the glare the failing nerves
Provoke but vain regrets.

The timid snick, the nasty jab:
Time and again an innings proves forlorn;
Confidence wastes away, and
Adulation dwindles into scorn.

The temperament confounds the natural skill:
Forget the glory of the net-time shots.
The fatal flaw will ever tell
The same sad story –
How can the leopard change his spots?

Gerald Brodribb

Here I stand umpire, doomed
For a space to suffer, flung
To and fro upon the
Indiscretions of the young.

The team is mine. I am the
Ball, the wicket and the bat.
Now is the contest. Though I am
Umpire, I am more than that.

I know each weakness better
Than my own: who'll miss the catch,
Utter the foolish call, throw wide,
Lose patience – possibly the match.

Here comes the opening batsman
Cloaking a slopping heart with pale smile.
Dry-mouthed, I give him guard,
Call 'Play!', and set my life on trial.

What irony to call this 'play';
'Torment' would be a better name:
Surely no Test Match wrings the heart
More fiercely that this House Colts game.

An hour or so will shape the fates:
Render the evening grave or gay.
Perhaps we lack the natural touch
To look upon it in this way,
Truly I wish I did not care
So much.

Chris Sparkes

And not let Channel 4's
terrestrial carnival this summer
– while our English Lions fight
in front-lines for the Ashes,
at that Victorian pavilion'd
battle-field in St John's Wood,
against their ancient enemy
Australia – interrupt the war
with Dobbin fun-races and jumps,
goggled at by Surrey looking-glass
Alices and rabbits, wearing
ten and six top-hats
on, say, a Lady's Day
that's spoofed up by a commentator
who gargles all his jazz
along so quick
you'd hope he's got a bus
or train to catch
across some final fence:
Ascot might be royal,
but Lord's is, ah, divine.

G. F. Wilson

An instant, poised in air,
A rosy light delayed;
Dropt, and willow blade
Flashed like a golden share,
Flashed – and a throbbing star
Waned to a spark, afar.

Simon Armitage

Forget
the long, smouldering
afternoon. It is

this moment
when the ball scoots
off the edge

of the bat; upwards,
backwards, falling
seemingly

beyond him
yet he reaches
and picks it

out
of its loop
like

an apple
from a branch,
the first of the season.

Neil Rollinson

The infield is for wisecrackers, pepper-pots, gum-poppers:
The outfield is for loners, onlookers, brooders . . .
Stuart Dybek, 'Death of the Right Fielder'

I like it here, where the meadows of Kent
lap at the boundary rope, redundant
with apples and hops. You can ponder
the subtler things: the way a summer
ripens with every innings, sycamores moving
through deeper and deeper greens.
A man could drop dead out here
in the long grass, and no one would know.
They never found Blenkinsop, fielding
at deep-square-leg. They found some bones
the following year, his name carved in a tree,
but nothing more. We're a different breed.
Not for us, the tense excitement
of silly-point or forward-short-leg,
the flamboyance of bowlers
with their googlies and flippers.
I do bowl sometimes, for an over or two,
a languid, deceptive leg break;
but I pine for the stillness,
the silence of lost cricket balls
rotting like toadstools under a fence.
Nothing else happens, for months.
A whole season can pass
like a lifetime. I lounge in the sun,
practice my golf or read a book.
You lose touch out here.
I watch the weather: the clouds,
the twelve degrees of turquoise
you find in an August sky,
and I love the rain, the way it soaks the hills,
the orchards, the whole of England.
One of these days they'll find me

dead among the dandelions,
the red smudge of a cricket ball
gracing my head, or maybe I'll disappear
into the unmown grass, the oaks
and elm trees, the last day of summer,
into memory, and beyond.

Alexis Lykiard

Retiring in both sense, the old groundsman spoke:
I still recall my first big game
of cricket for the County team.
I was our youngest would-be pro
though all of us went in some awe
of Walter Hammond, skipper then.
(General, you might say, to enlisted men!)
Sent out to field, it proved no joke,
the batsmen hammered us and I let through
several hard shots which flew for four.
That endless afternoon nothing was good,
Gloucester turned Hell under the sun.
I froze, some sweated, others swore.
Blushing in the Pavilion, I tried to apologize:
"Really I'm sorry, Mr Hammond sir, I should
have kept my legs together." "No
lad" the Great Man answered, slow
and loud his timing sweet fire in his eyes:
"That's what your mother should have done."

John Snow

Standing
on a summer's day,
eye watching swallows
earth-hugging
insect chasing way,
wondering what to do,
knowing that it always happens
and now it's happened to you.
What not again? Yes.
Feeling like laughing at the fable
yet not being able
because you have no middle
and life waits watching behind
having given you the casual twiddle.
Yet as your world revolved
it spun you through a wider sky,
opened further open eye,
it's a game.
So come on, who's king of the castle
now I'm the dirty rascal,
standing,
on a still summer's day
eye watching swallows
insect-chasing way.

Des Wilson

Few in cricket know our name
Because we play the committee game.
Not for us picture in the paper
Raised bat to cheering crowd – all that caper,
Instead our pitch is on the top floor
Our test behind the committee door.
Not for us bowled, stumped and caught
Our challenge is of another sort:
Hire the cooks, balance the books
Buy a roller, find a fast bowler.
Winter comes, mist rolls in,
Torn-up programme in the season's bin,
The gates to the ground are firmly shut
They've locked the door of the scorers' hut.
But wait . . . in the pavilion there's a light
Who's still there at nine at night?
Up the stairs, open the door
– Climb up to the committee floor
And here we still are, minutes and files
Devising ways to get crowds thro. stiles
Of course even for us there's spin . . .
Persuading auditors the money's in.
Ten becomes 11, then 12, then one
(How time passes when you're having fun.)
But at last the plans are made
Books are balanced, players paid.
We can go to Christmas without fear,
The county's safe for another year.
So, in that room of thankless toil
Of quiet debate, of battle royal
We do all know the other's name
Because together we've played – and won –
The committee game.

John Tripp

'Pitch it up!' the captain said
as I trundled to the crease:
'Stop bowling bumpers.'
What he wanted was a loss
of speed, more slow left-arm
spin. I tried to oblige
but the language cherry reared up
again, wide of the off-stump.
'No ball' the umpire muttered.

I got more shine on it,
judged angle of flight and the in–
swing, curved it as a craftily
concealed googly. The atmosphere was quite
heavy, good for medium pace as I sent it
scattering the bails half-way
to the sight screen. My mind ached
from the effort. 'That's better,'
the captain said. 'You're coming on.'

Irving Rosenwater

A title takes our fancy:
Should we enter and enquire?
Or should we hover on the threshold
Like some indecisive buyer?
Far wiser to embark upon
Some leisured exploration,
Where Walter Scott and Andrew Lang
Excite our admiration.
Or better still perhaps
To climb the literary scale,
And find the names that *really* count –
Like Nyren and Fred Gale.
What has happened to that volume
On the Yorkshire pros of old?
"Oh, that book, sir, only yesterday,
Just yesterday was sold."
In that case we must make our choice
From things more up to date,
Like Hendren's reminiscences
Or those of Maurice Tate.
I very much would like to buy
That book on Hirst and Rhodes –
An infinitely better prize
Than that dreamy Keats's odes.
Gibbon makes us, true enough,
Enjoy *Decline and Fall*;
But from today my reading shall
Be more of bat and ball.

Yes. I *have* made up my mind:
Bennett and Wells must go.
And so must G.K. Chesterton
And Edgar Allan Poe.
And so must Mrs. Humphry Ward
And Conrad and Defoe:
And Shaw and Pope and Conan Doyle,
All of them must go.

And in their stead there soon will reign
A different set of names,
Of men who tell of pads and stumps,
Who tell of cricket games.

Simon Rae

Sightscreens, beer tents, empty stands;
    The first few streaky fours;
Fielders blowing on chapped hands;
    Echoey applause.

Bowlers doing a 'little bit';
    A sharp, half strangled cry:
The batsman gets the benefit,
    And trots an easy bye.

Nervous taps to check the box –
    The bowling looks quite quick;
The bat against the toecap knocks,
    And then a little flick.

A member sets aside his beer
    And cheerfully applauds;
Will this one be the golden year,
    With glory won at Lord's?

Joe Public stolidly unpacks
    His thermos from his bag;
A fiercely gusting wind attacks
    The country's sun-bleached flag.

Four o'clock sees queues for tea,
    Rock cakes and sticky buns;
The diehard faithful hope to see
    A few more hard-earned runs.

A middle order bat departs;
    The sun goes in again.
And so another season starts
– And stops, of course, for rain.

Malcolm Wroe

My old school, a crab
with pincers outstretched
to the 1st XI field,
crouches still at the city's edge.

By the pavilion,
self-appointed, as a Junior, I
used to break in cricket bats with
a wooden mallet, at the Season's start:
make gentle pockmarks – not to
split the pallid skin, put
hair-line cracks upon
the pure-grained meat.

An old rag steeped
in linseed oil was used
to soothe the willow's punished flesh,
drinking voraciously
its first two applications –
the wooden 'V', where blade met handle
never to be wet.

In the morning, glistening,
sticky-dry, a shade darker,
the rested warrior and I were ready;
for yet another day
of discipline,
of learning how to take the knocks.

Michael Mendel

Then the 'phone goes on Saturday morning
And I clamber, cursing, from bed.
'Hello, this is Mendelson speaking,
Who's ringing to waken the dead?'

'This is Peter from cricket, remember?
We haven't seen you for a while,
We've missed your dressing-room banter
Which sent us all off with a smile.
You were playing pretty well the last time,
Don't worry 'bout missing that catch
Or the shot you played to get out to,
We all thought you had a good match.
So I thought I would ring you and ask you
Whether you might like to play?
At home to Old Templetonians.
That's right, two-thirty today.'

'Look, I'm sorry Peter I have told you
That I'm not keen to play anymore,
Trying to broaden horizons,
I'm sorry to be such a bore.
Well, no Peter, not anything settled,
So, yes, I suppose I am free,
But give me a truthful answer,
The real reason you're asking me?
I see, so you've tried all the usuals,
You'd given up hope and then
You thought you would ring me and tell me
You're playing and only got ten!'

David Phillips

Falling asleep in a chair in the sun,
detached from the game, unimpressed by the play;
a clack of the ball and a scampering run
the only distractions – we're losing (hooray!)

Stretched out on the balcony, boots on the rail,
the lounger reclined, the *Silk Cut* out;
this is the sentence for daring to fail,
they give you your money for arsing about.

The lad who took over from me gets a duck,
shouldered arms at a straight one that cannoned his knee;
of course you could say it's a bit of bad luck,
but bad luck for him must be good luck for me.

The skipper and Chairman sit huddled and glum,
let's try plan B and rejig all the places;
and is that a glance at the discarded bum?
It's quite hard to tell with egg on their faces.

Perhaps they'll relent and forgive me, who knows?
Before I can wonder what anyone thinks
a jockstrap is dangled in front of my nose –
it's time for the twelfth man to carry the drinks.

David Phillips

Off the mark;
the greatest innings
always start from small beginnings.

Ten runs;
double figures in my score,
from where they came there's plenty more.

Twenty runs;
well, I can say
I made more than the boss today.

Thirty runs;
no one can shout
if I now get myself out.

Forty runs;
would please most men,
but I would like another ten.

Fifty runs;
the crowd applaud
the big five-o up on the board.

Sixty runs;
this season's best,
let's see if I can make the rest.

Seventy runs;
the singles flow,
only three more tens to go.

Eighty runs;
I'm steaming on,
surprised that all my nerves have gone.

Ninety runs;
they've all come back,
I push, I prod, I poke, I hack.

A century!
I raise my bat,
now let the buggers chew on that.

David Phillips

You ask if my wife comes to watch me play?
When we first got together she thought it was great
that I played in the League and might play for the County one
day.

She came to the matches, palled up with the blokes
and helped the girls with the lunches and teas
and ironed my kit (which was one of our jokes).

When I signed for the County and cash seemed less tight
we got married and moved to a house near the ground.
We were happy then and our life was . . . well, all right.

We started a family – both wanted kids,
I thought I could juggle my home and my job,
but my love for the game put our love on the skids.

Too often away fixtures did nothing to fix
a relationship glued in resentment and pain –
she wanted a Joe who would come home at six.

She thought I was stupid to stay in a game
which loved you or hated you, dropped you at will,
favoured the lucky and gifted the same.

And I felt the pressure of having to give
a 100% for my place in the team
as home life grew tougher, less rewarding to live.

We split up last Christmas, agreed not to tell;
I still see the kids and we play out a game
to convince everyone we're as happy as hell.

You ask if my wife comes to watch me play?
I do send her tickets but she never comes –
cricket's a dull game when love's gone away.

David Phillips

I watch those sods sip G & T,
late cut a ball and scamper two,
but then they have their backs to me
like red-arsed monkeys in a zoo,
these business geeks are bloody rude.

What actor on stage would play
before ill-mannered oiks like these?
For every player worth his pay
is driven by the need to please
with something given in return.

The Chairman says they bring in loot;
I think indifference breeds disdain,
and if an arsehole in a suit
wants corporate junkets let him drain
his Bolly glass elsewhere I say.

I miss a straight one, there's a sound
of thudded pad below the knee,
but in the boxes round the ground
men still stand with their backs to me
and miss what they might like to see.

David Phillips

At the end of September they give me the shove,
a steep plunge in profits has stricken the Board,
the club is in crisis; the fat has to go,
the Chairman sees me as a starter for slimming:
so sorry, but cricket's a business, old boy –
there's all sorts of angles and all kinds of reasons,
but thanks for the previous twenty-three seasons.

I hadn't enjoyed the brightest of summers:
a hamstring in April was not a good start,
the weather was dreadful in June and July,
some umpiring calls I could hardly believe,
and the captain could never decide where to play me.
It seemed that my batting was devilled by fate –
but most of the time I wasn't that great.

What can I say? I'd a run of cheap scores
but was I washed up as a County player?
Everyone thought so; nobody batted
an eye when I got my cards at the close
and a silver salver with the wrong dates engraved.
So I cleaned out the locker and left my address,
farewell to celebrity, hello DSS.

And then the overseas signing fell through,
our all-rounder was banned for unauthorised drugs,
and the opening bat was poached by TV.
So suddenly there on the mat, a new contract
with a grovelling note from the Chairman's PA.
But do I need all the blood, sweat and pain –
and can I face that dressing-room again?

Simon Rae

A red ball spins, a swallow's flight,
That every generation follows
From rituals first performed in meadows
To epic Tests in packed arenas.

Shadows signal the close of play
Then slip through turnstiles into light:
Another match, another day.
Around the world the red ball spins.

Simon Rae

Sundial tall
the day revolves
around his presence
at the crease.

Fielders run his errands,
bowlers sweat in his service
as shadows point the passing hours
towards his century
and an ocean of applause.

*

Now he's becalmed;
drops anchor,
goes into his shell.

Fathoms down
all he can hear
is the steady hum
of concentration
in his own eardrum.

He's a barnacle
stuck to the hull
of the afternoon.

Spectators,
the vaguest murmur
of a distant rumour
a world away.

They could be keel-hauled
one by one
over the unyielding
contours of his will.

He is there for good.
Won't give an inch.
Nothing matters
but holding on
holding on
holding on.

Simon Rae

A fisherman's patience
hour after hour

*

The blur of a bite
volts from the palm
leap right up the arm

hold up the prize
back-slaps
high fives

*

Hour after hour
a fisherman's patience

Simon Rae

Think twice
and then don't

Zero tolerance
that's me

Step out of line
and I'll have you

sprawled in the dust
as the warning shot

screams past your ear
into the gloves

A sniper's brain
a hair-trigger arm

Take me on?

Make my day

Simon Rae

A whole day's play
shot from above
with some new technique
for tracking the ball
wherever it goes
like a tracer bullet
and relayed like radar
on a giant screen
of air-traffic controllers'
aquarium green,
hour by hour
a firefly frenzy
a cat's cradle of arcs
and then speeded up
like a time-lapse sequence
of the lights of cars
lasering around
Manhattan's grid
or Spaghetti Junction.
What would you have?
A steady pulsing
between wicket and wicket,
an etched penumbra
of dabbed defence,
then far-flung corona
of drives and pulls
while behind the stumps
fairy lights strung
to link up the slips
as the ball makes its way
back to the bowler.

Can you imagine
Lara's five tons
all rolled into one
played through in a minute,
the fire-flies gone crazy,
the cat's-cradle electric;
and then the same thing
for each game of cricket
that's ever been played,
every ball's flight path
every delivery
hit, missed or blocked –
millions and millions
since the game first began,
each one unique
within the pattern
repeated for ever
on ever more screens
filling ever more acres,
till time does its loop
or whatever it does
when it comes to the end
and space contracts
(or is it expands?)
and somewhere for sure
an atom collides
with something or other
which sets the ball rolling
all over again?

Simon Rae

Looks over his shoulder
always. His world is side on,
is angles of attack,
Blitzkreig, ambush

or the long penance
of attrition:
the drawbridge
slammed shut between
the battlements of pads
impenetrable
astride the crease.

It's a batsman's game.

What are the odds –
a bit of stuffed skin
against a great plank of wood?

The pitch is a runway
for jumbos to launch
their flightpaths into the sky
while the bowler stands
earthbound
watching the dot
fast disappearing
over his shoulder

Simon Rae

Brisk as a barber,
the purr of his gossip
running like clippers
up the nape of your neck;

a tic-tac of gestures
at the edge of your vision:
attentively bobbing,
he'll put you at ease.

Relax, let your hair down –
his cosy confessional
is always indulgent;
you're safe in his hands:

errors of judgement,
chance indiscretions,
nothing goes further.
It all stops with him.

A close shave! He whistles;
Saved by a whisker!
sharp as a razor
stropped close to your ear.

Then the lightest of nicks
and he raises his arms
admiring his handiwork
with a casual *How's that?*

Colin Shakespeare

As a player, he would
Have liked to be
First in and last out,
Now he's first out
And last in,
What a turnabout
Is umpiring.

Retiring
From the game left a gap
Like an ache; what he knew best
He knew best what to do,
To give back to the game
What the game had given him:
So to umpiring.

Now he occupies the field of play
All day, has a player's instinct
For the game, the judge's impartiality,
And summers are green again,
He can mix with crowds unrecognised
But knows that in the first-class games
TV can freeze a frame
And show to millions
The human frailties of the game.

XII

CLOSE OF PLAY

(End of Season)

~

There is a mood of reflection as the season comes to an end, nostalgia for what has been, repining for what could have been. As Chris Sparkes reminds us in 'The Plunderer', 'the whole of life's a net'. As it ebbs away – life, that is – cricket's constituents and conclusions make natural metaphors. For so many, the game itself has made life worth living and for them, in the words of Herbert and Eleanor Farjeon, 'memory will play again many and many a day again, the game that's done, the game that's never done . . .'

D. R. A.

Thomas Moult

How shall we live, now that the summer's ended,
And bat and ball (too soon!) are put aside,
And all our cricket deeds and dreams have blended –
The hit for six, the champion bowled for none,
The match we planned to win and never won? . . .
Only in green-winged memory they abide.

How shall we live, who love our loveliest game
With such bright ardour that when stumps are drawn
We talk into the twilight, always the same
Old talk with laughter rounding off each tale –
Laughter of friends across a pint of ale
In the blue shade of the pavilion.

For the last time a batsman's out, the day
Like the drained glass and the dear sundown field
Is empty; what instead of summer's play
Can occupy these darkling months ere spring
Hails Willow once again the crowned king?
How shall we live so life may not be chilled?

Well, what's a crimson hearth for, and the lamp
Of winter nights, and these plump yellow books
That cherish Wisden's soul and bear his stamp –
Time's ever changing, unalterable score-board,
Thick-clustered with a thousand names adored:
Half the game's magic in their very looks!

And when we've learnt those almanacs by heart,
And shared with Nyren . . . Cardus . . . the distant thrill
That cannot fade since they have had their part,
We'll trudge wet streets through fog and mire
And praise our heroes by the club-room fire:
O do not doubt, the game will hold us still!

Herbert and Eleanor Farjeon

Soft, soft the sunset falls upon the pitch,
The game is over and the stumps are drawn,
The willow sleeps in its appointed niche,
The heavy roller waits another dawn –
Bowled is the final ball again,
Hushed is the umpire's call again,
The fielders and the batsmen cease to run –
But memory will play again
Many and many a day again
The game that's done, the game that's never done.

In happy dreams we'll see each ball re-bowled,
And mend the fault that robbed us of some prize,
In dreams we'll hold the catch we failed to hold,
And see our duck-eggs swell to centuries –
In dreams we'll take the field again,
In dreams the willow wield again,
And see the red ball spinning in the sun –
Ah, memory will play again
Many and many a day again
The game that's done, the game that's never done.

VALEDICTION: TO THE CRICKET SEASON

Gavin Ewart

As a boy who has lost a girl so sadly
tears up a photograph or her early letters,
knowing that what has gone is gone for ever,
  a lustful bustful,

the exchange of confidences, the hours of cuddling,
the paraphernalia of what some call sharing,
so we mourn you; televisually prepare for
  their filthy football,

professional fouls and the late late tackle
breakaway forward held back by a jersey,
the winning or losing almost equally nasty.
  The English summer

is never perfect, but you are a feature
as pleasing to us as a day of sunshine,
to spectators at least a calm, straw-hatted
  Edwardian dandy.

Not really a game of physical contact,
the batsman pardons the ungentlemanly bouncer,
the only foul would be leg theory,
  bodyline bowling;

as nostalgic as those old school stories
the plock of bat on ball penetrates outfields,
calming to the mind. Warm pints of bitter
  and county cricket

are long married in our friendly folklore
of white marquees, the spires of cathedrals,
pitch-wandering dogs, boys on the boundary,
  mystified girlfriends,

all of it as much a myth and a ritual
as the fairy stories written by learned
elf-haunted dons who invent a cosmos
  neat but escapist,

where the rules are forever, can never be broken,
and a dragon, as it were, can be l.b.w.
if he puts a foot the wrong side of the mountain.
    You are the bright one

that shines in the memory; as old fashioned writers
say 'she was a maid of some seventeen summers',
we don't reckon age by the passing of winters,
    by happier seasons

we count up the final inescapable total,
remember huge sixes by maverick sloggers –
compensating, like love, for the field that's deserted,
    the padlocked pavilion.

John Snow

Sometime, when I'm older
perchance my mind will range
over days when I was a cricketer
unaware of time's colder ways,
then perhaps in a dusty corner
amongst the jumble of life
I'll recover cobwebbed memories
of past summers and friendly strife.

The vicarage lawn and village green,
church tower shimmering in high summer scene,
honeysuckle days of horses pulling harvest machines,
backyard centuries and boyhood dreams.

Later, in far flung places, meeting idols galore,
F. S., George, Wes and many more,
playing amongst them, as a minnow 'midst whales,
gathering impressions and numerous tales . . .

From clambering Caribbean palm-fringed ovals
with Sobers strong and smooth as Mount Gay rum,
casually batting, rummaging through bowling,
dimming even the tropical sun;
To writhing, wracking Bangladesh birth,
all riots, hardship and blood on dry earth,
matches played on political whim,
Bhutto's anthem, Ayub Khan's funeral hymn;
The schizophrenic Australians, bottles and cans,
Pommy bastard, 'on yer mate, let's shake hands,
Lillie and Thomson, the Chappells and Co.,
white flannelled undertakers happy you should go.

Laced through these winters, back at home,
Count games, facts and figures for *Wisden*'s tome,
and Lord's on historic Test match days,
the 'Egg and Bacon' and traditional ways.

Finally, after it all, in later years,
games played to assuage some of life's tears,
Lord Taverners friendship, more fun and show,
hoping for others things we were lucky to know.

Sometime, when I'm older . . .

Anon

An old man by the fire will dream of all
The little things he did when he was young
He will remember early walks among
The woods and fields, when barley was as tall
As he himself was then. He will recall
A thunderstorm, a poem, a linnet's song
And cricket, too, and he will dream and long
For the sweet singing sound of bat and ball.
He will remember how he held a catch,
Or how he stayed two hours at the crease,
And by his stubborn effort saved the match
When none but he could still defend their wicket
Against such bowlers. Dreaming thus of cricket,
While the fire crackles, he will be at peace.

TEST MATCH

Ian McDonald

When cricket is playing
This place has a special mood.
Naturally, in the town there's little else.
For miles and miles and miles around
Attention centres on the Test Match ground:
Stands besieged from early morning;
Transistored cyclists weave one-handed
Risking crashes every wicket down.
Heroic men are just down there
And the greatest heroes are our own.
Latest score is all that counts.
There is a feel of fair-ground in the air.

It catches on in Mercy Ward,
The excitement rises in the days before.
The desperate centring on self departs.
The subject concentrated on is changed.
The endless question unexpressed:
How much time have I got left?
Now other questions supervene:
The boys in trouble or the boys on top?
Their minds, diverted and released,
Fly out to where the cricket plays.
For a little while at least
Those broken on the wheel of life
Feel at their throats a different knife.

Howard Fergus

(parson, politician, teacher, cricketer)

They say you were a little hasty
your balls were quickies as they hurried
off the wicket as you 'came through'
Teacher George; but you also bowled
the moderate stuff. Thought you'd use them
when playing for the Pearly Gates.
You didn't stay for trifle (there is dessert
in heaven but that's not what I mean)
like waiting for a friend's return
to watch your innings close and celebrate
your trophies, man of the match and the moment.

You were not too nice with protocol
so towels of lamentation
will do your memory wrong. Rather a conch shell
a peal of hands and a standing ovation
as you enter the pavilion to pad up
for a higher order of service.

Death did not intimidate you
but its very quick delivery left us reeling
with a bloody blow. You went for 67,
short of a life-run, but you cheated time
of a prolonged match with sickness
and a slow crossing. We have no substitute
for you. Your team well-knit by blood
and brotherhood must limp along without you
but we will join you on a golder field
not Lord's but at Elysium where there is no appeal.

Michael Laskey

I shall play cricket in heaven
in return for the afternoons
gladly given to the other
pleasure of other's leisure.

I shall walk, without haste, to the wicket
and nod to the angels kitted
in their whites waiting to discern
the kind of batspirit I am.

And one stroke in heaven, one dream
of a cover drive will redeem
every meeting of bat
and ball I've done without.

And I'll bowl too, come on to bowl
leg-breaks with such control
of flight and slight changes of pace
that one over will efface

the faint regret I now feel.
But best of all I shall field:
alert in the heavenly deep,
beyond the boundary of sleep.

Humphrey Clucas

Age could not weary him, nor steal his skill.
He was a working legend – Vulcan, perhaps,
Or Joshua, for whom the sun stood still;
And death was a false stroke, an untimely lapse.

Lie on him lightly, earth that knew his tread;
And smile, and clap him in, illustrious dead.

Chris Sparkes

The whole of life's a net. You
Never make it to the middle.
For Death, the international harvester,
Who's never lost its form, has roped it off.
Everything is pitched against the batsman:

With one arm raised, and Death's round eye
Aiming down the barrel of its shoulder, Death
Has fixed its all-uprooting eye on every innings.
Only God and love can ever be not out.
So, we take our Death-defying guard,

And crooked and hunchbacked at the crease,
We make our timid stance, and hook
The loose deliveries at the mesh. But when
You think you've sorted out its googlies,
Flight, and swerve, and the more you're sure

That you're entrenched, and think you've seen it off,
Death rolls up its sleeves, marks the turf out
With its spiky boots, and Death runs up,
And sprays a yorker through the gate.
For Death, when it's decided, bowls flat out

And never misses. No wonder how we cherish,
For a thin applause, every glance and pull,
There being no refund till the grave
To which the Death-cart rumbles,
With its bell, and pale flags and ensigns

On the ropes and tents of every ground.
Life's already got its finger up.
The donkey drops are few. Yet undeterred
But nerved, we make our crossbat hoiks,
And drives and swipes, outside the on and off,

Till the ghostly umpire calls us out,
And the scorer chronicles your deeds.
And unless the not-out Infinite has heard
Your call, and is ready with the stretcher,
And unless we enter through the narrow wicket

To the Lord's pavilion, then we've had it
Middle-stump – until the second innings, afterwards.
That rattle. The stumps spring back. Another puts the whites on.
Then the gloves. Death's wide gates invite the crowd;
Then it takes collections round the boundary.

CODA

~

At the end as at the beginning, there is but a single poem. We come full circle with William Douglas-Home's paean to cricket. There could be no more fitting benediction.

D. R. A.

William Douglas-Home

Though we sit tired out by the hours of play
When the shadows of evening fall,
We have watched through the dancing heat of the day
The struggle 'twixt bat and ball:
For we love the changes and chances of cricket
Though the bat succeeds or fails.
Though the ball is striking the fatal wicket
Or the white pavilion rails;
For cricket's a glorious game, say we
And cricket will never cease to be.

Yes, cricket will live till the trumpet trumps
For the wide pavilioned sky.
And time, the umpire, lays low the stumps
As his scythe goes sweeping by –
Till the mighty seed of humanity fails
At the light of another birth.
And God stoops down to remove the bails
From the dark deserted earth;
Yes, cricket's a glorious game, say we
And cricket will live in eternity.

ABOUT THE POETS

The great majority of poets in this book are noted below. There are however, a few whose identity has remained hidden. Several of these were contributors to 'Poets Corner' in *The Cricketer*, whose files were destroyed when ceasing publication. Any biographical information on poets who have their compositions in the text and who are not to be found in this section, will be gratefully received by the publishers for inclusion in possible further editions.

DANNIE ABSE (1923–)
Abse was born in Cardiff. At the same time as his first collection of poems was being published, he was studying Medicine in Wales and then at King's College. He qualified as a doctor in 1950, and went on to have a distinguished career specialising in chest complaints. Many of his poems reflect his medical and indeed Jewish background.

JOHN AGARD (1949–)
Playwright, poet, short story and children's writer, Agard was born in British Guiana (now Guyana). He worked for the Guyana *Sunday Chronicle* newspaper as sub-editor and feature writer before moving to England in 1977, where he became a touring lecturer for the Commonwealth Institute, travelling to schools throughout the UK to promote a better understanding of Caribbean culture. In 1993 Agard was appointed Writer in Residence at the South Bank Centre, London, before becoming, in 1997, Poet in Residence at the BBC. His work includes *Man to Pan* (1982), winner of the Casa de las Américas Prize.

C. A. ALINGTON (1872–1955)
Dr. Cyril Argentine Alington was educated at Marlborough (he was in the Cricket XI), and Trinity College, Oxford.

He became headmaster of Shrewsbury (1908–16) and later Eton (1916–33), then Dean of Durham (1933–51). Legend has it that in contemplative mood he would stroll down the nave of Durham Cathedral considering whether or not it would take spin! Alington was an accomplished classicist and a witty writer, especially of light verse.

DRUMMOND ALLISON (1921–1943)
Educated at Bishop's Stortford and Oxford, Allison served as an intelligence officer with the West Surrey Regiment and was killed in action in Italy. He had poems published in *Poetry from Oxford in Wartime*, and posthumously in *The Yellow Knight* (1944).

M. J. C. ALLOM (1906–1995) AND
M. J. L. TURNBULL (1906–1944)
This tribute to Frank Woolley's style from the two famous cricketers, comes from *The Book of the Two Maurices*, a log of the MCC tour to Australasia in 1929–30. As a bowler, Maurice James Carrick Allom played five times for England between 1930 and 1931, his finest hour being on his debut, when he achieved 5 for 38 against New Zealand, including four wickets in five balls. Maurice Joseph Lawson Turnbull appeared nine times for England between 1930 and 1936. Batting in the middle order for most of his Test

career, he averaged just over twenty.

JOHN ARLOTT (1914–1991)
Leslie Thomas John Arlott was many things – a poet, author, wine connoisseur – but above all, the greatest sports commentator there has ever been. Born in Basingstoke, he worked as a diet clerk in Park Prewett Mental Home, and then served in the Southampton Police. It was while still a policeman, during World War Two, that his early poetic works came to the attention of John Betjeman. Betjeman was one of his mentors, and it was he who was the catalyst to Arlott joining the BBC in 1945 as a literary programmes producer.

SIMON ARMITAGE (1963–)
Born in Marsden, near Huddersfield, in 1963, Armitage is one of the leading poets of today. He is also a novelist and playwright. While working as a probation officer in Oldham, Manchester, his first collection, *Zoom!* was published in 1989. Awarded the Lannan Literary Award for Poetry in 1994, he was shortlisted for the T. S. Eliot Prize in 2002; in 1993 he was named *Sunday Times* Young Writer of the Year, and in 1999 was commissioned to write the official Millennium Poem. Away from poetry, Armitage has written a stage play, *Mr Heracles*, updating the Greek myth, and a stereotype-crushing travel guide, *All Points North* (1998). He has also been a stand-in DJ on Radio One, presented poetry shows on Radio Four, and lectured at Iowa, and Manchester Metropolitan University.

ALFRED AUSTIN (1835–1913)
Born in Headingly, Leeds, and educated at Stoneyhurst and London University, for a time Austin was a barrister on the northern circuit, but left the legal world within three years in pursuit of a career in literature. He also tried to enter politics, and practised journalism. As a poet he could write simply in praise of the English and Italian countryside, and could claim to represent popular feeling, but it has been said that he 'lacked the gift of transforming it into true poetry'. Despite this, Austin succeeded Alfred, Lord Tennyson, as Poet Laureate in 1896. He died in Ashford in Kent.

R. WHIELDON BADDELEY (1840–1875)
Richard Whieldon Baddeley was born in Rocester, Staffordshire and later moved to Uttoxeter. BA at Brasenose College, Oxford, 1862. Practised as a solicitor. He has produced novels and volumes of poetry including *Cassandra and Other Poems. The Golden Lute and Other Poems* was a posthumous publication.

SIMON BARNES (1951–)
Barnes, the multi-award-winning chief sportswriter of *The Times*, is one of the few sports journalists to have been offered an honorary doctrate of letters. He has written 15 books, including three novels and several books on wildlife, one of them the best-selling *How To Be A Bad Birdwatcher*. The parodies in this anthology come from his *A la Recherche du Cricket Perdu* of 1989. He plans to write *Le Cricket Retrouve* on his deathbed but is in no hurry to do so.

CLIFFORD BAX (1886–1962)
Bax studied at the Slade and then the Heatherley Art School, before finishing his education in Germany. Chairman of the Incorporated Stage Society in 1929, he abandoned painting to concentrate upon literary and dramatic work. His first play commercially produced was *The Poetasters of Ispahan*. Bax founded the Phoenix Society (1919–26) to revive important Elizabethan and Restoration dramas. For many years he ran a cricket team called 'The Old Broughtonians', for which many famous writers played. He was the brother of Arnold Bax, Master of the King's Musick. He died in Knightsbridge in London.

CHRIS BENDON (1950–)
A self-employed poet, Bendon was born

in Leeds and worked as a courier for an archaeological cruise company going round the Mediterranean before taking a degree in English at the University of Wales, Lampeter. He has continued to live in the Principality, and from 1982 to 1985 he edited *Spectrum* magazine. Describing himself as an 'unorthodox amateur', as a boy Bendon enjoyed impromptu games of cricket with his friends on soccer fields in sight of Leeds University. He has won several prizes, including First Prize (the Hugh MacDiarmid Memorial Trophy) in the Scottish Open.

JOHN BETJEMAN (1906–1984)
Betjeman was the son of a well off London merchant and manufacturer who was of Dutch origin. Educated at Marlborough, and Magdalen, Oxford, he worked for a time as a schoolmaster. During part of World War Two, Betjeman was United Kingdom Press Attaché in Dublin. Early on he made a name for himself as a writer on architecture, and up until the late 1930s was probably better known as an expert on the nineteenth-century Gothic revival than as a poet. Unlike some of his modernist contemporaries, Betjeman was content to document with an eye towards place or buildings as markers of human connection or history. His control of formal verse was masterful, and the sometime comic overtones tempered with more serious consideration of childhood memories and lyric expression only added to its power. He attained huge popularity and was appointed Poet Laureate in 1972 in succession to Cecil Day Lewis.

W. A. B. (1856–1929)
Walter Ambrose Bettesworth was born in Horndean, Hampshire and educated at Ardingly College, where he returned as a schoolmaster. He became a middle order right-hand batsman, slow round arm bowler and good cover field for Sussex, for whom he played twenty-one matches between 1878 and 1883. A noted author and journalist, he was assistant editor of *Cricket* from 1896 to 1905, and cricket editor of *The Field* from 1906 to 1928. He also wrote several books on the game. Bettesworth died in Hampstead.

EDMUND BLUNDEN (1896–1974)
Poet, critic, scholar, and man of letters, Blunden's verses in the traditional mode are known for their rich and knowledgeable expression of rural English life. Educated at Christ's Hospital and Queen's College, Oxford, he joined the Royal Sussex Regiment on the outbreak of World War One. During the war Blunden fought at Ypres, and the Somme, and won the Military Cross for bravery. He taught in Japan throughout most of the 1920s and returned there in the late 1940s, after teaching at Oxford and serving on the staff of the *Times Literary Supplement*. He was Professor of English at Hong Kong University (1953–64) and Professor of Poetry at Oxford (1966–68). He died in Long Melford, Suffolk.

MARTIN BOOTH (1944–2004)
Booth was born in Whitstable, Kent. Booth's family moved to Hong Kong when he was six, and he stayed until 1964. It was there that he learnt Cantonese, and played with local children in the streets of Kowloon, and first encountered 'the Triads in an opium den at the tender age of seven'. He started out scriptwriting for BBC Radio and in his time was an Editor for the BBC and worked in their Comedy Development department; Deputy Controller, responsible for entertainment at the ITV Network Centre, an Executive Producer and a Vice President. He was a freelance writer for more than twenty years, and was shortlisted for the Booker Prize for *The Industry of Souls* in 1998. He also scripted several wildlife documentaries including David Attenborough's *Wildlife on One*.

G. F. Bradby (1863–1947)
Godfrey Fox Bradby was educated at
Rugby School and Balliol College,
Oxford, he was assistant master at Rugby
from 1888 to 1920. His published works
include *The Great Days of Versailles,
About Shakespeare and his Plays,* and
several novels, including *The Lanchester
Tradition.* He also a volume of verse,
Parody and Dust Shot (1931) which
contains three cricket poems including
'The Black Sheep'.

Kamau Brathwaite (1930–)
A major figure in Caribbean literature,
Brathwaite was born in Bridgetown,
Barbados. After attending Harrison
College in Barbados, Brathwaite won a
scholarship to Cambridge where he
read History. Later he earned a PhD
from Sussex University for his study of
'The Development of Creole Society in
Jamaica (1770–1820)'. For seven years,
from 1955 to 1962, Brathwaite taught in
Ghana where African customs,
traditions and literary forms had an
enormous impact on his subsequent
poetic output. He has won the Neustadt
International Prize for Literature in
1994, and is currently a Professor of
Comparative Literature at New York
University.

Jean 'Binta' Breeze (1957–)
Breeze was born in Jamaica. She studied
at the Jamaican School of Drama. A
'dub' poet, she began to write poetry in
the 1970s, performing and recording first
in Kingston, then in London. She has
worked as a director and a scriptwriter
for theatre, television and film, and is
joint-editor of *Critical Quarterly* in
London, where she works as a lecturer
and performance poet. Breeze has
performed her work throughout the
world, touring in the Caribbean, North
America, Europe, South-East Asia, and
Africa.

Gerald Brodribb (1915–1999)
Brodribb worked as a schoolmaster,
St Peter's, Seaford; Canford School and
Hydneye House, where he was
headmaster (1954-70). He was also the
author of several books including *The
English Game* (anthology); *Cricket in
Fiction; Next Man In; Hit for Six; The
Croucher* (biography of G. L. Jessop)
and *Maurice Tate.* One of his main
interests in cricket was researching the
life of Nicholas Wanostrocht (Felix).

Stewart Brown (1951–)
Brown was born in Southampton and is
Reader in African and Caribbean
Literature at the University of
Birmingham, having previously taught
in Jamaica and Nigeria. He has
published several volumes of poetry,
including *Elsewhere: New* and *Selected
Poems* (2000), and critical work on
major Caribbean and African poets.
Most recently he co-edited with Mark
McWatt *The Oxford Book of Caribbean
Poetry* (2004).

Gerald Bullett (1893–1958)
Gerald William Bullett was educated
privately and at Jesus College,
Cambridge. He was a prolific novelist,
short story writer and anthologist. He
worked as a freelance contributor and
reviewer for journals such as the *Times
Literary Supplement* and the *New
Statesman.* Between 1940 and 1943 Bullett
was a talks producer for the BBC
Overseas Service.

John Bunting (1932–)
Bunting was born in Eastbourne, where
he lived until wartime evacuation took
him to the Midlands in 1940. It was in
Nottingham that he learned how to play
cricket, and as an opening batsman played
for his school and several club teams. He
developed an early interest in verse writing
and was much influenced by John
Betjeman. He has worked in farming and
associated industries, and as a market
representative for a local authority.
Bunting now lives in North Yorkshire.

LORD BYRON (1788–1824)
George Gordon Byron, 6th Baron Byron, was among the most famous of the English 'romantic' poets, whose contemporaries included Shelley and Keats. He was a satirist whose poetry, personality, and extraordinary escapades captured the imagination of Europe. *Hours of Idleness* from which 'Cricket at Harrow' comes, was his first published collection of poetry. Byron died of fever and exposure while engaged in the Greek struggle for independence.

O. C. CABOT
O. C. Cabot was the pseudonym of E. N. McCulloch. Under this pen name he was a regular contributor of poems on a wide range of subjects in the well known *Bulletin* magazine. Some of his work is known to have been collected by such distinguished individuals as Australia's first Prime Minister, Sir Alfred Deakin.

LEWIS CARROLL (1832–1898)
Lewis Carroll, pseudonym of Charles Lutwidge Dodgson, logician, mathematician, photographer and novelist, is especially remembered for *Alice's Adventures in Wonderland* (1865) and its sequel, *Through the Looking Glass* (1871), and the poem *The Hunting of the Snark* (1876). Dodgson was the eldest son and third child in a family of seven girls and four boys, whose father was Charles Dodgson, Archdeacon of Richmond Cathedral. Dodgson was educated at Rugby and Christ Church, Oxford, and although ordained, he never entered the church, although he did occasionally preach. Besides his children's stories, Dodgson also produced humorous pamphlets on university affairs, and one of the best of these was *Notes by an Oxford Chiel* (1874), which includes 'The Deserted Parks'.

'CENTURY'
In his introduction to *Cricket Rhymes* (1899), the editor of *The Cricket Press*,

A. J. Fiettkau, thought it fitting to say a few words about the author. ' "Century" is not, as might be thought, the pen name behind which a masculine bard prefers to hide his identity. On the contrary, the personality which it conceals is that of a young lady. One might say, indeed, of a very young lady, for some of these verses, which have been written from time to time during a period of five years, date back to the era of long hair and short frocks.'

GEOFFREY CHAUCER (c. 1342/43–1400)
Son of a vintner, Chaucer was the outstanding English poet before Shakespeare. In 1357 he was in the service of the Countess of Ulster and by 1359 in the army in France with Edward III, who ransomed him after capture at the Seige of Reims. In 1366 Chaucer was appointed a Court official.

In the following years he travelled to Flanders, France and Italy on diplomatic missions and was given the job of comptroller of the customs. His first important poem was 'Book of the Duchesse' (1369 or 70), then followed the love-vision narrative poems 'Hous of Fame'; 'Parlement of Foules'; a prose translation of Boethius' 'Consolation of Philosophy'; and the romance *Troilus and Criseyde*.

In the 1390s, having retained his favour at court, he produced his great poetic masterpiece *Canterbury Tales* which was unfinished. He was buried in Westminster Abbey.

G. K. CHESTERTON (1874–1936)
Known for his exuberant personality and rotund figure, Gilbert Keith Chesterton was the author of verse, essays, novels, and short stories. He was educated at St Paul's School, and later studied art at the Slade School, and literature at University College, London. His preoccupations were social and literary criticism, and theology and religious argument. He converted from Anglicanism to Roman Catholicism in 1922. He is perhaps best

remembered for his 'Father Brown Stories'.

HERBERT E. CLARKE (1852–?)
Herbert Edwin Clarke was born in Scotland. A poet and author, his published works include 'Songs in Exile' (1879) and 'Storm Drift'. He was also a contributor to *Harpers New Monthly Magazine*.

CHARLES CLIVE-PONSONBY-FANE (1941–)
Born in Salisbury, Wiltshire, Charles E. B. Clive-Ponsonby-Fane is the great great grandson of Sir Spencer Ponsonby-Fane, Treasurer of the MCC 1879–1916 and co-founder of the I Zingari Cricket Club. Clive-Ponsonby-Fane is Patron of the Somerset Cricket Museum and Custos Rotulorum (Keeper of the Lists) I Zingari Cricket Club. He is also the author of *We Started a Stately Home, Wild Oats* and *The Totally Utterly Politically Incorrect Book of Verse*.

JEFF CLOVES (1937–)
Born in East Barnet, Hertfordshire, Cloves describes himself as a slow off-break bowler, poet, freelance hack. Apart from school, he has played for only one team in his life: the park side, Oakhill C.C. East Barnet. His champagne moments are getting a hat trick; once holding a full-length catch in the deep worthy of a Test Match; twice taking seven wickets; having an entry in *Wisden* (1984–85) – as a poet; and hearing Jeff Thomson read the poem he had written about him on *Test Match Special*.

HUMPHREY CLUCAS (1941–)
Clucas read English at King's College, Cambridge, where he was a choral scholar. Having taught English in schools for twenty-seven years, while maintaining a separate singing career, he finally gave up teaching on his appointment as a Lay Vicar (member of the choir) of Westminster Abbey, from which he retired in 1999.

W. N. COBBOLD (1863–1922)
Born in Long Melford, Suffolk, Cobbold was Captain of Cricket at Charterhouse in 1892 before going up to Cambridge, where he played lawn tennis for the University. Better known as a footballer, he played for England nine times. In partnership with W. R. Gray, Cobbold was involved in the tenth highest recorded stand for the first wicket in minor cricket. The game was between West Wratting and Fitzwilliam Hostel, at West Wratting in 1891. Cobbold and Gray put on 440. In his previous innings he had made 179, and in the next he made 104.

ALFRED COCHRANE (1865–1948)
Alfred Henry John Cochrane was born in Moka, Mauritius. He was educated at Repton and Oxford, where he won a blue in 1885, 1886, and 1888. His medium-pace left arm bowling won him a place for the Gentlemen at Lord's in 1886, and he later played for Derbyshire. His book of cricket stories *Told in the Pavilion*, 1896, is among several publications. He died in Batheaston, Somerset.

RICHARD CONGREVE (1937–)
Born in London, Congreve spent his early years in North Wales having been evacuated during World War Two. He completed his education in Eastbourne and then worked in the Far East in Malaysia in rubber planting and timber. His only connection with cricket was his maternal grandfather who was a cricketer by the name of Joseph Moore who captained East Molesey in 1920s. He instilled a passion for cricket in Congreve, who says that he was never any good at playing so he writes about it instead. Now retired, Congreve lives in London and publishes his own poetry.

WENDY COPE (1945–)
Born in Erith, Kent, Cope is one of the foremost poets of today. Educated at St Hilda's College, Oxford, and Westminster College of Education,

Oxford, she taught in primary schools in London (1967–81 and 1984–86). Cope became a freelance writer in 1986, and was TV critic for *The Spectator* magazine until 1990. She is a Fellow of the Royal Society of Literature, and lives in Winchester. In 1998 she was the listeners' choice in a BBC Radio 4 poll to succeed Ted Hughes as Poet Laureate.

ALBERT CRAIG (1849–1909)

Craig was born in Huddersfield into a poor working family whose employment was based on the local textile trade. He worked as a postal worker, married and, in his mid-thirties, moved to London to pursue his aptitude for versifying. He took up residence near Kennington Oval and wrote a number (over 200 are known) of rhymes/poems connected with cricket; also many on football. He styled himself as the 'Cricket Rhymester', but was also referred to as the 'Surrey Poet'. Craig produced his works in broadsheet form and sold them at the Oval and elsewhere. He was a born salesman and known for his badinage with the crowd.

SIMON CURTIS (1943–)

Son of a vicar, Curtis was born in Burnley, Lancashire and brought up in Towcester, Northamptonshire. He was educated at St John's, Leatherhead and St Catharine's, Cambridge. He later taught English and French at Manchester University, and was a visiting fellow at the University of New South Wales in 1989. He was editor of the *Thomas Hardy Journal* and chairman of the Hardy Society 2001–02. He is a regular contributor to *The Spectator*, the *London Magazine* and *Critical Quarterly*. Among his prolific *oeuvre* is the book *Twenty Sonnets and a Coda*.

Curtis is a fervent Northamptonshire Cricket supporter and looks back with nostalgia to the days of the Brookes, Oldfield, Livingstone Tribe – 1952 – the County Ground and Tyson, Andrew and Freddie Brown.

DONALD DAVIE (1922–1995)

Born in Barnsley, Davie studied at Barnsley Holgate Grammar School, and St Catharine's College, Cambridge. During the war he served in the Royal Navy, reaching the rank of Sub-Lieutenant. Afterwards he completed his Cambridge degree and embarked on a series of teaching posts and professorships on both sides of the Atlantic. Davie was a scholarly formalist poet, whose work concerned itself with traditions of dissent, various religious subjects, and social loss. In 1973 Davie was elected a Fellow of the Royal Academy of Arts and Sciences, and in 1987 was named as a Fellow of the British Academy. He died in Exeter.

D. A. DE SILVA (1927–?)

Douglas Alan 'Algy' de Silva was a left-hand bowler with the Singha Sports Club in Sri Lanka betweeen 1951 and 1953. He also wrote under the names Alan de Silva and Algy de Silva. A Deputy Director at the World Bank, Washington, he served in the Diplomatic Service of the Sri Lankan Government. He became Sri Lankan Ambassador to Belgium (EEC) and The Netherlands. Cricket, bridge and the English language were consuming interests throughout his life.

C. J. DENNIS (1876–1938)

Dennis was born in Auburn, South Australia. Christened Clarence Michael James, and afterwards given the confirmation name of Stanislaus, he preferred to be known as Den. After formal education in Gladstone, Laura and Adelaide, Dennis had a number of jobs, such as a solicitor's clerk, a staff member on *The Critic* (a weekly Adelaide journal), and as a hotel barman. A number of his early verses were published in *The Critic* in 1898, where he later became editor. 'Den' amusingly described himself as 'tall enough to look a small man straight in the eyes'. He died in Melbourne.

FELIX DENNIS (1947–)
One of the UK's most successful magazine publishing entrepreneurs, Dennis first made front page headlines in the early 1970s as one of the co-editors of *Oz*, the radical underground magazine. He founded his own publishing company in 1973, concentrating initially in the sport, entertainment and motorcycle fields. This led to the acquisition of *Personal Computer World*, Europe's first personal computing magazine and in 1991 he received the Marcus Morris Award, the highest accolade in UK magazine publishing. Following a life-threatening illness in 1999, Dennis developed a compulsion to write poetry. He found himself scribbling verse in the strangest situations, in business meetings, in aeroplanes, at social functions, and even in his sleep. This led to the publication of his first book of poetry, *A Glass Half Full*. In a period of under two years, Dennis wrote over four hundred poems on a wide variety of subjects in mostly informal meter (sonnet, villanelles, sestinas), which paid strict attention to rhyme and reader accessibility.

NEVILLE DENSON (1934–)
Born in Chadderton, Lancashire, Denson was educated at Chadderton Grammar School. He is a retired local authority Chief Executive. He was inspired to write poetry at an early age to fill in the gaps in the school magazine and has written for various publications including *The Cricketer International* and the *Guardian*. His interests include cycling and jazz. Denson says that he was once 'a fell walker, but now sticks to his armchair'.

MORGAN DOCKRELL (1939–)
Born in Dublin of Irish/Canadian parents, Dockrell was educated at St Columba's College and Trinity College, Dublin. His great grandfather, Sir Maurice Dockrell, D.L., was one of the last four Unionist MP's from Southern Ireland to be elected in the 1918 General Election. His first recollection of verse is his father reciting Macaulay's 'Horatius' to him during World War Two, with photos of family members also 'facing fearful odds', serving in the Army and RAF, looking down on him. This early exposure to rhyme and rhythm gave him a lifelong immunity from free verse.

He was first bitten by both the cricket and rhyming bugs at his cricket-mad prep school, Castle Park and became keenly interested in both the literary and statistical sides of cricket. Dockrell describes himself both as 'a craftsman-versifier' and 'a rhyming dinosaur'. His Poetical Pets' Corner includes Dryden, Pope, Byron, Erich Kästner, Heine and Tom Lehrer, all predominantly satirists, satire being his chief literary love. His verses have appeared in *The Cricketer, Cricket Lore* and several anthologies.

Dockrell left his family business, to teach English and German at St Columba's, 'graduating from being metaphorically a minder of tills to being a tiller of minds'. He refers to himself as 'a spoilt merchant'.

HUBERT DOGGART (1925–)
George Hubert Graham Doggart was educated at Winchester and Cambridge. An excellent all-round sportsman, he was awarded his blue for cricket (blue all three years) and for soccer, and also represented the university at squash, rackets, and rugby fives. He captained Cambridge at cricket in 1950, and Sussex in 1954, for whom he played a hundred and fifty-five matches between 1948 and 1961. He joined E. W. Swanton's tour to the West Indies in 1955/56, and also toured East Africa with MCC in 1957/58 and South America 1958/59. He played two Tests for England, and with J. G. Dewes put on 429* for the second wicket when at Cambridge in a match against Essex which constituted a new second wicket record in English first-class cricket. He became President of MCC

1981/82 and Treasurer in 1987. He was a housemaster at Winchester and subsequently headmaster at King's School, Bruton. His publications include *Oxford and Cambridge Cricket* co-authored with George Chesterton.

WILLIAM DOUGLAS-HOME (1912–1992) The third son of the Earl of Home, and younger brother of the former Prime Minister, William Douglas-Home was educated at Eton and then at Oxford. During World War Two he achieved some public prominence as an anti-war activist, which culminated in him being court-martialled for refusal of orders at the Siege of Le Havre. After the war, Douglas-Home had a distinguished career as a writer, particularly of plays and film scripts.

ARTHUR CONAN DOYLE (1859–1930) Best known for his creation of the detective, Sherlock Holmes – one of the most vivid characters in English fiction. Doyle practised medicine – he was an eye specialist – until 1891 after graduating from the University of Edinburgh, and the character of Holmes, who first appeared in *A Study in Scarlet* (1887), partly derives from a teacher at Edinburgh noted for his deductive reasoning. After giving up his medical career, Doyle became a full-time writer. Doyle's prowess as a sportsman is perhaps less well known. A capable amateur boxer, he played football at the highest level and had a golf handicap of ten. He also took a hat trick for MCC against Warwickshire, and once bowled W. G. Grace, which, of course, is the matter of 'Reminiscence of Cricket'. He was knighted in 1902 for his work with a field hospital in Bloemfontein, South Africa, and for other activities concerning the Boer War. In later life he dedicated himself to spiritualism.

RALPH WALDO EMERSON (1803–1882) American lecturer, poet, essayist and philosopher, Emerson was born in Boston, Massachusetts. After studying at Harvard and teaching for a brief time, Emerson entered the ministry. The death of his 19-year-old wife from tuberculosis led to a loss of faith and he resigned his pastorate in 1831.

He visited Europe and began a friendship with Thomas Carlyle which helped formulate Emerson's own philosophy on Transcendentalism, of which he became a leading exponent. On his return to New England, he was known in literary circles as 'The Sage of Concord'.

Emerson wrote a poetic prose, ordering his essays by recurring themes and images. His poetry, though, was often harsh and didactic. He died of pneumonia.

GAVIN EWART (1916–1995) Gavin Buchanan Ewart first published poems at the age of seventeen. Educated at Wellington College and Christ's College, Cambridge, his poetry combines an inventive use of form and technique with an irreverent sense of humour. After serving in the Royal Artillery between 1940 and 1946, he worked for the British Council, and then became an advertising copywriter until 1971. Subsequently he was a full-time freelance writer.

HERBERT FARJEON (1887–1945) and **ELEANOR FARJEON** (1881–1965) Herbert Farjeon was influential in the British theatre world from 1910 until his death. A drama critic, lyricist, librettist, presenter of revues, playwright, theatre manager, and theatre researcher, Farjeon came from a hugely creative family. His father was the novelist Benjamin Leopold Farjeon, his mother Margaret Jefferson, the daughter of the American actor Joseph Jefferson, his brother Joseph Jefferson Farjeon author of detective stories, and his sister Eleanor Farjeon, well known for her children's verse and stories. *Herbert Farjeon's Cricket Bag* has been produced in several editions.

HOWARD FERGUS (1937–)
Professor Howard Fergus holds a
Doctorate degree, and is a graduate of
the Universities of Bristol, Manchester,
and the University of the West Indies. A
former Chief Education Officer of
Montserrat, he was Speaker of the
island's legislative Council for over
twenty-six years and has periodically
deputised as Governor of Montserrat
over the past twenty-five years. Fergus
was knighted by HM the Queen in 2001.

J. S. FLETCHER (1863–1935)
Joseph Smith Fletcher was born in
Halifax. His mother, Rosamond, was
author of *The White Moth*. Fletcher was
a journalist who became leader writer
on several newspapers, including the
Leeds Mercury, *The Star* and the *Daily
Mail*, before he turned to writing
books. After writing history books, he
switched to the genre of crime fiction,
at which he was very successful. His
detective novels gained currency in
Great Britain and the USA, and were
translated into fifteen different
languages. *The Middle Temple Murder*
in 1918 was considered a classic British
mystery. Initially his verse was privately
circulated and attracted the attention
of luminaries such as Thomas Hardy,
Cardinal Newman and Clement
Shorter. Eventually his *Collected Verse
(1881–1931)* was published as such in a
volume in 1932.

NORMAN GALE (1862–1942)
Dubbed the 'cricket poet', Norman
Rowland Gale played cricket with the
Rugby Club. He is remembered for his
publications, notably *Cricket Songs* (1890
and 1894); *More Cricket Songs* (1905); and
Close of Play (1936), with which he
ended:

> Run out:
> To cricket played without a crease,
> Its scorers, umpires and police,
> A harrowing farewell:
> All that I had to sing is sung,

And now, being very far from young,
I have no more to tell.

DANNY GARDNER (1953–)
Gardner was born in Tasmania, but
apart from a three-year sojourn in the
US and the UK in the early 1960s he has
lived in Sydney continuously since 1975.
Apart from his work as a poet he is also a
freelance journalist and novelist.
Gardner has had two books of poetry
released in the UK, *Hope in Progress*
(1980) and *Made in Public* (1982) and has
been published in several magazines and
newspapers and done countless reading
performances in Australia, the UK and
the USA. Since 1990 he has been co-
organiser (now Convenor) of Live Poets'
Society, Sydney's longest-running
performance venue. In 1997 he was
awarded a 'highly commended' citation
in the Northern Territory's Red Earth
Poetry Prize.

In 2001 he shared first prize in a
World Congress of Poets competition
and also received a Centenary of
Federation Medal for services to the
North Sydney community. Live Poets'
Press has published seven books of
poetry and Gardner has co-edited three
of them. The last (*Open Boat – Barbed
Wire Sky*) has currently raised over 7000
dollars for assistance to refugees seeking
asylum.

J. A. GIBNEY (1883–1950)
James Aloysius Gibney was born in
Brisbane, Queensland, the son of Irish
immigrant parents. He was educated at
Enoggera State School and later by the
Christian Brothers at St Joseph's College,
Gregory Terrace. He was employed by
Queensland civil service and served in
the Department of Justice and the Stamp
Duties Office. For many years he held
the position of Chief Inspector of
Totalisators.

He wrote both verse and prose as Jas.
A. Gibney or Ajax and was a regular
contributor to the daily papers in
Brisbane and Sydney, particualrly during

1920–1935. From boyhood, Gibney was a great lover of nature and the bushland surrounding outer Brisbane. As an adolescent he took a great interest in all sports, particularly cricket and horse racing. Gibney married Jean Stark who arrived in Australia from Glasgow at the age of 17. They had 5 children and 22 grandchildren.

The poem 'C. V. Grimmett' was first published in the *Brisbane Daily Mail* in 1925. Gibney produced several other amusing poems on cricket.

WILLIAM SCHWENK GILBERT (1836–1911)

Born in London, Gilbert was universally-known for his collaboration with Sir Arthur Sullivan in fourteen comic operas.

A playwright and humourist, he began his working life in the civil service and then was called to the bar. However, his collections of The Bab Ballads for the magazine *Fun* were the germ of his future dramatic career. From 'Thespis' (1871) to 'The Grand Duke' (1896) covered an extraordinarily prolific and successful quarter of a century in a partnership with Sullivan that was not without strain and tribulation.

Gilbert's gift was to develop a genuinely artful style that burlesqued contemporary behaviour.

He died from a heart attack brought on by rescuing a woman from drowning in the lake on his Grim's Dyke estate at Harrow Weald.

F. A. J. GODFREY (1893–1940)

Frederick Augustine John Godfrey contributed to many magazines with his poems, including *The Cricketer*.

WILLIAM GOLDWIN (1682–1747)

Goldwin was a native of Windsor, and went from Eton to King's College, Cambridge in 1700. A parson and a schoolmaster – he was Master of Bristol Grammar School (1710–17) and Vicar of St Nicholas, Bristol, from then until his death. A proficient Latin scholar, there is no evidence that Goldwin himself played cricket. His poem '*In Certamen Pilae*' is the earliest description that is known of a cricket match. Goldwin's wife expired within half an hour of his death.

ROBERT GRAY (1945–)

Gray was born in Sydney and grew up on the north coast of New South Wales near Coffs Harbour. He worked in a variety of jobs including as an editor, advertising copywriter, buyer for bookshops, and teacher of creative writing.

DENIS GRIFFITHS (1920–)

Born in Mortlake, London, Griffiths attended St Michael's and All Angels School, Paddington, where 'I was taught to read and write'. He lived in Jersey until the outbreak of World War Two, when he joined the Sherwood Foresters. POW of the Japanese in Burma/Siam, he worked on the 'Death Railway'. Subsequently, he worked on a farm at the Verney Estate in Buckinghamshire and married at Buckingham. Griffiths returned to Jersey before becoming Gate and then Head Porter at Jesus College, Cambridge, where he captained the Staff cricket team against High Table. He enjoys exploring different poetic forms. On his retirement as head porter to Jesus College, Cambridge, his poems were gathered together and published privately in book form. The collection attracted such interest that it was later made generally available. In his foreword to the book, the Master of Jesus College, Sir Alan Cottrell, states that this book 'has been produced as a mark of esteem and affection'.

JOHN GROVES (1926–)

Groves was born in London's East End. Following four years in the Grenadier Guards during and after the war, he re-embarked on a career in public service, progressing through various departments of Government, specialising in information services and publicity across a broad spectrum of the media. After a short sabbatical in Hollywood he resumed life with the Post Office, a qualified PR specialist in films and broadcasting. Liaising with virtually every news and documentary programme on the air, from *The Nine O'Clock News* to *News at Ten*, from *Blue Peter* to *Panorama*, he also became in the late sixties and early seventies Government Media Spokesman on National Broadcasting Policy. He was later Deputy Director of Public Relations, Post Office, then eventually a PR consultant and City correspondent. A novelist and anthologist, he produced a controversial book of prose and poetry incorporating wide-ranging environmental philosophy, *Naked Heaven, Naked Earth*, and three collections of verse.

JAMES NORMAN HALL (1887–1951)
Hall was born in Colfax, Iowa. At the outbreak of World War One he joined the British Army, serving in the 9th Battalion Royal Fusiliers, and took part in the Battle of Loos. Hall re-enlisted in 1916 as a member of the Lafayette Flying Corps, which was later incorporated into the United States Air Service. In 1918 Hall was shot down behind the German lines and he spent the last six months of the war in a prison camp. He is perhaps best known as being the co-author of the book *Mutiny on the Bounty* (1932) which has been filmed three times.

GEORGE ROSTREVOR HAMILTON (1888–1967)
Born in London, Hamilton was educated at Exeter College, Oxford. For his services to the Inland Revenue, for which he worked for most of his adult life, he was knighted in 1951. A Fellow and Member of the Council of the Royal Society of Literature, his prolific writing included eighteen volumes of poetry. Together with John Arlott, he produced

a book of topographical verse of England and Wales entitled *Landmarks* in 1943.

BARCLAY HANKIN (1919–)
Hankin was an Engineer (in communications) and spent World War Two in North Africa and Italy in long distance communication. He then became a staff officer at the War Office and was later an adjutant of the Signals Regiment in Germany. Hankin left the army at the end of World War Two and did operational research, using scientific methods to study management problems. The inspiration for 'A New Lawn for Cricket Buffs' was reading about the removal of the original turf from Lord's.

BASIL MacDONALD HASTINGS (1881–1928)
Hastings wrote much cricket verse, which appeared mostly in *The Cricket Star*.

A. P. HERBERT (1890–1971)
Alan Patrick Herbert was a novelist, playwright, poet, politician and author of more than fifty books. He was also a witty lyricist who wrote many highly successful comic operas and musicals. Among these were *La Vie Parisienne, Tantivy Towers, Derby Day, Big Ben* and *Bless the Bride*. As a Member of Parliament for Oxford University, he advocated the abolition of the Entertainments Tax, and the reform of the laws of divorce and obscenity. Herbert was knighted in 1945 and made a Companion of Honour in 1970.

PHILIP HODGINS (1959–1995)
Hodgins was born in Shepparton, Victoria, Australia, where he experienced a country childhood that was to be a major source of his poetic themes. His awards included the Wesley Michael Write Prize for Poetry, the Bicentennial Poetry Book Award, the New South Wales Premier's Award, the Grace Leven Prize, and the National Book Council

Poetry Prize. From his mid-twenties, Hodgins suffered from chronic myeloid leukaemia, and his own illness became a major theme of his poetry which includes *Blood and Bone* (1986) and *Seeing Things* (1995).

THOMAS HOOD (1789–1845)
Son of a bookseller and apprenticed to an engraver, Hood's humanitarian verses served as models for a whole school of social-protest poets. He was widely translated in Germany and Russia. Hood was also a notable writer of comic verse, particularly 'black comedy', and is famous for his punning which has been described as 'almost a reflex action, serving as a defence against painful emotion.'

Later work included the grim ballads 'The Dream of Eugene Aram, the Murderer'; 'The Last Man'; 'The Song of the Shirt'; 'The Lay of the Labourer' and 'The Bridge of Sighs' – they are protests against sweated labour, unemployment and duplicitous sexual behaviour.

Hood suffered throughout his life from rheumatic heart disease. He was born and died in London.

BOB HORNE (1948–)
Horne was born in Halifax, West Yorkshire and educated at Hipperholme Grammar School. He gained an MA in Poetry from Huddersfield University. He was a teacher and, until recently, Head of Drama at Brighouse High School. Having retired Horne is now a secondhand book dealer. In a Bradford League match in 1970, he boldly hooked Roy Gilchrist for six.

A. E. HOUSMAN (1859–1936)
Best remembered as the author of immensely popular *A Shropshire Lad*, Alfred Edward Housman was educated at Bromsgrove School, and St John's College, Oxford. Most of his working life was spent as a classical scholar, which led to appointments as Professor of Latin at University College London, and then later as Kennedy Professor of Latin at Cambridge.

GERALD HOWAT (1928–)
Howat was born in Dennistoun, Glasgow. In a varied career, Howat has been a schoolmaster, visiting university professor, and a journalist with the *Daily Telegraph*. He has written widely in the fields of history, biography and cricket. Since 1989 he has served on the MCC Arts and Library Sub-Committee and the Membership Committee, and is currently Chairman of the MCC's Publishing Working Party. Howat has played cricket for MCC, and for his village club until 2005, being (in 2002) the oldest player in the country in the third round of the National Village Competition.

TED HUGHES (1930–1998)
In 1979, Hughes led a poll as Britain's best poet. In 1984, at age 54, he was appointed Poet Laureate – the youngest to hold this post since Alfred, Lord Tennyson. Hughes won many honours, including a Guggenheim Fellowship (1959), the Somerset Maugham Award (1960), the Premio Internazionale Taormina (1973) and the Queen's Medal for Poetry (1974). Hughes' verse is markedly passionate and deeply engaging. Throughout his prolific career the negotiation between the acceptance and denial of our animal nature appears as a constant theme. Hughes died just thirteen days after receiving the Order of Merit.

THOMAS HUTCHINSON
Hutchinson's *Little Book of Cricket Rhymes* contained seventeen poems on the game that were reproduced in the *Morpeth Herald* in 1923, and printed by J. & J. S. Mackay. The booklets, admiringly dedicated to members of Morpeth Cricket Club, were available to be bought from his Pegswood residence, which was in the town. He was an avid collector of books, particularly in the minor byways of nineteenth-century

poetry and essays. He published two volumes of adult verses at his own expense, as well as a life of Burns. A prolific correspondent, Hutchinson seems to have been tolerated, if not respected, by such contemporaries as Swinburne, Tennyson, the Cowden Clarkes and Coventry Patmore. There is conflicting information as to the year of his death: some sources give 1919.

GEOFFREY JOHNSON (1893–)
Johnson was a schoolmaster and poet with many publications to his name. Much of his work first appeared in *The National Review*.

FRANK KEATING (1937–)
Born in Hereford, Keating was for many years the sports correspondent for the *Guardian* and although officially retired, still continues to write for the newspaper. He was Sports Writer of the Year no less than four times, Sports Features Writer of the Year twice, and in 1980 was Columnist of the Year in the What The Papers Say Awards. Keating has written many books in a humorous and original style.

JOHN KEATS (1795–1821)
Born in London, Keats was a Romantic lyric poet whose expression was marked by vivid imagery and great sensuous appeal. The vehicle for his philosophy was classical legend.

His father who leased a livery stable died in a riding accident and after the break-up of his mother's second marriage, he lived with his widowed grandmother at Edmonton, Middlesex. Went to school at Enfield where he formed a lasting friendship with the headmaster's son, Charles Cowden Clarke. After he left school, Keats was apprenticed to the family doctor and later became a dresser at Guy's Hospital, London. Poetry, however, became his passion and he forsook his medical career.

At the age of 25, he died of tuberculosis while seeking a cure in Rome.

PAUL KEENS-DOUGLAS (1942–)
Keens-Douglas was born in San Juan, Trinidad and spent his early childhood in Grenada. He gained a degree in Sociology from Sir George Williams University (Concordia), Canada and has done two years of post-graduate work at the Univeristy of the West Indies, Jamaica. Active in drama from an early age, Keens-Douglas has a wide and varied background in theatre and the creative arts. A self-published author, he has to his credit nine volumes of written work, fifteen albums, seven CDs and three videos. A founding member of the Association of Black Storytellers of America, he has won many international awards. Keens-Douglas works within the advertising industry, and makes regular tours of the Caribbean territories and metropolitan countries, lecturing, performing and doing workshops. He is now a much sought after motivational speaker and presenter.

CHRISTOPHER KEMP (1936–)
Son of a Methodist minister, Kemp was born in Corbridge, Northumberland. Attended Kingswood School, Bath, and then read English at Magdalen College, Oxford. National Service in the RAF in Egypt and Aden, before teaching at Mexborough Grammar School and lecturing at Worcester College of Higher Education. All-rounder in club cricket, he has played for Kingswood Cuckoos and The Stragglers. Described as 'a man of great erudition and a vivid raconteur', Kemp's interests range from the Church, War in the Vendée, and Renaissance literature to the history of cricket and allotment gardening. Kemp is delighted to be able to say that he saw Hammond bat.

COULSON KERNAHAN (1858–1943)
Kernahan was a man of letters of wide range. The Triolet included in the text dates back to c. 1900.

OMAR KHAYYAM OF NISHÁPÚR
(1048–1122)
Ghiyath al-Din Abu'l-Fath Umar ibn
Ibrahim Al-Nisaburi al-Khayyami:
brilliant poet, methematician,
astronomer, and philosopher of Persia,
who, like the nineteenth-century
translator of his Rubáiyát, Edward
Fitzgerald, was 'a lounger in the flowery
ways of life' – in other words, somewhat
of a rustic hermit. Rubáiyát is the
plural of the Persian for 'a poem of four
lines'. Fitzgerald's version distills the
spirit rather than extracting the specific
meaning of the original. The colourful,
exotic and remote imagery lent itself to
the Victorian interest in the Oriental. Its
Epicurean motifs linked it with the
Aesthetic Movement and its romantic
melancholy presaged the pessimism of
such literary figures as Hardy.

ROGER KNIGHT (1946–)
Roger David Verdon Knight was born in
Streatham, London and educated at
Dulwich College and St Catharine's,
Cambridge. Knight was a top order left-
hand batsman, and a right-arm medium
pace bowler, who played for Cambridge
University, Surrey, Gloucestershire,
Sussex and MCC. He toured with
Derrick Robins' side to South Africa in
1972/73; MCC to West Africa, 1975/76;
MCC to East Africa, 1973/74; and played
in the Bengal Golden Jubilee match in
India, 1980/81. He worked as a
schoolmaster at Eastbourne College; his
alma mater – Dulwich College, and
became housemaster at Cranleigh and
later headmaster at Worksop College.
He much enjoys the writings of Ogden
Nash. Roger Knight was MCC's
Secretary & Chief Executive from 1994
until 2006.

R. D. LANCASTER (1892–1963)
Lancaster had three poems published in
London Magazine, volume no. 12, March
1962.

ANDREW LANG (1844–1912)
Son of the Sheriff-Clerk of Selkirkshire,
born in Selkirk and educated at the
Edinburgh Academy and at the
Universities of St Andrews and Glasgow,
he also won a Snell Exhibition to Balliol
College, Oxford. Fellow of Merton
College, researching anthropology there
until 1874, he was associated with the
Rondelier group of poets.
   One of the most popular journalists of
his day, writing for the Daily News and
Longman's Magazine, Lang is mostly
remembered for his translations of
classical literature. His vast output
included books of poetry, biographies,
histories, and children's stories. He was
also known as an essayist and belletrist.

MICHAEL LASKEY (1944–)
Born in Litchfield, Laskey read English at
Cambridge and taught in Spain and
England for ten years. He lives in
Suffolk, where he works as a freelance
writer, leading workshops with adult
groups and in schools. An associate tutor
at University of East Anglia, he also
teaches regularly for the Arvon
Foundation and the Open College of the
Arts. Well known as a champion of
contemporary poetry, he founded the
International Aldeburgh Poetry Festival
in 1989, and directed it through its first
decade; and he has co-edited the poetry
magazine Smith's Knoll since 1991.
   He has published two pamphlets –
Cloves of Garlic (1988) and In the Fruit
Cage (1997) – and two full collections,
both Poetry Book Society
Recommendations: Thinking of
Happiness (1991) and The Tightrope
Wedding (1999) which was also
shortlisted for the T. S. Eliot Memorial
Prize.

ROBIN LINDSAY (1928–)
Lindsay was educated at Clifton College
(where he was top scholar and captained
the cricket XI) and Trinity Hall,
Cambridge. After National Service in
Nigeria (4th Battalion, Nigeria

Regiment) he taught at Sherborne Preparatory School (owned by his parents) and subsequently became headmaster and proprietor.

He has written or spoken on many subjects including the teaching of Mathematics and other educational matters, appreciations in verse on Jonty Rhodes, Sir Donald Bradman, Archbishop Robert Runcie, and has contributed to the obituary columns of national newspapers. In August 1963 he took part in the Great March on Washington (wearing his MCC tie) and heard Martin Luther King make his 'I have a dream speech'. A year later he became one of the first to water ski across the Sea of Galilee; and a little more than ten years after that he lectured in Fort Worth/Dallas on the writings of Helen Waddell. Since retirement in 1998, Lindsay spends much time travelling and writing.

OSCAR LLOYD (1890–1956)
Lloyd was born in Newark, Nottinghamshire. His father was a Unitarian non-conformist minister. Following an early move to Gloucestershire, he attended Crypt Grammar School and proceeded to University College, Bangor, North Wales. During World War One, Lloyd was a Major in the Cheshire Regiment, and suffered severe injuries during the Battle of the Somme, which resulted in hospitalisation for two years. His health suffered as a result for the rest of his life. After the war he resumed teaching at Barry High School, and in 1925 accepted a post in Malaysia to work in the Colonial Education Service. Around this time he had already begun composing verse, some of which was accepted by *The Spectator* and *Punch*. He taught at the D. R. Gent School at Eastbourne and later at Chichester High School, where he was English and History master. Before World War Two he was on the staff at Huddersfield College. Having been injured in a motor accident the

previous year, Lloyd died in Bognor in 1956.

SAMUEL J. LOOKER
Anthologist and editor of the The Beechwood Books series including *The Chase, Float and Fly, On The Green* and *Cricket: a Little Book for Lovers of the Game*. The series of little volumes sought to present 'a selection from the best books on sport past and present'. In the 1920s Samuel Joseph Looker lived at South Green, Billericay, Essex.

E. V. LUCAS (1868–1938)
A scion of a Quaker family, Edward Verrall Lucas was born in Eltham, Kent. An early move to Brighton cemented his feeling as a native of Sussex. In the first twenty years of his life Lucas attended at least nine schools in various parts of the country, and he stated that disputes between his father and the headmasters over the fees were the main causes of his leaving most of them. At the age of sixteen, Lucas was apprenticed to a Brighton bookseller, which gave him a taste for literary exploration. Subsequently he became a journalist with the *Sussex Daily News*, and then, after an uncle had provided the necessary funds, he was able to attend lectures at University College, London. Continuing as a freelance journalist, he joined the staff of *The Globe*, and later that of *The Academy*, and eventually became assistant editor of *Punch* and Chairman of the publishing company, Methuen. Lucas was a hugely prolific writer, but found it very difficult to keep cricket out of his pages. The best of his cricket verses were included in *Willow and Leather* (1898). Lucas played cricket for the village team of Crockham Hill in Kent, and also for J. M. Barrie's famous team of authors and artistes, the 'Allahakbarries'. Barrie's unflattering description of Lucas's ability, 'E. V. Lucas had, unfortunately, a style' has never been forgotten. He received

honorary doctorates from St Andrew's and Oxford Universities, and having refused a knighthood, became a Companion of Honour, which he felt would be less conspicuous.

ALEXIS LYKIARD (1940–)
Born in Greece, Lykiard came to England when he was young, and won a scholarship to King's College, Cambridge, where he edited *Granta*. In the 1960s he became, briefly, a best-selling novelist. But, despite many commissions in prose and translation, poetry is his first love.

E. A. MARKHAM (1939–)
Edward Archibald Markham was born in Montserrat and arrived in Britain in 1956. He studied at the University of Wales and taught in London in the 1960s. Since then he has worked and lived in the Caribbean, France and Papua New Guinea, where he worked as a media co-ordinator from 1983 to 1985. Markham has worked in the theatre, published two collection of short stories, and has also written a number of 'Lambchops' and 'Philpott' books under the pseudonym Paul St Vincent. He is now a Professor of Creative Writing at Sheffield Hallam University.

G. D. MARTINEAU (1897–1976)
Born in Lahore, Gerard Durani Martineau was descended from the first King of Afghanistan. An Anglo-Indian child, he attended school in England at St Aldate's at Sevenoaks, and then at Charterhouse, before entering the Royal Military College, Sandhurst. During the First World War he served with the Royal Sussex Regiment in France and Germany. Never more than a moderate club cricketer, he was for a short period a Holiday Coach at the Aubrey Faulkner School of Cricket. A great lover of the game, he wrote copiously on it, and was the author of a number of books including *Bat, Ball, Wicket and All*, a history of cricket implements, and *The*

Valiant Stumper, a history of wicket-keeping, and also, appropriately, *A History of the Royal Sussex Regiment*. Martineau combined writing with work as a schoolmaster. He died in Lyme Regis, Dorset.

JOHN MASEFIELD (1878–1967)
Born in Ledbury in Herefordshire, Masefield was educated at King's School, Warwick. Apprenticed in the Merchant Navy, Masefield at seventeen deserted ship in New York, and for a short time, without any financial support, lived on the streets writing poetry. After obtaining work in a carpet factory, Masefield contracted both tuberculosis and malaria, which led to a reconciliation with his family and a return to England. He worked for a time as a journalist for the *Manchester Guardian,* and settled in London. During World War One Masefield served in the Red Cross in France, and on a hospital ship at Gallipoli. He was appointed Poet Laureate in 1930, and held the position until his death near Abingdon in Berkshire in 1967, a tenure unmatched by anyone except Tennyson.

ROGER MCGOUGH (1937–)
McGough is one of Britain's best known poetry voices. Following the success of his collection, *The Mersey Sound* (with Brian Patten and the late Adrian Henri), he has been captivating children and adults alike with his unique blend of heart and wit for four decades. Much travelled and translated, he is now an international ambassador for poetry, and was awarded an OBE for his work in 1997. In 2001 he was honoured with the Freedom of the City of Liverpool.

IAN MCDONALD (1933–)
Born in St Augustine, Trinidad, in 1933, McDonald was educated at Queen's Royal College, Port-of-Spain, and Cambridge University where he received an Honorary Degree in History. Since 1955 he has lived in Guyana and worked

in the sugar industry, where he is now CEO of the Sugar Association of the Caribbean. A tennis champion, he captained Cambridge and Guyana and subsequently the West Indies in the Davis Cup and played at Wimbledon. In 1984 he became editor of the literary magazine Kyk-Over-Al. He received the Golden Arrow of Achievement honour from the Guyana Government in 1987. He was awarded the Guyana Prize for Literature in 1992 for the collection of poems Essequibo and awarded an Honorary Doctorate of Letters in 1997 from the University of the West Indies. He is a Fellow of the Royal Society of Literature. During 1991/92 he was editorial consultant to the West Indian Commission under the Chairmanship of Sir Shirdath Ramphal. He has published short stories, four poetry collections, and his play *The Tramping Man* is often staged. His award-winning novel *The Humming Bird Tree* was first published in 1969; in 1992 it was made into a BBC film. He has written a weekly column for Stabroek News, often on cricket, since 1986.

R. J. O. MEYER (1905–1991)
Rollo John Oliver Meyer was born at Clophill, Bedfordshire. Educated at Haileybury and Cambridge University, he was an attacking middle order right-hand batsman and a right-arm slow medium bowler. At Cambridge he achieved a blue in all three years (1924–26) and also played for Western India (1930/31 to 1934/35); Bombay (1926/27); Somerset (1936–49 in 65 matches) and Europeans (1926/27 to 1934/35). Besides captaining Somerset in 1947, Meyer also played for Hertfordshire (1923–29) and Bedfordshire (1949–50). He is most famous as the founder and headmaster of Millfield School, where he promoted what for the time were pioneering and revolutionary ideas on education and sporting excellence.

A. A. MILNE (1882–1956)

Humorist, minor playwright, and originator of the immensely popular stories of Christopher Robin and his toy bear, Winnie-the-Pooh. Alan Alexander Milne attended Westminster School, London, and Trinity College, Cambridge, where he edited *Granta* for a year. At the age of twenty-four he became assistant editor of *Punch*, remaining there until the outbreak of World War One. As well as the two sets of stories about the adventures of Christopher Robin's toy animals, as told in *Winnie the Pooh* and *The House at Pooh Corner*, he adapted another children's classic, *The Wind in the Willows* by Kenneth Grahame for the stage as *Toad of Toad Hall*.

EGBERT MOORE (1904–1980)
Egbert Moore, also known as 'Lord Beginner', was born in Trinidad. He established himself as one of the pioneers of calypso, and became a popular singer in that genre, making many recordings. Moore's first well known calypso celebrated a West Indian victory over England in 1935; his most famous one though, recalls the feat of Ramadhin and Valentine in the memorable victory by the West Indies over England at Lord's in 1950.

JULIA A. MOORE (1847–1920)
Julia A. Moore was also known as 'The Sweet Singer of Michigan'. For almost two years in the late 1870s, this gifted writer of hilarious bad verse had a national following. Mark Twain based a character on her in *Huckleberry Finn*. Ogden Nash was said to have been not only a fan but a disciple. It was reported that Moore had inspired Ogden to become a great bad poet rather than a bad good poet!

R. W. MOORE (1906–1953)
Ralph Westwood Moore was educated at Wolverhampton Grammar School and Christ Church, Oxford. He was appointed as headmaster of Harrow in

1942, after periods teaching at Rossall School, Shrewsbury School and Bristol Grammar School.

DOM MORAES (1938–2004)
An international journalist and poet, Dominic Frank Moraes was born in Bombay, India and educated at the University of Bombay and at Oxford. As a child, Moraes travelled through Sri Lanka, Australia, New Zealand, and the whole of South-East Asia, and precociously began to write poetry at the age of twelve. His first book of poems, *The Beginning*, won the Hawthornden Prize in 1957 when he was only nineteen, the youngest poet ever so to do.

ANDREW MOTION (1952–)
Named Ted Hughes' successor as Poet Laureate in 1999, Motion was born in London and educated at University College, Oxford, where he won the Newdigate Prize for Poetry. Subsequently a lecturer in English at the University of Hull, where he met Philip Larkin; his exhaustive biography of Larkin won the Whitbread Award in 1994. Motion served periods as Editor at Chatto & Windus, *Poetry Review,* and Faber & Faber. In 1995, he became Professor of Creative Writing at the University of East Anglia and later Professor of Creative Writing at Royal Holloway College, University of London.

THOMAS MOULT (1895–1974)
Moult was educated at Marple, Manchester. Also known as Sidney Southgate, he was the founder of *Voices,* a monthly magazine primarily for young writers. Poet, novelist and critic, he wrote music criticism for the *Manchester Guardian,* theatre criticism for *The Athenaeum*, and book criticism for various English periodicals. He was also President of the Poetry Society. As far as cricket was concerned he was the editor of Jack Hobbs's *Playing for England* (1931); the miscellany *Bat and Ball*, and *New Book of Cricket* (1935), and author of

Willow Pattern – a Book of Cricket Poems (1936).

GEORGE MURRAY (1830–1911)
Murray was the son of *The Times* Foreign Editor, James Murray. Murray showed early literary distinction as a pupil of Greig's School, Walthamstow House, Essex. Soon after he entered King's College, London, and won the Chaplain's two prizes for English Verse and another for Latin Verse. At Hertford College, Oxford, he was equally successful, winning the Lusby Scholarship and the Lucy Exhibition. A critically acclaimed venture at Oxford was 'The Oxford Ars Poetica; or How to Write a Newdigate'. From 1859 to 1892 Murray was the senior classical master at the High School in Montreal.

HENRY NEWBOLT (1862–1938)
Newbolt was born in Bilston in Staffordshire and studied at Clifton School, and Corpus Christi, Oxford, he then became a barrister. Despite the jingoistic nature of his verses, Newbolt was a reserved scholar with a deep knowledge of Latin, Greek and English poetry. He was knighted in 1915 and awarded Companion of Honour in 1922.

NORMAN NICHOLSON (1914–1987)
Nicholson was a writer in the widest sense. He wrote novels, plays, short stories, topographies, criticism, essays, reviews and biographies, but he was first and foremost a poet. His writing was largely inspired by the landscape and industry of his native Millom, a small mining town in south-west Cumbria. Apart from two years in Hampshire whilst recovering from tuberculosis, he resided in the house where he was born for his whole life – 14 St George's Terrace, Millom. Nicholson was awarded the Queen's Gold Medal for Poetry in 1977 and the OBE in 1981.

WILLIAM PERFECT (1737–1809)
Dr. William Perfect of West Malling,

Kent, published a collection of verses called *A Bavin of Bays*. An amateur poet, Dr. Perfect was the local surgeon, apothecary, man midwife, and physician. He played his part in the history of psychiatric treatment, hence his being known by the rather uncomplimentary title of 'The Mad Doctor'.

ARTHUR PETERSON (1851–1932)
Born in Germantown, Philadelphia, Peterson was the son of Henry Peterson, a Philadelphia/Pennsylvania verse-writer and editor/publisher of *The Saturday Evening Post Magazine* and Sarah Webb Peterson, who was also a poet and editor of *The Lady's Friend*.

Peterson became an assistant editor of *The Saturday Evening Post* and editor of *Peterson's Journal* after which he entered the navy as assistant paymaster in 1877. Subsequently, he reached the equivalent rank of Lieutenant. He is the author of *Songs of New Sweden and other Poems* (1888); *Collected Poems* (1916).

DANIEL PETTIWARD (1913–1996)
Born in Polzeath, Cornwall, Pettiward grew up at Finborough Hall, Great Finborough, Suffolk. His father was Arthur Conan Doyle's secretary until inheriting this stately home, where servants would use a tunnel under the grounds rather than risk ruining the view by trailing across the gardens. Pettiward went to Eton, then University College Oxford.

Pettiward provided amusing verses about the English rural scene, which originally appeared in *Punch*. Eventually they were published in book form, *Truly Rural*, by Dent in 1939, illustrated with cartoons by his brother Roger under the pseudonym Paul Crum. Pettiward's poem 'Our Pond' is often used in anthologies. He wrote another book called *Money for Jam*. Pettiward also was a professional actor and president of the Studio Theatre, Salisbury, where latterly he lived.

His ashes are at Salisbury Cathedral but were the subject of some debate – he had said he wished for his ashes to be scattered in several places, but this was not allowed – so close friends set fire to his curtains and scattered those ashes at Finborough Hall instead.

DAVID PHILLIPS (1947–)
Phillips was born in Leicester, and raised in South-East London. In the 1970s, he moved to Margate, Kent, to teach music in a local primary school. At this time began to write and had poems published in the *New Statesman* and *The Spectator*, as well as having several plays broadcast on the radio. Phillips says that he did not dread retiring from teaching and now, 'When I'm not watching England caning Bangladesh on the telly, I occasionally write CD liner notes and articles for specialist classical music magazines.'

HUBERT PHILLIPS (1891–1964)
Phillips was educated at Sexey's School, Bruton, and Merton, Oxford, where he got a first class degree in history before serving in the army throughout World War One. He was Secretary to the Liberal Industrial Inquiry and Secretary and Advisor to the Liberal Parliamentary Party. He was well known by several pseudonyms, including 'Caliban' of the *New Statesman,* and 'Dogberry' of the *News Chronicle*, on whose magazine page 'An Englishman's Crease' first appeared. Phillips was a compiler of thousands of puzzles, as well as crosswords, quizzes and cyphers and appeared on many radio programmes. He was an accomplished player of contract bridge, captaining England in 1937 and 1938.

FRED PONSONBY (1815–1895)
Born in Marylebone, London, Frederick George Brabazon Ponsonby, 6th Earl of Bessborough, played cricket for Cambridge University, MCC, Surrey, and then finally for the Cambridge Town Club. His privately printed booklet, *Cricket Rhymes,* was dedicated to Harrow Colts. He died in Mayfair and was buried at Pilltown.

JOHN PUGH (1904–1964)
Born Radford, Coventry, Warwickshire, John Geoffrey Pugh was educated at Rugby School. He was an attacking middle order right-hand batsman who played nine matches for Warwickshire between 1922-27. He was the uncle of C. T. M. Pugh who captained Gloucestershire in 1961 and 1962.

Pugh played as an amateur and worked for the family ATCO company (responsible for evenly-striped lawns) founded by his father, Charles H. Pugh. John Pugh's 'Lines based upon John Keats' poem "The Mermaid Tavern"' were read during the annual dinner of the Buccaneers Cricket Club on 8 January, 1947, at Lord's. The Buccaneers had been formed in 1930. The annual dinner was held at various prestigious locations including the Connaught Rooms, Carr's, Simpson's, and on one occasion each – Lord's, the Oval and the House of Commons. Pugh produced a limited edition (250 copies) of *Poems* (1962).

JAY QUILL (1896–1974)
Jay Quill was the pseudonym of Hilarie (Hilaire) Jansz, the editor of the *Ceylon Observer*.

SIMON RAE (1952–)
Rae is a poet, playwright, biographer, librettist and broadcaster. After postgraduate work at Oxford, he turned freelance in 1985, writing for a number of publications, including the *Times Literary Supplement*, *New Statesman* and the *Guardian*. Rae later wrote and presented programmes for both Radio 3 and Radio 4, including the series *Poetry Please!* with which he was associated for five years. In 1999 Rae won the National Poetry Competition. His book, *W.G. Grace: A Life* was joint winner of the Cricket Society's Literary Award in 1998. In 1999-2000 he was Poet in Residence at Warwickshire County Cricket Club, and since then has taught at Warwick University and Oxford Brookes University as a Fellow of the Royal

Literary Fund. He runs a small theatre company, Top Edge Productions and lists his spare-time pre-occupations as cricket, and waiting to be paid.

R. W. RAPER (1842–1915)
Born in Llanwenarth, Monmouthshire, Robert William Raper was educated at Cheltenham College and then at Balliol College, Oxford. From 1866 he lectured in classics at Trinity College, Oxford. Ineligible to stand as he had not taken Holy Orders, Raper was generally accepted as the great President Oxford never had. An accomplished cricketer, rider, skater, keen on athletics and known as a genial host, Raper was a sympathetic, wise and witty counsellor. A passionate conservationist (serving on the National Trust) he helped save the Malvern Hills from being quarried. He is buried in Colwall.

TIM RICE (1944–)
Timothy Miles Bindon Rice was born in Amersham, Buckinghamshire and educated at Lancing College and, briefly, at the Sorbonne, Paris. His teenage passions were pop music, cricket and statistics, and his early ambition was to become a pop singer. Having met Andrew Lloyd Webber in 1965, he became part of one of the most legendary partnerships in the history of musical theatre, with *Joseph and the Amazing Technicolour Dreamcoat*, *Jesus Christ Superstar* and *Evita*. Taking a separate path, Rice wrote the lyrics for such shows as *Blondel*, *Chess* and *The Lion King*. In 1994 he was knighted for services to sport and the arts. In 1973 Rice formed his own cricket side, Heartaches C. C., and has produced the Heartaches Cricketers' Almanack annually ever since. He has served two terms as President of the Lord Taverners and in 2002/03 was President of MCC.

R.C. ROBERTSON-GLASGOW
(1901–1965)
Raymond Charles Robertson-Glasgow

was born in Edinburgh. He played cricket for Oxford University, gaining a blue for four consecutive years. He went on to be a fast-medium bowler, as an amateur with Somerset (1920–37) but 1923 was his only full season, when he took over a hundred wickets. Later Robertson-Glasgow was a schoolmaster at Hindhead and a cricket correspondent on *The Morning Post*. He appeared occasionally on BBC Radio and was Chairman of the Cricket Writers Club. Adopting the nom de plume 'Crusoe', he was a skilful author of a number of books on the game which are laced with shrewd observation and wry humour. He died by his own hand at his home in Pangbourne, Berkshire.

NEIL ROLLINSON (1960–)
Rollinson was born in Yorkshire and published his first collection of poetry, *A Spillage of Mercury,* in 1996.

IRVING ROSENWATER (1932–2006)
Born in London, Rosenwater, (in his own words), enjoyed a wide and varied career as writer, essayist, collector, editor, bibliographer, researcher, reviewer, obituarist, spectator, crossword-compiler, publisher's reader, indexer, speaker (and minor player). He was a former assistant editor of *The Cricketer*; founder and first editor of the Cricket Society *Journal*; former contributor to *Wisden* (including Records section); television scorer-statistician for BBC (nine seasons) and for Channel Nine, Australia (ten seasons and one season in UK); organiser and manager of W. S. Surridge's side in Bermuda, 1961. He was made a full member of MCC in 1966 (life member, 1997) and was the author of numerous books and limited editions.

Rosenwater had verses published in publications, too numerous to recall, in England and Australia, including *The Cricketer, Sussex Life, The Twelfth Man, The Journal of the Cricket Society*, down to his own specially produced Christmas cards. He wrote approaching 100 cricket poems (mostly destroyed!) and on occasions wrote personal letters to friends in verse (and likewise letters to the press). Versification is a family trait: his late mother wrote only one poem (non-cricket), a World War Two poem which was promptly published; his elder sister has written frequent verse, and has been a runner-up in a nation-wide National Poetry Day competition. His mother's great-aunt was a professional playwright.

ALAN ROSS (1922–2001)
Ross was an author, publisher, journalist and editor of *The London Magazine*. Born in Calcutta, India, he was educated at Haileybury, and St John's College, Oxford. He served in the Royal Navy (1942–47), seeing service in the Arctic and North Sea. Ross acted as an interpreter to British Naval Commander-in-Chief, Germany in 1946. He served on the British Council (1947–50), on the staff of the *Observer* (1950–71) and toured Australia, South Africa and West Indies as a correspondent (1954–68). Among his many publications are *The Cricketer's Companion* and an autobiography *Blindfold Games* (1986).

KRISHNA A. SAMAROO (1954–)
Samaroo was born in Belmont, Trinidad and Tobago. He holds a BA and an MA in English from the University of the West Indies, and had his first collection of poetry published in 1985. Samaroo has been a teacher of English language and literature since 1979 at the Pleasantfield Senior Comprehensive School, San Fernando, USA.

SIEGFRIED SASSOON (1886–1967)
Born into a wealthy Jewish family in Kent, Sassoon initially lived the pastoral life of a young squire: foxhunting, playing cricket, golfing, and writing romantic verses, much influenced by the Pre-Raphaelites. He had been educated at Clare College,

Cambridge. Following his brother's death from his wounds, Sassoon embarked on almost suicidal acts of bravery on the battlefield during World War One, and in 1916 was awarded the Military Cross for rescuing an injured soldier whilst under heavy fire. Subsequently he became one of the most famous war poets, although attracting criticism for what was felt at the time to be flagrant anti-patriotism. Sassoon's later poems returned to his pre-war affinity with the Pre-Raphaelites.

R. C. SCRIVEN (1907–1985)
Born in Sheffield. In spite of being handicapped by deafness and blindness for much of his life, Ronald Charles Scriven made a name for himself both as a poet, radio playwright, author and journalist.

OWEN SEAMAN (1861–1936)
Educated at Shrewsbury and Clare College, Cambridge, Seaman was best known as editor of *Punch* magazine from 1906 to 1932. After being knighted in 1914 he was made a Baronet in 1933. He was also a member of J. M. Barrie's famous 'Allahakbarries' side.

ROBERT WILLIAM SERVICE (1874–1958)
Born in Preston, Lancashire, England of Scottish parents, Service spent his childhood in Scotland and attended the University of Glasgow. His vagabond career took him throughout the world, with a diversity of jobs from cook to clerk, from hobo to correspondent. He emigrated to Canada in 1894 and took a job with the Canadian Bank of Commerce and was stationed for eight years in Whitehorse, Yukon. It was while in the Yukon that he published his first book of poems that was to make him famous – *Songs of a Sourdough*.

He was a correspondent for the *Toronto Star* during the Balkan Wars of 1912–13 and an ambulance driver and correspondent in France during World War One. He settled in France after the war and married a French girl, Germaine Bougeoin. He returned to Canada during World War Two, living in Hollywood and Vancouver. He wrote two autobiographical words, *Ploughman of the Moon* (1945) and *Harper of Heaven* (1948) and six novels, including *The Trail of '98* (1912) about the Klondike Gold Rush, and more than forty-five verse collections containing over 1,000 poems. Several of his novels and his poem 'McGrew' were adapted to movies. He made a brief appearance with Marlene Dietrich in the 1942 film *The Spoilers*. After World War Two he returned to France, where he lived for the remainder of his life mainly in Brittany and on the French Riviera.

COLIN SHAKESPEARE (1929–)
Born in Pontefract, West Yorkshire, Shakespeare was educated at Hemsworth Grammar School. He qualified as a pharmacist from Bradford Technical College in 1950. He has published five books of poetry, the last one being 22 *Cricket Poems*. The poetic impulse for Shakespeare began when the West Indies beat England at Lord's in 1950. 'Lord Beginner's Victory Calypso made a big impression on me, and being passionate about poetry and cricket, I vowed to try to write the occasional cricket poem when commanded by the muse to do so', says Shakespeare. 'I tried and found it difficult. You have to spend a lot of time in the poetry nets. I spent years heeding the advice of W. B. Yeats to poets to... learn your trade/Sing whatever is well made.'

WILLIAM SHAKESPEARE, OR SHAKSPERE (1564–1616)
The Bard or Swan of Avon was baptised at Stratford-upon-Avon. Poet, dramatist and actor, often called the English national poet, he is generally considered to be the greatest dramatist of all time. His plays have been performed more

often and in more countries than those of any other playwright.

Shakespeare attended the local grammar school in Stratford and had three children by his wife, Anne Hathaway – a daughter Susanna and twins Hamnet and Judith. By 1584, he had emerged as a rising playwright in London. He enjoyed fame and relative prosperity as a member of the Lord Chamberlain's Company (afterwards known as the King's Men), which was the leading theatrical group in the capital. It is thought that Shakespeare spent some time in Lancashire, before retiring to his birthplace and living the life of a country gentleman. He was buried in the parish church at Stratford.

Rikki Shields (1942–)
Born on a riverboat in Katherine, near Darwin, Northern Territory, Australia, Sheilds was raised at a Catholic Mission, Garden Point, Melville Island. He left school at the age of twelve and for many years 'walked the land'. He worked as a docker and spent time in Tasmania where Shields claims the ancient Aboriginal rock *Mantrika* put him in touch with his ancestors and released his spiritual energies. He began making a photographic record of Aboriginal culture and his work was later exhibited. He left Australia in 1985 to travel to Germany and Denmark before finally settling in Britain.

In his broadcasting career, Shields has made a film entitled *A Journey of the Spirit*; participated in *BBC's Heart of the Matter* and has been a storyteller for BBC Radio. Shields has also been investigating Aboriginal human remains in British museums and campaigns for their return to traditional burial grounds in Australia.

John Snow (1941–)
John Augustine Snow was born in Worcestershire. Making his debut for Sussex in 1961 as a fast bowler, he played

260 matches for the County before retiring in 1977. Snow first played for England in 1965, and went on to take 200 Test wickets in 49 appearances. His most successful series was probably in Australia in 1970/71, when Ray Illingworth's side brought back the Ashes. Snow finished with thirty-one wickets in five games. He has produced two collections of poetry.

Sandy Solomon (1948–)
As an American who discovered cricket as an adult, Solomon realised she had passed an invisible boundary when she heard herself explaining the game to casual (English) observers of a Trojan Wanderers game at Jesus College, Cambridge and heard herself saying the word 'exciting'. Her prize-winning book, *Pears, Lake, Sun*, is published in the UK by Peterloo Poets; individual poems have appeared in such magazines as *The New Yorker, The New Republic, The Times Literary Supplement* and *Poetry Review* (the Thrumpton poem first appeared in *The Southern Review*). Solomon was the Bunting Fellow in Poetry and later Visiting Poet at Harvard University's Radcliffe Institute from 1997–99. She lives part of the year in Princeton, NJ, where her English husband is Professor of History, and part of the year in London. They are usually in Britain in time for the first Test Match each year.

Chris Sparkes (1951–)
Sparkes was born in Birmingham. The son of an English and drama teacher who had unsuccessful trials for Worcestershire and Warwickshire, Sparkes played club cricket at League level. After completing an MA in Creative Writing at Chichester University, he lectured there on the same subject and in linguistics. He now teaches at a further education college and runs writing groups. He was inspired to write poetry by reading the works of John Keats. He has published poetry and read his work widely. He is

co-author of forthcoming books on grammar and creative writing.

DR. SATYENDRA SRIVASTAVA (1935–)
Srivastava was born in Azamgarh, Uttar Pradesh, India, but has lived in the UK for nearly four decades. After gaining a Ph.D. from London University he has taught at Toronto University (Canada), London University, City University in London, and lectured for twenty-five years at the Faculty of Oriental Studies, Cambridge University. A well known Hindi writer, he has received several international prizes and honours, and has published many collections of poetry, plays, travelogues, and academic articles in both Hindi and English.

RICHARD STILGOE (1943–)
Born in Surrey and educated at Clare College, Cambridge where he was a member of Footlights. Stilgoe made his name on the BBC television programme *Nationwide*, followed by Esther Rantzen's *That's Life!* His ability to write a song from almost any source material and at prodigious speed is part of his cabaret act, and he has also written lyrics for musicals such as *Cats* and *Starlight Express*. He has written and presented numerous BBC radio programmes, including *Hamburger Weekend*, *Used Notes*, and *Who Pays the Piper*. He founded the Orpheus Trust in 1998, offering performing arts experiences to young people with various disabilities, and the Stilgoe Family Concerts series at the Royal Festival Hall, which feature young performers and regular commissions of new music. Stilgoe has two Tony nominations, three Monte Carlo Prizes, a Prix Italia, an honorary doctrate and an OBE to his name. He is well-known for his love of architecture (both building and demolishing it), having designed and built his own house more than once, and cricket, he was appointed President of Surrey County Cricket Club in 2005.

JOHN STUART (1944–)
Born at Lismore on the far north coast of New South Wales, Australia, John Keith Stuart has spent most of his life as an English teacher in this area, known as the Rainbow Region. He is the author of secondary textbooks, and has written extensively on English literature. Stuart did not start to write poetry until his retirement from teaching five years ago. Travelling widely to over twenty-five mainly under-developed countries, he found himself commenting in poetic form on a number of important social issues. He is currently living in Byron Bay, where *In That We Share* was written during the wet months of the winter of 1999. *Sharing In That* was written that same year and completed the following summer. This was later followed by *The Spirit Ascending*, to complete the series.

K. V. V. SUBRAHMANYAM
The appelation 'Eminent Poet' was conferred on the author by the International Poetry Association at Madras, India. Subrahmanyam has written poetry over three decades, and much of his work deals with the burning problems of the day – social, political, academic – as well as with the lighter side of life.

H. P.-T. (1866–1931)
Born in Woolwich, Percy Francis Thomas produced a number of thoroughly researched and learned booklets on cricket including a series of six pamphlets concerning the game prior to the days of Hambledon embraced under the title *Old English Cricket*. A man of much humour, he wrote under abbreviations and nicknames, 'H. P.-T.', 'Pott' and 'Hippo-Pott-Thomas'. He died in Cricklewood, London.

ALFRED, LORD TENNYSON (1809–1892)
Often regarded as the chief representative of the Victorian age in poetry, Tennyson was raised to the

peerage in 1884. The fourth of twelve children, Tennyson was born into an old Lincolnshire family and the influence of the surrounding countryside is evident in much of his poetry. He was educated at Louth Grammar School, and Trinity College, Cambridge, where in 1829 he won the Chancellor's Gold Medal with a poem called 'Timbuktu'. Tennyson's position as the national poet was confirmed by his 'Ode on the Death of Wellington' (1852) and the famous poem on the charge of the Light Brigade at Balaclava, which was published in 1855. Tennyson was appointed Poet Laureate in 1850.

DYLAN MARLAIS THOMAS (1914–1953)
Born in Swansea, Glamorgan, Wales, Thomas probably had more myths spun around him than any other poet since Byron. 'Bewilder 'em', he once said, and some of his verse certainly did, because of its dense imagery. But his writing which is known for its comic exuberance, rhapsodic lilt and pathos, is ultimately comprehensible.

Thomas attended the grammar school where his father taught English, and he edited and wrote for the school magazine. His first book *18 Poems*, appeared in 1934 and announced a strikingly new and individual voice. The overt emotion in his work, its primitivism and the allied importance of sound and rhythm, create a powerful effect. In his compositions he was much concerned with the subjects of sex and death, sin and redemption, creation and decay.

Attempts to finance his liking for alcohol with work for the BBC and as a film scriptwriter were not sufficiently remunerative and he took to borrowing from friends. *Portrait of the Artist as a Young Dog* (1940), *Deaths and Entrances* (1946), and *Under Milk Wood* (1954) are signature works. The latter, which evokes the lives of the inhabitants of a small Welsh town, is richly imaginative in language, totally realistic in characterisation and fertile in comic

invention.

A reckless drinking bout and the incompetence of a local doctor led to his early death in New York City.

FRANCIS THOMPSON (1859–1907)
Thompson was born in Preston in Lancashire. A poet of the Aesthetic movement, whose most famous poem 'The Hound of Heaven', describes the pursuit of the human soul by God. Educated in the Roman Catholic faith at Ushaw College, Thompson studied medicine in Manchester but failed his degree three times. Moving to London, poverty reduced him to selling matches and newspapers, and ill health drove him to opium. During this period a Leicester Square bootmaker accosted him in the street, gave him light employment in his shop, and – what proved a more enduring gift – old account books for scribbling paper. A painful recovery was helped by a growing literary sense, and Thompson wrote the 'Ode to the Setting Sun' and the 'Essay on Shelley'. Despite his mystical prepossessions, Thompson found recreation in watching cricket matches and wrote odds and ends of verse in honour of the game. He died in St John's Wood, London.

JOHN TRIPP (1927–1986)
A farrier's son, Tripp was born in Bargoed and raised in Cardiff. He was a journalist in London for several years before returning to Wales in 1969 to work as a freelance writer and poet. Much concerned with the condition of modern Wales and the historical roots of that condition, he observed critically what he saw as empty materialism. Although his poetry has a colloquial style, the idiom remains resolutely contemporary.

TONY TURNER (933–)
An amateur cricketer and MCC Life Member, Turner is now retired from a career as an industrial chemist.

Chairman of Metroland Poets, Amersham, he has over 150 poems published in a variety of poetry magazines, books, papers and anthologies. He has five published collections of his own poems, the most recent being *How Far Away Australia Is* (2005). The collections included fifteen cricket poems.

G. H. VALLINS (1898–1956)
George Henry Vallins was a schoolmaster, lecturer and frequent parodist for *Punch*. Two of his most notable works were a parody of Browning, and an excellent Chaucerian cricket parody. He was the author of *The Making and Meaning of Words* (1949), *Good English* (1951), *Better English* (1955), *The Pattern of English* (1957) and *The Wesleys and the English Language* (1957). He was formerly senior English master at Selhurst Grammar School in Croydon before becoming principal of a teacher training college in Liverpool. Vallins was an Assistant Examiner in English for the University of London School Certificate Exam board.

ARNOLD WALL (C. 1870–1966)
Arnold Wall, CBE, MA, graduated from Cambridge in the early 1890s and later became Professor of English Literature at the University of Canterbury, New Zealand. He wrote *The Queen's English* in 1959. His poem 'A Time Will Come' was written during the 1914–18 war. During the *Bodyline* series, Douglas Jardine was said to have praised it effusively. The poem originally appeared in Wall's volume of verse *The Pioneers*.

PAUL WESTON (1949–)
The son of a violinist in the London Philharmonic Orchestra, Weston studied trumpet at the Royal Academy of Music (1966–70) before embarking on a teaching career in the London Borough of Newham. A lifelong member of the Salvation Army, Weston commenced writing comic verse to enliven dreary

coach journeys when the Brighton Congress Hall Band were playing away. His first cricket poems were published in *Cricket World* and thereafter in *Wisden Cricket Monthly* and *The Cricketer*.

WALT WHITMAN (1819–1892)
Born in Long Island, New York, Walter Whitman was a journalist, essayist and poet whose publication in 1855 of *Leaves of Grass*, which asserted the beauty of the human body, physical health and sexuality, created a sensation. Almost overnight he was seen as a revolutionary figure in United States literature. The work was revised and enlarged many times over a period of thirty-seven years.

At various stages of his life Whitman was a journeyman printer, teacher, newspaper editor, storekeeper, builder and real estate speculator. The quality of Whitman's poetry was equally variable and could move from oratorical excitement to a mood that was quietly plangent to efforts that were verging on the maudlin.

Whitman's avowed aim was to eschew normal aesthetic form and inaugurate language in a way that was natural, strong, and yet sentimental. Many found his championing of the common man too idealistic, and yet he came to be considered one of the great American poets of his time, because he had sufficient universality and seemingly never compromised his own personality.

He was partly paralysed by a stroke in 1873. Whitman died in Camden, New Jersey.

JOHN WHITWORTH (1945–)
Born in Nasik (Bombay Province) India, Whitworth was educated at the Royal High School, Edinburgh, and then Merton College, Oxford. For fifteen years he taught at the Centre of Economic and Political Studies in London, 'the sort of thing people do when they haven't got a respectable job', he remarks. Subsequently, he has been a teacher of Creative Writing at Kent

University. Whitworth first started writing verse in his twenties, and has had published a Faber *Anthology of Blue Verse*, a book of poems for children, and seven other books for adults. A keen cricketer, he equates himself to 'Boycott without the talent, but more hair. Like him, I also used to keep my collar up.'

HUGO WILLIAMS (1942–)

Hugo Mordaunt Williams was born in Windsor. An Old Etonian from a theatrical dynasty (father and brother both actors – Hugh Williams and Simon Williams respectively), Hugo Williams eschewed the family business and became a poet. His verse reflects his passion for pop music, his obsession with the past, and the vicissitudes of an unconventional marriage. At various times he has worked as an assistant editor for *London Magazine*, a television critic for *New Statesman*, a theatre critic for *Sunday Correspondent*, *TLS* columnist, and film critic for *Harpers & Queen*. His poetry publications include *Symptoms of Loss* (1965), *Sugar Daddy* (1970), *Dock Leaves* (1994), *Billy's Rain* (1999), and in 2002, *Collected Poems*. Williams was awarded the T.S. Eliot Prize (1999).

DES WILSON (1941–)

Wilson was born in Oamaru, New Zealand. He began his career as a cricket writer in New Zealand and since has become well-known as founder Director of 'Shelter' and for his involvement in the voluntary sector. He was a member of the Management Board of ECB and former Senior Vice-Chairman of 'Sport England'.

G. F. WILSON (1869–1935)

Educated at St Paul's, where he played for the XI, George Francis Wilson wrote several volumes of verse including *Cricket Poems* (1905).

P. G. WODEHOUSE (1881–1975)

Comic novelist, short-story writer, lyricist, and playwright, best known as the creator of Jeeves, the 'supreme' gentleman's gentleman. Pelham 'Plum' Grenville Wodehouse was the author of more than ninety books, collaborated in more than thirty plays and musical comedies, and wrote more than twenty film scripts. Educated at Dulwich College, he worked in a bank, before taking on a job as a humorist columnist on the *London Globe* in 1902. He also wrote freelance for many other publications. During World War Two, Wodehouse was interned in Germany. Later he settled in the United States, becoming a citizen in 1955. He delighted in vivid, far fetched imagery and in slang, with plots that are complicated and carefully planned, and based in the social atmosphere of the late Edwardian era. He was knighted in 1975.

J. HICKORY WOOD (1859–1913)

Born in Manchester, Jay (/John J.) Hickory Wood was originally an insurance clerk before establishing a niche as a creator of scripts for pantomimes. Writer of soliloquies, monologues, and lyricist of many music hall songs, including, in collaboration with Herman Finck, the popular 'You Could Hardly Notice At All'. Wood wrote many of the Drury Lane pantomimes in which the comedian Dan Leno starred, and, in fact, it was Wood who became Leno's first biographer in 1905. In 1911, no fewer than thirty-three of Wood's pantomimes were being presented by professional companies throughout the English-speaking world.

WILLIAM WORDSWORTH (1770–1850)

Wordsworth was a major English Romantic poet and Poet Laureate of England (1843–50). His *Lyrical Ballads* (1798), written with Samuel Taylor Coleridge, helped launch the English Romantic movement. Having spent what he called 'fair seed-time' for his soul, as a boarder at a grammar school at Hawkshead near Windermere, Westmorland, Wordsworth went to St John's College, Cambridge on a scholarship. Early in his life he spent time on the Continent, mainly France, where youthful republican sympathies were nurtured. His most creatively productive periods were spent in the West Country and in the Lake District.

RALPH WOTHERSPOON (1897–1979)

George Ralph Howard Wotherspoon was a writer, journalist and playwright who was born in 1897. He went to Eastbourne College, then Merton College, Oxford. Having served in the Queen's Royal West Surreys (TF) and Royal Garrison Artillery during World War One, he was one of the original Cherwell Editorial Staff 1920-21. Went on to become Private Secretary to the dramatist Henry Arthur Jones, then Colonel Hon. Angus McDonnell, and was later Secretary of the Primrose League.

He contributed extensively in prose and verse to leading journals, magazines, and newspapers and first wrote for *Punch* in 1924. Wotherspoon co-wrote books, such as *Ready-Made Rhymes* in 1927, *The Underground Fairy Tale* in 1932, and *Some Sports And Pastimes Of The English* in 1937, which was a humorous look at many sports including rugby, cricket, darts, bridge and foxhunting. He also wrote many sketches for BBC West Regional, and a one-act play, *All In The Day's Work*. His light verse appeared in *The Cricketer*.

He saw active duty in World War Two, until invalided out in 1941, when he worked for the Ministry of Supply for a year, then the Ministry of Information, before becoming Regional Press Officer for London and the South East. He was a Director of Smith and Whiley Theatrical Productions, which was the first backer of *The Mousetrap* in 1951.

KIT WRIGHT (1944–)

Poet and children's author, Wright was educated at Oxford University. He lectured in Canada, before working as Education Officer at the Poetry Society in London (1970–75) and was Fellow Commoner in the Creative Arts at Cambridge University (1977–79). He was awarded an Arts Council Writers' Award in 1985. His books of poetry include *The Bear Looked Over the Mountain* (1977), which won the Geoffrey Faber Memorial Prize and the Alice Hunt Bartlett Award, and *Short Afternoons* (1989), which won the Hawthornden Prize and was joint winner of the Heinemann Award. His poetry is collected in *Hoping It Might Be So: Poems, 1974-2000* (2000).

MALCOLM WROE (1945–)

Born in Nuneaton, Wroe went to St Peter's, York, and the Royal College of Music where he studied singing. He worked as an actor and stage manager on West End productions and provincial tours, before retiring to run a youth club and play-reading group. Being invited to read poetry in public encouraged Wroe to start writing himself. He has written a one-act play, *The Student and the Cockatoo* and five books of poems. *Smoke Secrets* is the third of a trilogy, *Sparks and Embers* and *Kindling* being the others.

PETER YOUNG (C. 1930–1995)

Born in Kyneton, Victoria, fifty miles from Melbourne, as a young man, he learned the trade of a cooper, but then moved to the Northern Territory and joined the police force, rising to the rank of Superintendent. Always a keen sportsman, he became an ardent member of the (now defunct) Wave Hill Cricket Club. Later in his life he was crippled by illness. Young enjoyed a mordant wit. On returning from the theatre after the loss of his leg in an operation, his urgent message to his wife was: 'Please tell Frank Dalton (the club's skipper) to get someone else padded up.'

INDEX OF FIRST LINES

INDEX OF POETS

ACKNOWLEDGEMENTS

I would like to express my gratitude for the help and support of MCC throughout the preparation of this anthology, particularly Colin Maynard, Stephen Green, Adam Chadwick, Glenys Williams, Ken Daldry and the late Michael Wolton. Anne and Michael Chapman also gave great practical assistance, notably in applying for copyright clearances and this task has been carried on with considerable charm and aplomb by Emma Larsson.

At Methuen, MD Peter Tummons and in-house editors Emma Musgrave and Nina Woods have never let a smile disappear from their faces even when the route was rocky. And with this edition Nina in particular has been quietly punctilious, incorporating recent information and much necessary minutiae into the text. I am in her debt.

Initial research of much-needed biographical information by Kevin Locke and then Amanda Ripley was complemented latterly by startling finds in unexpected places due to the unassuming detective qualities and expertise of Camilla Lake. To all three grateful thanks are a very poor reward.

In Australia John Cordner has been tireless in finding out the details of cricket poems written by fellow-countrymen. In this he has been helped by Danny Gardner. In New York, Jane Magidson likewise went to a great deal of trouble searching for data on nineteenth-century American poets who had composed on cricket. Again, much gratitude in triplicate. To Claire Westall, at Warwick University, not so far away up the M40, similar gratitude for her comprehensive help with the Caribbean contribution.

I should also like to thank Thiwiye Banafu Khumalo for the courage and devotion with which she undertook the challenge of translating 'Ngxatshoke Qonce!' which is written in Xhosa A (in effect the equivalent of mediaeval English): understandably this took a great deal of time.

And special thanks too to Sir Tim Rice for allowing the first public printing of his libretto to 'Cricket (Hearts and Wickets)', and to David Phillips, Richard Stilgoe, Simon Rae, Irving Rosenwater and Colin Shakespeare for being so readily receptive and enthusiastically supportive of the plunder of a goodly quantity of their work.

Many people took the trouble to send in poems they had composed on cricket in the hope of inclusion in these pages. I am grateful to them too, if only because of their interest in this project, and it is no reflection on the quality of their work that for one reason or another such inspiration was sadly put aside when it came to the final choice. In the last few months of compilation, the book continued to expand, but it proved impossible to pick all the baubles from the display boxes. Perhaps a more apt analogy would have come from my old Chemistry master who, while waggling his jowls in an alarming fashion would say, 'A saturated solution is one which cannot take any more stuff!' So again, may I thank all of those who fall into this category.

The standard phrase at the end of most acknowledgement sections in books is to apologise for any inadvertent omissions of copyright clearance. May I say that, in my experience, never has the tracing of copyright holders been more assiduously pursued than for this anthology, and in the very few cases where contact has not been made, it is not for want of trying. If you are one of those very few, please do get in touch with the publishers – if only for inclusion in any future editions.

Finally, a huge thank you to the following, all who have helped in a variety of ways. Space precludes the separate paragraph which each deserves:

John Agard; Pat Arlott; Richard Anthony Baker; Simon Barnes; Chris Bendon; Martin Booth; Robert Brooke; John Bunting; Kamau Brathwaite; Stewart Brown; Charles Clive-Ponsonby-Fane; Jeff Cloves; Humphrey Clucas; Richard Congreve; Wendy Cope; Guy Curry; Felix Dennis; Morgan Dockrell; Howard Fergus; Danny Gardner; Yvonne Gavan; John Goulstone; Denis Griffiths; John Groves; Barclay Hankin; Bob Horne; Ann James; Dr. Gerald Howat; Frank Keating; Paul Keens-Douglas; Christopher Kemp; Roger Knight; Tony Laughton; Robin Lindsay; Kevin Locke; Giles Lyon; Dr. Ian MacDonald; E.A. Markham; Roger McGough; John McKenzie; Geoffrey Moore; Andrew Motion; Bryony Newhouse; André Odendaal; Roger Packham; Said El-Ghaithy at The Centre for African Language Learning; Staff at the Poetry Library at the Royal Festival Hall; Staff at the Poetry Society; Mick Felton and Seren Books staff; Janet Reeve; Jonathan Rice; Christopher Saunders; Dominique Shead; Rikki Shields; John Snow; Sandy Solomon; Chris Sparkes; Staff at Cultural Section of Sri Lankan Embassy; Dr. Satyendra Srivastava; Paul Weston; John Whitworth; Des Wilson; Kit Wright; Malcolm Wroe.

The editors and publisher wish to thank the copyright holders for permission to reproduce the poems in this book.

A

A.B.C.: 'Ngxatshoke Qonce!' *Imvo Zabantsundu* newspaper, 1884.

Dannie Abse: 'Cricket Ball'. Reprinted by permission of The Peters Fraser and Dunlop Group Limited on behalf of: Dannie Abse. Copyright © Dannie Abse 1996; *New and Collected Poems*, Hutchinson 1996.

A gallant Anglo-Indian poet: 'Ladies' Cricket, as you know' (*Calcutta Times*) 1895; *The Lady Cricketers' Gazette*, 1899.

John Agard: 'Prospero Caliban Cricket' (*New Writing* 2), ed. Malcolm Bradbury and Andrew Motion, Minerva, 1993.

C.A. Alington: 'Lord's', 1928 (*Eton Faces, Old and Young*), John Murray, 1933.

Drummond Allison: 'Verity' (*The Poetry of Cricket*), Frewin, Macmillan, 1964.

M.J.C. Allom & M.J.L. Turnbull: 'Frank Woolley' (*The Book of the Two Maurices*.

M.C.C. Team in Australasia 1929–1930), London, 1930.

Anon: 'An Old Man Dreams' (The Poetry of Cricket), Frewin, Macmillian, 1964.

Anon: 'Bodyline – is it cricket?' (Brisbane Courier), 23 January 1933.

Anon: 'Futuristic Cricket' (The Poetry of Cricket), Frewin, Macmillan, 1964.

Anon: 'I am going to Bombay' (India's Hambledon Men), Bombay, Tyeby Press, 1986.

Anon: 'Loyal Cricketers' (Bell's Life in London), 18 September 1831.

Anon: 'On the Second Cricket Match between Mitcham and Coulsdon' (Cricket), 1905.

Anon: 'Something about a Cricket Match', by a Sunburian, MCC Library.

Anon: 'Stumps Drawn' (The Poetry of Cricket), Frewin, Macmillan, 1964.

Anon: 'The Duck's Egg', Amersham Hall, 1886.

Anon: 'The Game of Cricket' (The Gentleman's Magazine, Volume XXVI), 1756.

Anon: 'The Great Cricket Match, Brewers v Publicans' (Ironbark's Southerly Busters, Sydney 1878), John Sands, 1878.

Anon: 'The Kentish Cricketer' c. 1815 (Scores and Annals of the West Kent Cricket Club, 1812–1896), Philip Norman, Eyre and Spottiswoode, 1897.

Anon: 'Victor Trumper' (The Cornstalk); (Bat and Pad) ed. Derriman and Mullins, Choice Books, 2001.

John Arlott: 'Cricket at Swansea', 'To John Berry Hobbs on his seventieth birthday, 16th December 1952' (The Albemarle Book of Modern Verse for Schools, Vol 1), Murray, 1962; 'On a great batsman' (The English Game: an anthology), ed. Brodribb, Hollis and Carter, 1948; 'Stonewall Jack', MS; BBC Radio Sounds of Summer, 1979. All poems copyright © the estate of the late John Arlott.

Simon Armitage: 'The Catch 1992', (Kid), Faber & Faber Ltd., 1992. Copyright © Simon Armitage 1992.

Alfred Austin: 'Song', Macmillan and Co. Ltd.

B

W.A.B.: 'Clement' (Cricket: A Weekly Record of the Game), c. 1900

R. Whieldon Baddeley: 'The Stout Cricketer' (Cassandra, and other poems), Bell & Daldy, 1869.

Simon Barnes, 'Prologue to the Teste Matche Tales', 'Part Two of The Tragedy of Prince Botham' (A La Recherche du Cricket Perdu), Macmillan, 1989.

Clifford Bax: 'Cricket Days' (Farewell my Muse), Lovat Dickson, 1932.

Chris Bendon: 'Cricket' (Staple Issue 16); (Perspective Lessons, Virtual Lines…), Rockingham Press, 1992.

John Betjeman: 'Cricket Master' (Collected Poems), John Murray, 1966.

Edmund Blunden: 'Couplets for Learners as They Might Have Been Written in 1753', A. D. Peters; 'Hammond (England) a Cricketer' (After the bombing, and other short poems), Macmillan, 1949.

Martin Booth: 'Four' (The Cricketer), May 2000.

G.F. Bradby: 'The Black Sheep' (Parody and dust-shot), Oxford University Press, 1931.

Kamau Brathwaite: 'Rites' (The Arrivants), Oxford University Press, 1973.

Jean 'Binta' Breeze: 'On Cricket, Sex and Housework' (The Cricketer), November 1991; (The Arrival of Brighteye and other poems), Bloodaxe, 2000.

Gerald Brodribb: 'The Colt', 'House Match' (The Bay and other new poems), The Mountjoy Press, Ltd. Ed. 30 copies, 1953.

Allan Brodrick: 'The Match' (The History of South African Cricket), ed. M. W. Luckin, W. E. Hortor & Co. Ltd., Johannesburg, 1915.

Stewart Brown: 'Cricket at Kano' (Elsewhere: New and Selected Poems), Peepal Tree Press, Leeds, 1999.

Gerald Bullett: 'Poem' (News from the Village), Cambridge University Press, 1952.

John Bunting: 'Can We Know Too Much?' (At Riverside), D.C.C.C., 2002.

Lord Byron: 'Cricket at Harrow' (Hours of Idleness, a series of poems, original and translated), S. & J. Ridge, Newark, 1807.

C

O.C. Cabot: 'At Poverty Point' (*The Bulletin*), Melbourne, 1912; (*Six and Out*) Lansdowne Press, Melbourne.

Lewis Carroll: 'The Deserted Parks' (*Notes by an Oxford Chiel*), Parker, Oxford, 1865–1874.

'Century': 'Choosing an All-England XI in 1896', 'Ode to Gunn in 1896' (*Cricket Rhymes*), Cricket Press, 1899.

G.K. Chesterton: 'Lines on a Cricket Match', A. P. Watt Ltd. on behalf of the Royal Literary Fund.

Herbert E. Clarke: 'Cricket'.

Charles Clive-Ponsonby-Fane: 'Caught Out' (*Wild Oats*), 1993.

Jeff Cloves: 'A Floral tribute to the fast and furious Australian bowler, Dennis Lillee' (*Line and Length*), The Dodman Press, 1984; 'Double or Quits' MS, 2004; 'Picture of a Yorkshire Gritter in Six Overs'.

Humphrey Clucas: 'History', 'Old Pro' (*Unfashionable Songs*), Hippopotamus Press, 1991. Reprinted by the permission of the author.

W.N. Cobbold: 'A Village Cricket Match (A True Story)'.

Alfred Cochrane: 'Arma Virumque', 'Luck of the Toss', 'Monotonous Ballade of Ill-Success' (*Best Poems of* 1927), ed.Thomas Moult, Jonathan Cape, 1928.

Richard Congreve: 'Test Match Cricketers', Elm Park Books.

Wendy Cope: 'The Cricketing Versions' (*Serious Concerns*), Faber & Faber Ltd., 1992.

Albert Craig: 'Dedicated to the Famous Notts and Surrey Elevens', broadsheet, 1892; 'A Vacant Place at the Oval', broadsheet, 1893.

Simon Curtis: 'At Coogee Oval' (*The Chronometer*), Paper Bark Press, Sydney, 1990.

D

Donald Davie: 'Barnsley Cricket Club' (*Events and wisdoms: poems 1957–1963*), Routledge & Kegan Paul, 1964.

C.J. Dennis: 'Dad on the Test' (*Bat and Pad*), ed. Derriman and Mullins, Choice Books, 2001.

Felix Dennis: 'The Don' (*A Glass Half Full*), Hutchinson, 2002. Copyright © Felix Dennis 2002.

Neville Denson: 'Cricketing Compassion' (*The Cricketer*), 1995. Copyright © Neville Denson 1995.

Alan de Silva: 'Cardus' (*The Cricket Spring Annual*), 1988.

D.A. de Silva: 'On First learning of Sri Lanka's 1st Test Victory', MS, 1985.

Morgan Dockrell: 'In Memoriam Dudley Nourse', 'Last Instructions of a Cricketer', 'Popularity', MS, 1982; 'A Famous Victory' (*Tales From Far Pavilions*), Pavilion Books, 1984.

Hubert Doggart: 'Lord Be Praised', MS, 1988.

William Douglas-Home: 'A Glorious Game Say We' (*Half-term report*), Longmans, Green, 1954.

Arthur Conan Doyle: 'A Reminiscence of Cricket' (*The Poems of Arthur Conan Doyle*), Murray, 1922.

E

Gavin Ewart: 'A Pindaric Ode on the Occasion of the Third Test between England and Australia, played at Headingley, 16th–21st July, 1981' (*The Ewart Quarto*), Hutchinson 1984; 'Valediction: to the cricket season' (*The Collected Ewart 1933–1980*), Hutchinson.

F

Herbert & Eleanor Farjeon: 'The Game That's Never Done' (*Herbert Farjeon's Cricket Bag*), MacDonald, 1946. Copyright © Ann Harvey and David Higham Associates for the Farjeon Estate.

Howard Fergus: 'Death of a Friend', 'Lara Rains' (*Lara Rains and Colonial Rites*), Peepal Tree Press, 1998.

J.S. Fletcher: 'Cricket', 'The Old Stumper Recites a Piece of his Own Composing' (*Collected Verse 1881–1931*), George G. Harrap and Co. Ltd., 1931.

G

Norman Gale: 'Duck' (*Cricket Songs*), George E. Over, 1890; 'The Church Cricketant' (*Cricket Songs* – second edition), Methuen, 1894; 'Tit for Tat' (*Messrs. Bat and Ball*), Norman Gale, 1930.

Danny Gardner: 'The Batsman', MS. Copyright © Danny Gardner 2003.

J.A. Gibney: 'C.V. Grimmett' (*Brisbane Daily Mail*), 7 March, 1925.

F.A.J. Godfrey: 'The Vital Question' (*The Poetry of Cricket*), Frewin, Macmillan 1964.

William Goldwin: 'A Cricket Match' (*In Certamen Pilae – Musae Juveniles*), A. Baldwin, 1706. Translation, H.P.-T. Early Cricket (*Old English Cricket*), C.H. Richards, 1923.

Robert Gray: 'Curriculum Vitae' (*The New Oxford Book of Australian Verse*), ed. Les A. Murray, Oxford University Press, 1991.

Anthony Greenstreet: 'The Old Boys' Match' (*The Cricketer*), November 1984.

Denis Griffiths: 'Villanelle for Cricket' (*Gate Hours and other Poems*), ed. Arthur Gibson, Jesus College Cambridge, 1985.

John Groves: 'Cricket Encapsulate', 'The Game' MS; 'A Gentle Obliquity', 'Lovely Cricket' (*The Learning Curve of Love*), United Writers Publications, 1999.

H

James Norman Hall: 'The Cricketers of Flanders' (*A Treasury of War Poetry*), ed. George Herbert Clark, Houghton Miffin Company, Boston, 1917.

George Rostrevor Hamilton: 'Cricket' (*The Carved Stone: Small Poems and Epigrams*), Heinemann, 1952.

Barclay Hankin: 'A New Lawn for Cricket Buffs' (*Topical Rhymes*), 2002.

Basil MacDonald Hastings: 'The Lay of the Fast Bowler'.

Daniel Healey: 'The Game of Cricket' (*Bat and Pad*), ed. Derriman and Mullins, Choice Books, 2001.

A.P. Herbert: 'Luncheon to the New Zealand Cricketers, 1958', 'Luncheon to the Pakistan cricket team, 1954', 'Luncheon to the South African cricket team, 1960', 'Ninth Wicket', reprinted by permission of A.P. Watt Ltd. on behalf of the Estate of Jocelyn Herbert and Teresa Elizabeth Perkins.

Louis Herzberg: 'Cricket Circus' (*The Cricketer*), 1994.

Philip Hodgins: 'The Practice Nets' (*The Longest Game: a collections of the best cricket poetry from Alexander to Zavos, from the Gabba to the Yabba*), Heineman Australia, 1990.

Bob Horne: 'The Cricketers at Keswick', MS, 1997.

A.E. Housman: 'A Shropshire Lad' (*The Collected Poems of A.E. Housman*), Jonathan Cape, 1939.

Gerald Howat: 'Metamorphoses' (*Cricket Medley*), Sports History Publishing, 1993. Copyright © Gerald Howat 1993.

Ted Hughes: 'Sunstruck' (*Remains of Elmet*), Faber & Faber Ltd., 1979.

Thomas Hutchinson: 'A Straight Bat', 'Flannelled Fools' (*A Little Book of Cricket Rhymes*), Morpeth Herald, J. & J.S. Mackay, 1923.

J

Geoffrey Johnson: 'Rabbit' (*The Poetry of Cricket*), Frewin, Macmillan, 1964.

K

Frank Keating: 'Geoffrey Boycott World Record', 'We Three Tweaks' (*Guardian*), 1982.

Paul Keens-Douglas: 'Tanti at De Oval' (*Selected Works of Paul Keens-Douglas Vol. 1*),

Keensdee Productions Ltd, 1992. keensdee@carib-link.net.

Christopher Kemp: ' "Our Constitution is the Post True Batsmen Will Defend" (Dibdin)' (*The Journal of the Cricket Society*), Vol. 12, No. 4, 1986.

Coulson Kernahan: 'Cricket Triolets' (*Adventures in Poetry: Book II*), Macmillan, 1943.

Roger Knight: 'Anniversary Dinner' MS, 1997.

L

R.D. Lancaster: 'The Hayfields' (*London Magazine*), 1957.

Michael Laskey: 'On Having Given up Cricket' (*Thinking of Happiness*), Peterloo Poets, 1991.

Robin Lindsay: 'Some Thoughts on Sachin Tendulkar' (*Bombay Times*), 5 March 2001.

Oscar Lloyd: 'Grace at Gloucester' (*The Poetry of Cricket*), Frewin, Macmillan, 1964.

Samuel J. Looker: 'England v Australia', Spellmount, 1988.

E.V. Lucas: 'If Every-' (*This Wicket World*), Number 1, July 14, 1922, ed. Present Etonians, Eton College, 1922.

Alexis Lykiard: 'The Art of Captaincy' (*Safe Levels and other Poems*), Stride, Exeter, 1990.

M

E.A. Markham: 'On Another Field, An Ally: A West Indian Batsman talks us towards the Century' (*Empire Windrush: Fifty Years of Writing About Black Britain*), ed. Onyekachi Wambu, Phoenix, London, 1999.

G.D. Martineau: 'Recollections of "Ranji"', 'Six and Out (A Street Impression)', 'Tom and Pamela or The Ballad of the Incorrigible Cricketers' (*A Score, A Score and Ten*), Methuen, 1927; 'To the Shade of William Clarke' MS, 1938.

John Masefield: 'Eighty-Five to win' (*The Times*), 29 August 1956; (*The Bluebells, and other verses*), Heinemann, 1961; (*The Cricket Quarterly*), Rowland Bowen, 1964. Reprinted by permission of the Society of Authors.

Ian McDonald: 'Massa Day Done' (*Between Silence and Silence*), Peepal Tree Press, 2003; 'Test Match' (*Mercy Ward*), Peterloo Poets, 1988.

Roger McGough: 'The Railings' (*Defying Gravity*), Penguin Books, 1992. Copyright © Roger McGough 1992. Reprinted by permission of Peters, Fraser and Dunlop.

Michael Mendel: 'Selected for the First Eleven' (*The Cricketer*), May 1989.

R.J.O. Meyer: 'Cherihews' (*The Cricketer*), November 1995.

A.A. Milne: 'To an Old Bat'.

Egbert Moore: 'MCC v West Indies, 1935', John Cowley; 'Victory Calypso, Lord's 1950' (*The Penguin Book of Light Verse*), ed. Gavin Ewart, Penguin Books, 1980.

Julia A. Moore: 'Grand Rapids Cricket Club' (*The Sweet Singer of Michigan: Poems by Mrs. Julia A. Moore*), ed. Walter Blair, Pascal Covici, 1928.

R.W. Moore: 'The Air is Hushed' (*Trophy for an Unknown Soldier*), Oxford Press, 1952

Dom Moraes: 'Green is the grass' (*Green is the grass*), Asia Publishing House, 1951.

Andrew Motion: 'Cricket' MS, 2002.

Thomas Moult: 'Close of Play' (*The Willow Pattern*), 1936; 'The Names'.

Mo Muir: 'Close of Play' (*The Cricketer*), 1995.

George Murray: 'The Gentlemen Cricketers' Team' (*Poems*), ed. John Reade, Edward G. O'Connor, Montreal, 1912.

N

Henry Newbolt: 'Vitai Lampada' (*Admirals all, and other verses*), Elkin Matthews, Shilling Garland, 1897.

Norman Nicholson: 'Millom Cricket Field' (*Field Days: an anthology of Poetry*), ed. Angela King and Susan Clifford, Chelsea Green Publishing Co., 1999.

P

William Perfect: 'Around the Level Dale' (*A Bavin of Bays: containing various original essays in poetry, by a Minor Poet*), Privately printed, 1763.

Arthur Peterson: 'The Cricket Field at Germantown' (*Collected Poems, 1873*), G.P. Putnam's Sons, 1916.

Daniel Pettiward: 'The Song of the Pitch' (*Truly Rural*), Dent, 1939.

David Phillips: '14th April', 'Chinese Cricket', 'The Rasumovsky Quartets', 'Twelfth Man', 'No Such Thing as a Bad Hundred', 'Suzanne', 'Hospitality Boxes', 'Running on Empty' (*Man in the Long Grass*), Iron Press, 2001.

Hubert Phillips: 'An Englishman's Crease' (*The Poetry of Cricket*), Frewin, Macmillan, 1964.

Fred Ponsonby: 'Bowling' (*Cricket Rhymes*), Privately printed, 1877.

John Pugh: 'Lines based upon John Keats' Poem, "The Mermaid Tavern"' (*Poems*), The Author, 1962.

W. Puttock: 'Little John' (*Bell's Life in London*), 15 August 1847.

Q

Frank Quarterman: 'The Swan of Kent' (*Afterthoughts*), Broadway Publishers, 1989.

Jay Quill: 'How's That' (*Ceylon Observer*).

R

Simon Rae: 'Do Not Go Gentle into that Pavilion' (*Poetry Review*); 'Dr. Owen Playing Cricket', 'The New Season' (*Guardian* and *Soft Targets*), Bloodaxe Books Ltd., 1991; 'Failing the Test' (*Guardian* and *Rapid Response*), Headland, 1997; 'A Red Ball Spins', 'Batsman', 'Bowler', 'Cover', 'Keeper', 'Overview', 'Slip' (*Caught on Paper*), Renn & Thacker, 2001.

R.W. Raper: 'The Innings' (*Echoes from the Oxford Magazine: being reprints of Seven Years*), 1890.

Tim Rice: 'A Model English Cricketer' (Westminster Abbey), 2001; 'Cricket (Hearts and Wickets)' MS, 1986.

A.M. Robertson: 'The Cricket Match', 'A Nightmare Innings'.

R.C. Robertson-Glasgow: 'The One-Way Critic' (*The Cricketer Spring Annual*).

Neil Rollinson: 'Deep Third Man' (*Spanish Fly*), Jonathan Cape, 2001.

Irving Rosenwater: 'Of Adelaide and its Oval', 'The Lane – A Farewell', 'Yorkshire Reverie', 'G.S.C., In Tribute', 'The Literary Scale', 'D.G.B.: In Memoriam'. Various Publications. Reprinted by permission of the author.

Alan Ross: 'Cricket at Brighton', 'J.M. Parks at Tunbridge Wells', 'Watching Benaud Bowl' (*To whom it may concern: poems 1952–1957*), Hamish Hamilton, 1968.

S

Krishna A. Samaroo: 'A Cricketing Gesture' (*Crossing Water; Contemporary Poetry of the English-speaking Caribbean*), ed. Anthony Kellman, Greenfield Review Press, 1992.

Siegfried Sassoon: 'The Extra Inch' (*First Lines; Poems Written in Youth, from Herbert to Heaney*), ed. Jon Stallworthy, Carcanet, 1987. Copyright © Siegfried Sassoon by kind permission of George Sassoon.

R.C. Scriven: 'Cricketer' (*Collected Sporting Verse*), ed. Caroline Sheldon and Richard Heller, Hutchinson 1986.

Owen Seaman: 'A Missionary Game' (*The Poetry of Cricket*), Frewin, Macmillan, 1964.

Colin Shakespeare: 'Cricket Calendar', 'Brian Close' *(The Five Seasons)*, Oak Press, 1988; 'Frank Tyson at Sydney, 1954', 'Mike Brearley', 'The Umpire', 'England v Australia, Headingley, July 20th, 1981, Tribute to Ian Botham', 'Sonny Ramadhin'*, 'To Sir Len Hutton'* (*22 Cricket Poems*), Oak Press (Bradford) Ltd., 1983. * First appeared in *Wisden Cricket Monthly*.

Rikki Shields: 'The Last Over' MS, 1996.

John Snow: 'Bahawalpur Ground', 'On being dropped', 'Sometime When I'm Older' (*Contrasts*), Fuller d'Arch Smith Ltd., 1971. All poems © J. A. Snow. Publication by permission of the author.

Sandy Solomon: 'Annual Game, Thrumpton Cricket Ground' (*The Southern Review*), ed. James Olney and Dave Smith, 1995. Copyright © Sandy Solomon 1995.

Chris Sparkes: 'Donkey Drops', 'The Plunderer' MS, 2001.

Dorothy Spring: 'Slip-up from Somerset' (*The Poetry of Cricket*), Frewin, Macmillan, 1964.

Dr. Satyendra Srivastava: 'Bob Shillington Plays Cricket Alone' Cambridge University, 1998. Copyright © Satyendra Srivastava 1998.

Richard Stilgoe: 'It All Began at Hambledon' MS, 1989; 'The Heavenly Host' MS, 1994; 'Out For A Dyke' MS, 1985; 'Two Hundred Years of Cricket' (*A Song For Cricket*), ed. David Rayvern Allen, Pelham Books, 1981. All poems by permission of the author.

John Stuart: 'And Quiet Flows the Don' MS, 2001.

K.V.V. Subrahmanyan: 'In Defence of Cricket' (*A Ray of Hope and other poems*), Sterling Publishers Private Ltd, 1989.

Peter Swan: 'Lament from Lord's' (*The Cricketer*), May 1988.

T

Alfred, Lord Tennyson: 'The Princess (A Medley) Prologue', 1847.

Francis Thompson: 'At Lord's', 'Rime o' Bat of O my sky – Em' (*Francis Thompson's Cricket Verses*), E.V. Lucas, Oxford University Press, 1937.

John Tripp: 'Cricket at the National Library' (*John Tripp Selected Poems*), ed. John Ormand, Seren Books, Poetry Wales Ltd., 1989.

Tony Turner: 'The Coliseum comes to Lord's', T.W.M. Publishing, 2002.

U

Unknown: 'Some Cricket Suppositions'.

V

G.H. Vallins: 'After Wordsworth', 'Alfred, Lord Tennyson Umpires a Village Cricket Match', 'To a Batsman Bowled First Ball' (*After a Manner: a book of parodies*), Epworth Press, 1956.

Alan Vidern: 'Hero Worship' MS, 2002.

W

Arnold Wall: 'A Time Will Come'.

Paul Weston: 'Sri Lankan Soliloquy' MS; 'Kiwi Juice' (*The Cricketer*); 'Ranji's Hairloom' (*The Cricketer*), November 1991.

John Whitworth: 'Coarse Cricket', 'Lovely Cricket', 'Sporting Print of a Young Athlete'.

D.A. Williams: 'Brentwood' (*Journal of the Cricket Society*), Vol. 12, No. 1, Autumn 1984.

Hugo Williams: 'Boy at a Cricket Match'.

Des Wilson. 'The Committee Game' MS, 2004.

G.F. Wilson: 'A Sixer' (*Cricket Poems*), Simpkin Marshall, London, 1905.

P.G. Wodehouse: 'Missed' (*Unauthorised Versions*); 'The Outcast: A Tale of a Ladies' Cricket Match' (*Daily Express*).

J. Hickory Wood: 'The Cricket Club of Red Nose Flat' (*Recitations, Comic and Otherwise*), James Bowden, 1898.

William Wordsworth: 'Sonnet' (*Poems*), 1807.

Ralph Wotherspoon: 'The Band At Play' (*The Poetry of Cricket*), Frewin, Macmillan, 1964.

Kit Wright: 'Cricket Widow', 'I Found South African Breweries Most Hospitable', 'The Captain', 'Versions of Dr. Tyerley' (*Hoping It Might Be So: Poems, 1974–2000*), Leviathan, 2000.

Malcolm Wroe: 'Preparing Cricket Bats' (*Smoke Secrets, Poetry Library*), Outpost Publications, 1982.

Y

Peter Young: 'Wave Hill Cricket Club'.